CERVANTES'S NOVEL OF MODERN TIMES

CERVANTES'S NOVEL
OF MODERN TIMES

A NEW READING OF *DON QUIJOTE*

David Quint

PRINCETON UNIVERSITY PRESS

PRINCETON AND OXFORD

COPYRIGHT © 2003 BY PRINCETON UNIVERSITY PRESS

PUBLISHED BY PRINCETON UNIVERSITY PRESS,

41 WILLIAM STREET, PRINCETON, NEW JERSEY 08540

IN THE UNITED KINGDOM: PRINCETON UNIVERSITY PRESS,

3 MARKET PLACE, WOODSTOCK, OXFORDSHIRE OX20 1SY

SECOND PRINTING, AND FIRST PAPERBACK PRINTING, 2005

PAPERBACK ISBN 0-691-12227-X

THE LIBRARY OF CONGRESS HAS CATALOGED THE CLOTH EDITION
OF THIS BOOK AS FOLLOWS

QUINT, DAVID, 1950–

CERVANTES'S NOVEL OF MODERN TIMES : A NEW READING OF

DON QUIJOTE / DAVID QUINT.

P.   CM.

INCLUDES BIBLIOGRAPHICAL REFERENCES AND INDEX.

ISBN 0-691-11433-1 (ALK. PAPER)

1. CERVANTES SAAVEDRA, MIGUEL DE, 1547–1616. DON QUIJOTE. I. TITLE.

PQ6352.Q57 2003

863′.3—DC21   2003049791

BRITISH LIBRARY CATALOGING-IN-PUBLICATION DATA IS AVAILABLE

THIS BOOK WAS SUBSIDIZED BY THE PROGRAM FOR CULTURAL COOPERATION
BETWEEN SPAIN'S MINISTRY OF EDUCATION, CULTURE AND SPORTS,
AND UNITED STATES UNIVERSITIES.

THIS BOOK HAS BEEN COMPOSED IN SABON

PRINTED ON ACID-FREE PAPER. ∞

PUP.PRINCETON.EDU

PRINTED IN THE UNITED STATES OF AMERICA

3   5   7   9   10   8   6   4   2

To the Memory of Maurice J. Bennett
and David M. Jones

CONTENTS

PREFACE

LIKE CERVANTES, I came to *Don Quijote* from the experience of reading Renaissance and medieval romances of chivalry. These works are given to intricate multiple plots, digressive episodes, and stories within stories. On first reading they are "baggy monsters." Further reading invariably brings out connections and correspondences among the seemingly unrelated parts, and the strong sense of a deliberate design. *Don Quijote* presents a similar first impression, reinforced by the novel's conspicuous debt to picaresque narrative as well as to the chivalric romances themselves.

The existing criticism of Cervantes's novel has mostly interpreted it in parts, episode by episode, and treated the book as the sum of those parts. Some parallels between episodes have been noted, and a larger unity has often been suspected, but rarely documented. The great editor Martín de Riquer could conclude that the famous tale of the "Curioso impertinente" interpolated into Part One "has nothing to do with the plot and action of the book."[1] More peversely, Vladimir Nabokov, citing Salvador de Madariaga's view of the "bewildering succession of episodes" in *Don Quijote*, characterized them as "the padding of a tired author," and the novel itself as a confused "meat pie" made up of disparate and incongruous ingredients.[2]

I have written with the aim of refuting such judgments. In making a case for the artistic integrity of *Don Quijote*, I am arguing that what holds for the romances that Cervantes satirized and sought to supersede holds for his novel as well. I will show a close relationship to the rest of the novel—in details of plot and wording—not only of the "Curioso impertinente" but of all of the intercalated stories and individual episodes. In doing so, I also argue for and practice a method of reading Cervantes's book.

Cervantes's Novel of Modern Times offers a map of the structure and meaning of *Don Quijote*. My goals are twofold: to demonstrate the formal unity of *Don Quijote*, especially of its 1605 Part One—*how* the novel fits together; and to illustrate its thematic coherence—*why* its assembled features add up the way they do. Cervantes's book evinces a carefully studied plan carried out in great, if not to the last, semantic detail. Its episodes connect with and comment upon other episodes, and they do so through a repetition of motifs, parallel actions, and direct verbal echoes. This is particularly true of the interpolated tales, whose inclusion has caused puzzlement from the first reception of the novel and which modern readers are still liable to dimiss or skip over. Through the juxtaposition of episodes that recalls and adapts the narrative interlace ("entrelacement") of medieval and Renaissance romance, Cervantes carefully plays these interpolated stories off against Don Quijote's chivalric career and against one another. The meaning of the novel is thus created *relationally*, and a reading of any part of *Don Quijote* will be incomplete if it is not placed within this corresponding whole.

This unified *Don Quijote* recounts a story of historical transition. Critics have perceived in a general way that the realism against which the mad idealist Don Quijote opposes himself is tied to a newly emergent world of money.[3] I argue that *in the very structure and narrative progress* of *Don Quijote* Cervantes mimics and charts the arrival of this modern world that is beginning to succeed the feudal aristocratic order—the latter celebrated in the fantasy literature of chivalry that Don Quijote consumes and tries to reenact. In a carefully laid out sequence, the knights and monks of the older world Don Quijote imagines at the beginning of Part One have been succeeded at its end by their present-day equivalents, the professional soldier, Captain Viedma returned from captivity in Algiers, and his brother, the *letrado* Judge, on his way to Mexico City—their mobility symptomatic of a newly fluid society. As these brothers attest, theirs is a society of career choices and making one's way toward material acquisition: a society of money. Thus *Don Quijote* throughout tells and retells a master narrative of early-modern Europe: the movement from feudalism to the new order of capitalism that will become the realistic domain of the modern novel, the genre this book does so much to invent.

In Part One, the character Don Quijote is himself divided, more than he knows, between these two historical formations. This division is expressed in erotic terms. Though he has made his stand against modern times by going mad and seeking to revive the chivalric past, Don Quijote can also imagine chivalry as a career, and his love for the idealized Dulcinea coexists with a rival fantasy of rising to wealth and power by marrying an emperor's daughter. Cervantes depicts a shift in the nature of erotic desire as the measure of a historical change from feudal to proto-bourgeois values, and he writes it large in the narrative organization of Part One. A reflection of Don Quijote's own twofold amorous fantasies—for Dulcinea and for the princess-heiress who briefly seems to materialize as "Princess Micomicona"—Part One sets old-fashioned love stories (driven by jealousy and male rivalry) against stories of a modern love (which seeks marriage for money and social advancement). The "modern" love stories come later in the narrative sequence and gradually displace the stories of an older kind of love. This is a way in which the novel's form reflects the historical movement it describes. As for the two great interpolated tales of Part One, the "Curioso impertinente" and the Captive's Tale, they fall respectively into these two groups. If René Girard's classic account of triangular desire in *Don Quijote* and in the "Curioso impertinente" in particular fits the first cluster of stories, the Captive's Tale tells of another desire, raised and then renounced, that would put a price on the beloved. My reading of the Captive's Tale further suggests just how much energy Cervantes may have invested in making his auto-biographical counterpart, Captain Viedma, into an alternate hero of the novel. Cervantes's fiction, I seek to show, meditates on the relation of the new social mobility it portrays to the mixture of genres that constitutes its own novelistic form.

Part Two of *Don Quijote* is at once more straightforwardly and less tightly organized. Cervantes wanted to make the fiction easier for the readers puzzled by Part One, and the result, I think, is less daring writing. The meaning still depends on the interconnections among its episodes, and now it depends as well on the way that they recall and rewrite episodes in Part One. But the narrative keeps a steadier focus on Don Quijote and Sancho Panza. It is, in fact, through a dramatic change in Don Quijote's character that Part Two recasts the social and historical scenario explored by Part One; Cervantes himself seems to change his mind about the moneyed society that is emerging beside a stagnant aristocratic class.

Criticism of the novel has noted a greater emphasis in Part Two on Don Quijote's new inwardness, melancholy, and self-doubts. I am interested less in the character's interiority than in his new ethical actions and disposition. He gives up most of the aggression and anarchic violence that marked his attempt to revive feudal chivalry in Part One, and adopts a new moderation, peaceability, and Christianity. These characteristics are bound up with his acceptance of having to use money in his transactions with the world, and they align him in no small part with the book's representatives of a new moneyed class.

Part Two presents a parade of social types. In its first half Don Quijote meets members of a moderately wealthy class and its moderate ethical values, Don Diego de Miranda and Camacho the Rich. He initially opposes himself to but subsequently, in an ironic turnaround, adapts their behavior, stepping into what we can recognize as the future middle class. Just how far Don Quijote has changed is measured late in the novel, when he preaches Christianity to the bandit Roque Guinart, who might incarnate the lawlessness and violence that the mad hidalgo himself exhibited in Part One.

This new behavior opposes Don Quijote, in turn, to the cruelty and injustice of the Duke and Duchess, who host Don Quijote and Sancho Panza for most of the remainder of Part Two and who transform this last section of the novel into a biting satire on the "knights" of the present day, the high nobility. Don Quijote may be capable of ethical reform, but these aristocrats are not, and their entrenched power and courtly idleness offer an explanation for national decline. This power extends over the novel *Don Quijote* itself, which the Duke and the Duchess try to appropriate and rewrite according to their enjoyment of the slapstick of Part One. Don Quijote and Sancho Panza become their prisoners, both virtually and literally. The eventual escape of Cervantes's characters from these surrogate readers-authors suggests the future orientation of the genre of the novel, away from an aristocratic audience and with a view to a more socially heterogeneous public.

Some caveats are in order. The social interpretation that I offer of *Don Quijote* is mostly derived from the novel itself. It does not depend on, although I certainly have learned from, historical and contextualizing works on Cervantes's Spanish culture and society. But the present study is not the place to look for accounts of economic inflation in the sixteenth century. My reading is intended to reorient, but also to complement, other critical approaches to this multidimensional novel. I give secondary and sometimes only incidental attention to many familiar topics of the criticism on *Don Quijote*: reality versus appearance, the mad versus the visionary, Don Quijote versus Sancho Panza, the metaliterary games Cervantes plays with fictional codes and with his narrator. These issues have been the center of interpretations and whole books, and I have not felt it necessary to go over old ground.

Some readers may be surprised that my study is not squarely focused on the character of Don Quijote, although he is rarely out of the picture for long. My argument is that the novel itself always looks at its hero in comparison and in relation to the other characters who surround him. In Part One, they occupy as much if not more of the space of the novel; in Part Two, he is faced with a series of mirror figures: Don Diego de Miranda, Basilio, Roque Guinart, the Duke. Moreover, while I acknowledge that the great overall achievement of the novel is its creation of the mythical figures of Don Quijote and Sancho Panza, I also believe that its greatest stretches of writing lie in the interpolated stories of the "Curioso impertinente" and the Captive's Tale. If my emphasis on these Don Quijote–less episodes may seem to draw attention to the background of the novel, I would argue that in the process the figure in the foreground begins to change. So in aiming for a different effect, it may be that this book presents the reader with a new version of Don Quijote as well.

For all its merriment, *Don Quijote* is typically read as a novel of disillusionment—"desengaño"—the discovery of a crass, real world that does not live up to Don Quijote's dreams and that tells of the decline of Spain after her great century of empire. This disillusionment intensifies in Part Two, where Dulcinea is "transformed" into an ugly peasant and Don Quijote's own imaginative powers fail him. It is hard to dispute this interpretation generally, but it tells only half of the story. We should not identify Cervantes's viewpoint with that of his hero. The old soldier Cervantes, veteran of Lepanto and commissioner for the Armada, may well be nostalgic for a Spanish military greatness that he could have felt was slipping away; hence his identification with Captain Viedma in Part One. But he was not equally nostalgic for a feudal past or sentimental about the present aristocratic order; hence his declared purpose of destroying the romances of chivalry and his satirical portrait of the Duke and the Duchess in Part Two. By Part Two, moreover, Cervantes has come to find virtues in the new society of money, however unglamorous and reduced in heroism he may admit it to be. He reshapes Don Quijote according to those virtues. The hero may be correspondingly disillusioned, and sadder than before, but, in compensation, he is now also a gentler and better man. The future may belong to the bland middling Don Diego de Miranda and to the new Don Quijote who has become more recognizably the hero of a genre dedicated to a world of money. When Don Quijote awakens from his chivalric delusion at the end of the book, he dies, but a long life remains for his descendants in the art of the novel.

ACKNOWLEDGMENTS

IN WRITING THIS BOOK I have especially benefited from the advice and support of two friends whose own distinguished criticism of Don Quijote has shaped my understanding of the novel. Timothy Hampton and Alexander Welsh have given me careful readings of the manuscript and, just as important, the encouragement to see the project through. I am also particularly indebted to the friendship and intellectual conversation of Lawrence Manley, whose comments on the manuscript have helped me clarify my thinking and grasp larger issues. I am thankful to many others. Maria di Battista, Diana de Armas Wilson, and Anthony Grafton also read the entire book and offered generous and incisive criticism. Alban Forcione graciously read the first chapter and set me on my course. David Bromwich helped me, as he has done before with other books of mine, to bring this one to a conclusion and to make a more shapely preface. Various friends read and commented on individual sections of the book: Edwin Duval, Ronald Levao, Alex Woloch, Annabel Patterson, Margaret Doody, Daniel Javitch. Moira Fraidinger painstakingly went over the Spanish citations in the text. Cindy Crumrine has expertly copyedited a manuscript that contained numerous inconsistencies.

My thinking about Don Quijote has been sharpened and challenged in the classroom. I taught the novel almost yearly at Princeton University in an undergraduate course headed by Robert Hollander, and I fondly recall our conversations about it. Students in my graduate seminars at Yale University taught me about the book, especially Leah Price, Steven Monte, Katherine Hoyle, and Duncan Chesney. I profited from collegial conversations about Don Quijote with Howard Stern and Roberto González Echevarría at Yale and with Ignacio Navarrete at the University of California at Berkeley.

An earlier version of material in Chapter Three was published as an article, "Narrative Interlace and Narrative Genres in Don Quijote and the Orlando Furioso," Modern Language Quarterly 58, no. 3 (September 1997).

DON QUIJOTE, PART ONE

ONE

CERVANTES'S METHOD AND MEANING

Interlace

CERVANTES indicates to his reader how to read *Don Quijote*, as a whole and not as the sum of it parts, in the story of Leandra in Chapter 51, the last of the interpolated tales in Part One of *Don Quijote*. It is a kind of laboratory case set inside the novel to demonstrate one of the book's salient literary techniques, for it picks up echoes and details of *all* the other interpolated tales that precede it.

The charlatan soldier Vicente de la Roca, who runs off with Leandra, her jewels, and her father's money, is a debased version of the Captive, Captain Viedma, who recounts his escape from Algiers with his beloved Moor Zoraida, (Chapters 39–41). When the beautiful Leandra is compared to a miracle-working image ["imagen de milagros" (502; 506)] we are reminded of Zoraida, who brought about the Captive's "miraculous delivery" ["milagrosa libertad" (429; 431)], and who is closely associated with the Virgin Mary, whose name she takes as her own and whose images ["imágenes" (430; 432)] she recognizes when she first enters a church in Spain.[1] The phrase also anticipates Don Quijote's last exploit in the First Part, his attack on the disciplinants who are carrying an image of the Virgin Mary in the following Chapter 52. In its pastoral setting, and in the behavior of those lovers of Leandra who accuse her of disdain without ever having spoken to her, the episode obviously repeats the first of the interpolated stories, the episode of Grisóstomo and Marcela (Chapters 12–14). The songs that Vicente sings to Leandra evoke the story of Luis and Clara (Chapters 42–43). Leandra, the rich farmer's daughter who is seduced and abandoned, resembles Dorotea, dishonored and abandoned by Fernando (Chapter 28). The narrator of the tale, Eugenio, has a rival, Anselmo, whose name recalls the Anselmo of the "Curioso impertinente" (Chapters 33–35). When Eugenio, who has decided to blame the fickleness of women for his loss of Leandra, brawls with Don Quijote and Sancho in the next chapter, we should be reminded of Cardenio, who, similarly inveighing against the supposed falseness of Luscinda, fights with the hidalgo and his squire in the Sierra Morena (Chapter 24). Finally, when the braggart Vicente is said to claim that his right arm is his father, his deeds his lineage, and that as a soldier he owes nothing, even to the king (504; 507), he becomes a parodic mirror of Don Quijote himself, who in Chapter 4 had made the proverbial declaration that every man is the son of his own works (76; 57) and at the end of Chapter 45 had asserted to the police force of the Holy Brotherhood that he and other knights-errant were exempt from all jurisdiction (462; 465).[2]

As it recapitulates the episodes of Part One of Cervantes's novel, the story of Leandra suggests how these episodes interpolated into the adventures of Don Quijote and Sancho Panza are themselves interconnected. The stories of characters whom Don Quijote meets on his way (Marcela and Grisóstomo, Cardenio, Dorotea, Eugenio), the stories of the characters who arrive at the inn (the Captive, Don Luis, and Clara), the story of the "Curioso impertinente" that is labeled precisely as an interpolated tale, drawn out of a trunk and read at the inn, and, not least of all, the miniature chivalric romance that Don Quijote tells to Sancho in Chapter 21, itself another inset tale—these are all thematically linked not only to the deeds of knight and squire, but to one another. They take up the larger part of the narrative space of the first installment of the novel, and for long stretches can seem to crowd Don Quijote out of his own story.[3] The first readers of the novel appear to have objected particularly to the "Curioso impertinente"; Sansón Carrasco tells us in Chapter 3 of Part Two that they complained that the story "is out of place and has nothing to do with the history of his worship, Don Quijote" ["por no ser de aquel lugar, ni tiene que ver con la historia de su merced del señor don Quijote" (549; 562)]. Still later in Chapter 44, Cervantes seems to be answering his critics when the narrator Cide Hamete links the "Curioso impertinente" with the Captive's Tale as digressions and episodes that seem detachable from the rest of the book ["como separadas de la historia" (833; 848)].[4]

Cervantes is being ironic. These first critics were not strong readers. And it is still one of the weaknesses of the tradition of criticism on *Don Quijote* that it has generally treated the novel's episodes individually rather than as integral parts whose mirroring relationship creates its larger whole.[5] In doing so, such criticism may have emphasized the picaresque elements of *Don Quijote* over its inheritance from the chivalric romances the novel sets out to destroy and replace.[6] To accomplish this satirical demolition, Cervantes treats the picaresque and the chivalric romance as inversions of one another, transforming the quest of his mad knight-errant into a series of picaresque wanderings. He signals the overlay and reciprocity of the modern and the medieval genres early on in Chapter 3 of the novel, when the first innkeeper whom Don Quijote meets poses as a retired knight and describes his own earlier picaresque career as thief and criminal as a series of chivalric adventures (69; 49).[7] Cervantes thus gives his novel the formal appearance of a picaresque narrative, a collection of disparate episodes, one thing after another. Claudio Guillén writes that the picaresque "novel is loosely episodic, strung together like a freight train and *apparently* with no other common link than the hero."[8] In *Lazarillo de Tormes*, the ur-picaresque novel that Cervantes evokes in Chapter 22, the hero, as his name implies, appears to die and be reborn from one episode to the next as if to denote the discrete quality of each and the discontinuity of his human experience. (So, to a certain extent, does Don Quijote dust himself off after each defeat, assess the damage to his body, and ride off to his next adventure.) Guillén is careful to suggest, however, that despite appearances, even the picaresque narrative finds ways to link its parts together.

For the purpose of making such connections, *Don Quijote* turns back to the model of chivalric romance itself. Cervantes's method of playing one episode of the novel off against another derives from and is inspired by the technique of narrative *interlace* ("entrelacement") that organizes the great chivalric romances of the Middle Ages such as the prose *Lancelot*.[9] The romance follows the careers of some eight or ten questing knights, telling a segment of one knight's story before turning to a segment of another's, and thus keeps multiple plots going at once. The plots parallel one another and may share common motifs, and the reader begins to realize that the romance coheres and generates meaning not so much from the endings of the knights' stories, which are hardly in sight, as from the juxtaposition of the stories and their reflection upon one another.[10] Narrative strands that initially seem to be discrete can turn out to be symbolically related. To take an example from the *Lancelot*: when one knight fights a giant in his story line, and another knight kills a villainous baron oppressing a damsel in his, we are invited to see the baron as a kind of giant.[11]

So, in a rather clear-cut Cervantine adaptation of this technique in Chapter 29 of *Don Quijote*, Dorotea, cast by the Curate and Barber in the role of Princess Micomicona, tries to kiss the hands of Don Quijote after he has promised to champion her against the giant who persecutes her (295; 295). A few pages earlier Dorotea has in her own person tried to kiss the feet of Cardenio, who has promised to defend her honor against her seducer Don Fernando (290; 291). The reader sees the parallel between Dorotea's real-life situation and the chivalric scenario invented for the benefit of Don Quijote—Don Fernando is like a wicked giant, she is a genuine damsel-in-distress. Cervantes gives this narrative juxtaposition his typical psychological twist when Dorotea improvises upon and embroiders this scenario in Chapter 30: she seems quite conscious of the parallel and to be indulging in autobiography beneath the fiction that she is an exotic princess.[12] We may be led to a secondary reflection that if one inverts the parallel, the fantastic stories of chivalry may contain disguised versions of lived human experience in the first place.[13]

Interlace is the principle of narrative organization in Ludovico Ariosto's *Orlando furioso* (1516), the literary work that most deeply influenced Cervantes in *Don Quijote*.[14] Not only does Ariosto juxtapose, contrast, and compare the adventures of the myriad knights and ladies who zigzag across the map of his romance; he also introduces interpolated tales, often in the form of Bocaccian novellas, into its sprawling narrative. The "Curioso impertinente" is a rewriting of the two novellas in Canto 43 (9–46; 72–143) of the *Furioso* that recount husbands testing the fidelity of their wives, and Cervantes signals his debt by giving his overly curious husband Anselmo the same name as the jealous husband in Ariosto's second tale. It is important to emphasize that Ariosto builds these tales into the larger interlace structure of his poem: thus these stories of Mantuan and Ferrarese husbands and wives comment on the climactic marriage of the heroes Ruggiero and Bradamante, who will found the Este dynasty that produced Ariosto's patrons, the Cardinal of Ferrara and the Duchess of Mantua. In a more pointed example, the notorious, salacious novella that Ariosto advises his lady readers to skip in Canto 28 describes sexual intercourse with the conventional metaphor of horseback riding; in the next canto the mad Orlando rides the horse of his beloved Angelica to death in what is clearly a symbolic substitution for rape; in between, the woman-hating Rodomonte, for whom the novella was told, journeys by boat to save wear and tear on his own horse: the juxtaposition tells us something about men who treat women like horses, horses like women, horses better than women.[15]

Cervantes masters his own version of interlace in Part One of *Don Quijote*. While he does not present a series of concurrent stories and jump from one to another—though he *will* do something of this sort in Part Two when he alternates chapters between Don Quijote's experience in the castle of the Duke and Duchess and Sancho's tenure of his "governorship" (44–53)[16]—he makes full use, as I have already suggested, of the interpolated stories of other characters and of the interpolated tale itself. He establishes connections among them and between them and the main plot of Don Quijote's madness with an artistry that can be dizzying. Thus he requires his reader not only to understand a given episode of *Don Quijote* on its own terms, but to juxtapose it with other episodes that may at first appear unrelated to it. A motif central to one story will turn up displaced in a peripheral position in another, as seemingly out of place ("no ser de aquel lugar") as the entire interpolated tale of the "Curioso impertinente." But in this scheme, nothing, in fact, may be out of place in the novel; the apparently extraneous detail, no less than an entire digressive episode, can be found to fit into a larger web of meaning. The reader or critic does not need to share a romantic notion of the organic unity of the literary work of art or a classical aesthetic of the work's architectonic unity.[17] The practical experience of reading literature itself produces the axiom that precisely those elements of the text that on the face of it do not seem to fit—the digression, the subplot, the story-within-the-story—will almost always reward close attention and offer commentary, often through contrast and irony, upon a principal or central story. In Part One of *Don Quijote* the madness and career plans of Don Quijote reveal their full implications in the stories of the other characters that jostle for narrative space in the novel alongside his own. *Their* stories, reciprocally, are deepened by parallels among themselves—and to Don Quijote's motives, ideas, and behavior: an obvious, continuous irony of the novel suggests, sometimes gently, sometimes savagely, that these other characters are not much saner than the mad hidalgo.

Arms and Letters

The analyses that follow in this book seek to apply a method of reading *Don Quijote* by tracing and examining Cervantes's technique of interlacing his novel's episodes and of distributing its thematic motifs. They also propose an interpretation of the novel that emerges from this method. To suggest how one gets from the first to the second, I want to look now at two secondary instances of Cervantine interlace; they will give some idea of the technique in question. The first of my examples arches across nearly the entirety of Part One of the novel. It concerns the debate between arms and letters—that is, which is the nobler profession, that of the soldier or that of the man of learning?—a time-honored topos in Renaissance writing at least since the discussions of Castiglione's *Book of the Courtier* (1.42–46).[18]

Don Quijote, who is always ready to spout long passages from his reading, and who thereby repeatedly gains from those around him the opinion that he is a man of good sense when he is not pursuing his chivalric mania, gives an elaborate version of the debate of arms and letters in Chapters 37 and 38. The would-be knight naturally enough awards primacy to arms, whether or not he reflects the opinion of Cervantes, who could claim experience both as man of letters and as soldier. The author of *Don Quijote* had been wounded and lost the use of his left hand at the battle of Lepanto in 1571, as he tells us in the Prologue to Part Two, "the greatest occasion that present, past, or future ages have ever seen or can ever hope to see" ["la más alta ocasión que vieron los siglos pasados, los presentes, ni esperan ver los venideros" (526; 535)]. Cervantes weaves his character's version of this by now commonplace debate into a whole sequence of episodes in the novel, and we are invited to watch how its terms develop and change: the logic of this development will turn out to be *historical*, suggesting a movement from an earlier feudal social formation to the modern, money-driven society of Cervantes's age. This historical logic governs both the shape and the meaning of the first part of *Don Quijote*; it becomes a main subject of the larger novel.

The theme emerges as a joke that the Curate and Barber of Don Quijote's village make at Sancho Panza's expense when they greet him as he returns from the Sierra Morena on his mission to El Toboso and Dulcinea in Chapter 26. When Sancho tells them that he is to be rewarded with an island and governorship once his master rises through his prowess to become emperor or king, they play along and tell Sancho that it is very possible for Don Quijote "to become in time an emperor, as he had suggested, or at least archbishop, or something equally important" ["a ser emperador, como él decía, o, por lo menos, arzobispo, o otra dignidad equivalente" (260; 257)]. The offhand quip about the archbishop greatly worries the married Sancho, for he would be ineligible for the ecclesiastical benefices that Don Quijote in his capacity as archbishop-errant—one of the "arzobispos andantes," as Sancho calls them—would be able to bestow on him instead of the promised island. The Barber reassures him that Don Quijote will more easily become emperor than archbishop since he is "more of a soldier than a scholar" ["más valiente que estudiante"]. The contrast between Don Quijote's career options is thus cast explicitly in terms of the stereotyped opposition of arms and letters. Cervantes introduces this opposition in its most socially conservative form as one between martial aristocracy and church, in the feudal distinction between those who fight and those who pray.

These are the same backward-looking terms with which Don Quijote himself had already defined his mission as knight-errant much earlier in the novel in Chapter 13. When his traveling companion Vivaldo comments that the rules of knight-errantry appear to be stricter than those of the Carthusians, Don Quijote replies that "holy men, in all peace of tranquillity, pray to Heaven for the welfare of the world, but we soldiers and knights carry out what they ask for . . . not under shelter but under the open sky, exposed as target to the intolerable beams of the sun in summer and to the piercing frost of winter" ["los religiosos, con toda paz y sosiego, piden al cielo el bien de la tierra; pero los soldados y caballeros ponemos en ejecución lo que ellos piden . . . no debajo de cubierta, sino al cielo abierto, puesto por blanco de los insufribles rayos del sol en el verano y de los erizados yelos del invierno" (131–32; 118)]. Don Quijote thus claims for the soldier-knight a sacred calling—he is one of God's ministers on earth—even as he is careful not to pretend that the state of the knight-errant is as good as that of the monk: the two represent distinct but related careers. In the same passage Don Quijote lets himself think about just how high the chivalric career can aspire: some knights, he says, "rose to be emperors by the valor of their arms" ["algunos subieron a ser emperadores por el valor de su brazo" (132; 119)]. He returns here to his daydreams in the very first chapter of the novel, where he fancied himself "already crowned Emperor of Trebizond by the valor of his arm" ["ya coronado por el valor de su brazo, por los menos, del imperio de Trapisonda" (59; 38)]. When the Curate and Barber make their joke about Archbishop-as-opposed-to-Emperor Quijote, they thus pick up, without knowing it, the hidalgo's own opposition of religious and chivalric vocations. Even the joke itself has its precedent in the novel: back in Chapter 7, the delirious Don Quijote, recovering from his first sally, had addressed the same Curate as "arzobispo Turpín" (93; 76), evoking a character of the chivalric romances who had really been an archbishop-errant.

The same opposition of the religious versus the military life reappears in a very different context in Chapter 33 inside the interpolated tale of the "Curioso impertinente," in a prime example of Cervantes's technique of displacing the thematic motifs of his novel from one episode to another. In the tale, Lotario is responding to his best friend, Anselmo, who has asked him to test the chastity of Anselmo's wife, Camila, by pretending to court her. In urging Anselmo to consider what he may gain from this project, Lotario includes an odd and roundabout argument. There are, he says, three goals for human endeavors (none of which Anselmo can accomplish by his testing of his wife):

> Man undertakes arduous enterprises for the sake of God, for the world's sake, or for both. The first are undertaken by the saints, who strive to live as angels in human form; the second are accomplished by men who sail the boundless ocean and endure the vagaries of climates as they rove through far-off lands in quest of what are called the goods of fortune; the third, which are those that are undertaken for the sake of God and man, are the achievements of staunch soldiers, who no sooner see a breach in the enemy's rampart made by a single cannonball than, shedding all fear of the perils that threaten them from all sides and soaring on the wings of the desire to conquer for their faith, for their country, and for their king, they hurl themselves forward into the jaws of death, which awaits them in a thousand guises . . . but the project you would now attempt will earn you neither heavenly glory, nor goods of fortune, nor fame among men. (332)

> Las cosas dificultosas se intentan por Dios, o por el mundo, o por entrambos a dos: las que se acometen por Dios son las que acometieron los santos, acometiendo a vivir vida de ángeles en cuerpos humanos; las que se acometen por respeto del mundo son las de aquellos que pasan tanta infinidad de agua, tanta diversidad de climas, tanta estrañeza de gentes, por adquirir estos que llaman bienes de fortuna. Y las que se intentan por Dios y por el mundo juntamente son aquellas de los valerosos soldados, que apenas veen en el

contrario muro abierto tanto espacio cuanto es el que pudo hacer una re-
donda bala de artillería, cuando, puesto aparte todo temor, sin hacer discurso
ni advertir al manifiesto peligro que les amenaza, llevados en vuelo de las
alas del deseo de volver por su fe, por su nación y por su rey, se arrojan
intrépidamente por la mitad de mil contrapuestas muertes que los esperan
. . . Pero la que tú dices quieres intentar y poner por obra, ni te ha de alcanzar
gloria de Dios, bienes de la fortuna, ni fama con los hombres. (333–34)

Here, too, the man of religion and the man of war are opposed, even as
they are shown to share some common goals. We should note that the
soldier ["soldado"] in question is a modern one, apparently an infantry-
man and no longer Don Quijote's knight ["caballero"]. Like the saint, this
soldier pursues the glory of God as he fights for his faith, though he also
seeks for worldly glory. In the second formulation of the opposition, however, it is the latter—fame among men—that seems to characterize the soldier and to place him squarely in a secular realm. That realm is defined
further by the new, third term that the passage has meanwhile introduced:
the merchant whose ventures now take him to a literally New World, un-
dreamt of in earlier times, a world that Cervantes's Spain had taken a
leading role in discovering and colonizing. If there is a suggestion that
the merchant's hardships rise to a quasi-heroism—it is he who suffers the
changeable weather that Don Quijote had earlier ascribed to the soldier-
knight—Lotario's speech decidedly places the motive of commerce, the
mere gain of worldly wealth, beneath the goals of religion and military
honor that seek in complementary and divergent ways to transcend the
world. Heroism belongs most vividly to the soldier, and the speech expands
into a brief set piece to celebrate military courage in the face of death.

Lotario's speech has no place in its own context except to amplify his
admonishment to Anselmo not to pursue his "impertinent" curiosity about
the fidelity of his wife. Its larger function is to point forward in the novel,
as a kind of connecting bridge, to Don Quijote's long set speech defending
arms over letters in Chapters 37–38 and to the ensuing interpolated tale
of the Captive, Captain Viedma, newly come from Algiers with Zoraida.
Don Quijote's speech on arms and letters is, like so much of his discourse
in the novel, a piece of book-learning; the topic was a favorite for rhetorical
debate, and, as such, designed as much to demonstrate rhetorical and literary skill as to decide the issue. Lotario's vivid little scene of land battle
before a breach in the enemy ramparts has its counterpart in Don Quijote's
much expanded description of a sea battle in Chapter 38. Here, too, soldiers charge into near certain death into a tight space, on two planks of a
battering ram, to reach the enemy ship: "inspired by the honor that spurs
him on, he allows himself to be the mark for all their fire and endeavors
to force his way by that narrow path into the enemy vessel" ["llevado de

la honra que le incita, se pone a ser blanco de tanta arcabucería, y procura pasar por tan estrecho paso al bajel contrario" (391; 393)]. The passage evokes Cervantes's experience at Lepanto, and it is directly linked to Captain Viedma's ensuing narrative in Chapter 39, where he recounts how he was captured during Lepanto after he had jumped onto an Ottoman galley and found himself cut off from his own ship (396; 399)—turning Don Quijote's rhetorical example into true life-history.

If Don Quijote treats arms in a way consistent with the earlier appearances of the arms-versus-letters motifs we have traced in the novel, the same cannot be said for his discussion of letters. For the beginning of Don Quijote's speech in Chapter 37 now explicitly separates the vocation of letters from a religious calling:

> The aim and goal of letters—I am not now speaking of divine letters, whose sole aim is to guide and elevate the soul of man to Heaven, for with that sublime end none can be compared—I speak of human letters, whose end is to regulate distributive justice, to give every man his due, to make good laws, and to enforce them strictly: an end most certainly generous, exalted, and worthy of high praise, but not so glorious as the aim of arms, which is peace, the greatest blessing that man can enjoy in this life. For the first good news that the world ever received was brought by the angels on the night that was our day when they sang in the skies: "Glory be to God on High and peace and on earth to men of goodwill"; . . . This peace is the true end of war, and by war and arms I mean the same thing. (387–88)

> Es el fin y paradero de las letras . . . , y no hablo ahora de las divinas, que tienen por blanco llevar y encaminar las almas al cielo; que a un fin tan sin fin como éste ninguno otro se le puede igualar: hablo de las letras humanas, que es su fin poner en su punto la justicia distributiva y dar a cada uno lo que es suyo, y entender y hacer que las buenas leyes se guarden. Fin, por cierto, generoso y alto y digno de grande alabanza; pero no de tanta como merece aquel a que las armas atienden, las cuales tienen por objeto y fin la paz, que es el mayor bien que los hombres pueden desear en esta vida. Y así, las primeras buenas nuevas que tuvo el mundo y tuvieron los hombres fueron las que dieron los ángeles la noche que fue nuestro día, cuando cantaron en los aires: "Gloria sea en las alturas, y paz en la tierra a los hombres de buena voluntad"; . . . Esta paz es el verdadero fin de la guerra; que lo mesmo es decir armas que guerra. (389–90)

Don Quijote links the soldier, once again in the novel, to a higher, sacred calling. Here is an early formulation of the paradoxical idea espoused by military establishments that peace is their business. Arms may still bear some link to religion and to *divine* letters. But the thrust of Don Quijote's speech is to redefine—and in the process somewhat devalue—letters as purely human letters, and more specifically, to connect them to the career of the jurist and the magistrate.

Such was the usual construction given to the profession of letters by the end of the sixteenth century. "Letrado" perhaps primarily designated a lawyer, and the opposition of arms and letters evoked a social divide between a traditional martial aristocracy and a new legal elite that filled government positions in the early-modern state: what in France would be called the "noblesse de la robe," in Italy the "nobiltà della toga."[19] Like the church, this legal profession allowed some degree of social mobility: when Don Quijote takes up the subject again in Part Two of the novel (Chapter 24), he concedes that "more great families have been founded by letters than by arms" ["han fundado más mayorazgos las letras que las armas" (701; 718)]. He suggests as much here by describing the poverty of the student, even though he acknowledges that not all students are poor (388; 390). Through letters, the poor boy can make good.[20] And, Don Quijote concludes in Chapter 38, he is more likely to do so than the soldier who is most likely to meet his death, however honorable and glorious it may be, in battle (390; 391–92).

This redefinition of letters as a secular career leading to fortune and social position prepares the way for the Captive's Tale that immediately follows (Chapters 39–41) and the further story of Captain Viedma's brother and his family (42–45) that follows in turn. Just as Don Quijote's long set speech on the Golden Age in Chapter 11 precedes the pastoral episode of Grisóstomo and Marcela (12–14), so here his discourse on arms and letters precedes the Captive's story—which the Curate will later compare to an old wives' tale—of the three brothers of the Viedma family who set out to make their fortunes in the world. To be sure, they come of blue blood from León, and their father, a former soldier, lives the aristocratic life of liberality—that is, he lives beyond his means and is impoverishing himself. So the sons, who imitate their father's generosity by giving him back part of their inheritance, must find their own ways in the world.

The sons are instructed by their father to choose among the three vocations summed up in the Spanish proverb: "Iglesia o mar o casa real":

> If you want to be powerful and wealthy, follow the Church, or go to sea and become a merchant, or take service with kings in their palaces . . . one of you should pursue letters, another commerce, and the third should serve the king in his wars because it is difficult to obtain a place in his household, and although war does not bring much wealth it gradually brings great fame and renown. (394)

> Quien quisiere valer y ser rico, siga, o la Iglesia, o navegue, ejercitando el arte de la mercancía, o entre a servir a los reyes en sus casas . . . uno de vosotros

siguiese las letras, el otro la mercancía, y el otro serviese al rey en la guerra, pues es dificultoso entrar a servirle en su casa; que ya que la guerra no dé muchas riquezas, suele dar mucho valor y mucha fama. (396)

These three careers repeat the three callings described earlier by Lotario—ecclesiastic, merchant, and soldier—and we can see how that passage inscribed within the "fictional" tale of the "Curioso impertinente" now becomes actualized in the "real" world of the novel. The difference here is that all three—including the churchman's—are now described as worldly careers whose aim is wealth and power. The soldier's career may be distinguished on a higher level than the other two, but the fame and renown he seeks are worldly nonetheless—and Lotario's soldier, we also remember, was motivated by human fame as well as by heavenly glory.

The story of the Viedma brothers, moreover, conforms to Don Quijote's discourse on arms and letters by shifting the category of letters away from an ecclesiastical profession already conceived in primarily secular terms to the profession of law. One of the brothers (Cervantes is inconsistent as to whether it is the youngest or middle one) "said that he wanted to follow the Church or finish his studies in Salamanca" ["dijo que quería seguir la Iglesia, o irse a acabar sus comenzados estudios a Salamanca" (394; 397)]. The sentence is remarkably subtle and seems to enact the shift in which I am interested. Studies at Salamanca could lead to a career in the Church—Sansón Carrasco, bachelor of Salamanca, appears headed for one in Part Two. But the "or" suggests an alternative career in letters, and, in fact, when we meet this brother, who arrives at the inn shortly after the Captive has finished his tale, we find that he has studied the law and become a judge; he is on his way to Mexico, where he will sit as the king's "oidor" on the supreme court (42). The opposition between arms and letters is played out in the Viedma family in the careers of the gallant Captain, who returns penniless to Spain from his captivity in Algiers, and his brother the Judge who pursued "letters, in which God and my own exertions have raised me to the position in which you see me" ["las letras, en las cuales Dios y mi diligencia me han puesto en el grado que me veis" (435; 437)]. The Judge speaks of his worldly rise with the satisfaction of the self-made man.

What early in the novel thus begins, at least in the nostalgic imagination of Don Quijote, as a choice between two holy vocations—fighting knights and praying clerics—has, through the progressive unfolding of the motif of arms and letters, been reconfigured into a more modern choice among thoroughly secular careers. The noble father of the Viedma brothers, too, looks backward with his proverbial wisdom, but the Church is no longer the only—perhaps not even the primary—destination for the "letrado." The full extent of this secularization is suggested by the third, absent brother, the merchant.[21] He is absent from the scene of the novel, and he finds no place in Don Quijote's opposition of arms and letters as the two possible careers that a man of honor can follow. Yet this brother, and the worldly means—money—that he has at his disposal, are in fact crucial to Judge Viedma's story. In the next sentence, the Judge tells us:

> My younger brother is in Peru, so wealthy, that with what he has sent to my father and to me he has fully repaid the portion he took with him and has even given my father enough to satisfy his natural prodigality. Thanks to him, I have been able to follow my studies with more becoming fashion and authority, and so to reach my present position. (435)

> Mi menor hermano está en el Pirú, tan rico, que con lo que ha enviado a mi padre y a mí ha satisfecho bien la parte que él se llevó, y aun dado a las manos de mi padre con que poder hartar su liberalidad natural; y yo, ansimesmo, he podido con más decencia y autoridad tratarme en mis estudios, y llegar al puesto en que me veo. (437)

Having chosen the career whose aim—as Lotario earlier defined it—is the "goods of fortune," this brother has amassed a fortune in the colonial trade, money that, in fact, finances and makes possible both his father's generous way of life as an old-fashioned aristocratic man of arms *and*, perhaps more significantly, the Judge's own career as man of letters. The Judge did not live the life of the impoverished student described earlier by Don Quijote; his brother's money helped give him "authority" and it may have helped him to buy a lower court office (royal judgeships themselves were not for sale). Nor, he now acknowledges, is he entirely self-made: the repetition within two sentences, "me han puesto en el grado que me veis . . . y llegar al puesto en que me veo," leaves the reader to decide just how much of Judge Viedma's prominence in the legal profession is due to his own "diligencia," how much to the money that flowed in from the New World and allowed him to cut a dignified figure.

In the absent *perulero* brother the novel *Don Quijote* acknowledges, without quite being able to represent on its fictional stage, a modern mercantile capitalism that has brought about a new social fluidity. The moneyed economy has opened new avenues for social advancement, including Spain's colonial system that links together the two Viedma brothers, the soon-to-be Mexican Judge as well as the Peruvian merchant. In the third brother, the gallant Captain who goes East rather than West to fight the traditional religious enemy of Islam, Cervantes, the survivor of Lepanto, may still try to invest soldiery with higher, more disinterested values; if the soldier is not fighting as a crusader, he does at least pursue valor and fame. But, as I shall argue in Chapter Three, the money that ransoms the Captive and that he and his fellow Christians try to carry off from Zoraida's father in Algiers marks the novelist's simultaneous awarenesss of the extent to which wordly motives now infiltrate all professions.[22]

The debate between arms and letters that runs through through Part One of *Don Quijote*, taken up by apparently disparate episodes that are thus unexpectedly linked together, contains an implicit narrative of modernity. It eventually introduces commerce as a third term that cannot be fitted into the traditional opposition of martial versus clerical careers; yet the monetary forces and secular spirit of an emergent capitalism come to dominate and transform the nature of those careers and of the larger social order. The selfless knight and churchman, the imaginative projections of a receding feudal order cited by Don Quijote toward the opening of the novel, now have their modern, mercenary counterparts in the soldier and judge. Part Two of *Don Quijote* will take up this opposition of arms and letters in the opposition of Don Quijote himself to Sancho Panza, when the latter takes up his position as governor and judge and, as an illiterate "letrado," briefly accomplishes the most dramatic social ascent chronicled by the novel.[23]

Luscinda at the Window

My second example of how Cervantes links the motifs of Part One of *Don Quijote* is much more briefly told. It occurs in the space of two pages in the middle of Cardenio's story of his erotic woes in Chapter 27, and concerns two moments by the barred window of the house of his beloved Luscinda. The first records Cardenio's last conversation with Luscinda; she is troubled and her eyes fill with tears. Cardenio contrasts the moment with his recollection of earlier happier meetings by the window, always conducted, he notes, with propriety:

> the greatest freedom I permitted myself was to take, almost by force, one of her lovely white hands and to press it to my lips as best I could, despite the narrowness of the bars that separated us. (268)

> y a lo que más se estendía mi desenvoltura era a tomarle, casi por fuerza, una de sus bellas y blancas manos, y llegarla a mi boca, según daba lugar la estrecheza de una baja reja que nos dividía. (266)

The second passage comes a paragraph later, when Cardenio tells us how a letter from Luscinda was delivered to him: the bearer had passed by her window and been asked, as a Christian ["si sois cristiano"] to take the letter to the absent Cardenio. Luscinda added a further incentive:

> 'And in case you want money to do it, take what you find wrapped in this handkerchief.' 'With these words,' the messenger went on, 'she threw out of

the window a handkerchief in which were wrapped a hundred reals, this gold ring that I am wearing, and the letter that I have given you . . .' (269)

"y para que no os falte comodidad de poderlo hacer, tomad lo que va en este pañuelo."—Y diciendo esto, me arrojó por la ventana un pañuelo, donde venían atados cien reales y esta sortija de oro que aquí traigo, con esa carta que os he dado . . ." (267)

The memory of kissing Luscinda's hands through the railing, the handkerchief filled with coins she throws down from her window to the messenger: neither of these details is strictly necessary to Cardenio's story. But the first links the story backward in the novel to the model chivalric romance that Don Quijote tells to Sancho in Chapter 21, where a princess newly enamored by the knight-errant who has come to stay at her father's castle meets him for a nocturnal tryst; she will "give her white hands through the railing to the knight, who will kiss them a thousand times and bathe them with his tears" ["dará sus blancas manos por la reja al caballero, el cual se las besará mil veces, y se las bañará en lágrimas" (205; 198)]. The second looks forward to Chapter 40 and to the moment in the Captive's Tale when Zoraida lowers from *her* window a cloth ["lienzo"] filled with coins to Captain Viedma and his fellow companions in their captivity in Algiers; she, too, is searching for a Christian (405; 408).

The effects of this juxtaposition of episodes in the novel are complicated. First of all, it places the genre of the story of Cardenio, Luscinda, and Cardenio's rival, Don Fernando—an erotic novella—somewhere between the stereotypes of chivalric romance that fill Don Quijote's imagination and the "true history" of the Captive's Tale and, perhaps more specifically, to the reality principle that lends the tale its verisimilitude: the presence of money. Thus here, too, *Don Quijote* seems to be telling, on the level of literary history, a story of modernity, the transition of fiction itself from the fantasy world of chivalry, the literature of an outmoded feudal past, to the depiction of lived experience in a modern materialistic world, the new realm of the novel that Cervantes is inventing. Cardenio's kissing Luscinda's white hand is a gesture of old-fashioned romance and suggests something of the unreal, excessively literary quality of his love for her. It links him and the penitence he imposes upon himself to Don Quijote the lover of Dulcinea, the lady who is almost exclusively the creature of Don Quijote's literature-fed imagination. On the other hand, Cardenio is tied by money to the real world: the hundred reals that Luscinda wraps in her handkerchief ["pañuelo"] recall the very first appearance of Cardenio himself in the novel in Chapter 23, not in person, but in the form of his traveling bag that contains four shirts of Holland linen and a hundred "escudos" wrapped in a little cloth or handkerchief ["pañizuelo" (222; 216)], money—it may or may not be the same money—that Sancho happily appropriates. Here, too, Cervantine interlace is at work, for the first innkeeper whom Don Quijote meets in Chapter 3 advises him to carry money and clean shirts (70; 49), and the knight is careful to do so (96; 79) as he prepares in Chapter 7 for his second sally. Even when Cardenio goes mad for love, he is similarly prudent enough to pack the necessities. Cardenio's money, moreover, acquires a life of its own in the novel, for in Chapter 3 of the Part Two Sansón Carrasco states that many readers of Part One want to know what Sancho did with it: "for it is one of the substantial points that is missing in the work" ["que es uno de los puntos sustanciales que faltan en la obra" (551; 564). Money, Cervantes punningly asserts, is a matter of substance in his novelistic world.

The Two Loves of Don Quijote

These two examples of Cervantes's technique of interlacing together the thematic motifs and episodes of his novel are themselves related by the similar stories they tell about the arrival of a modern world reshaped and increasingly dominated by money. *Don Quijote* is a novel whose central character chooses to reject the modern world, to turn back the clock and to live in a idealized and fabulous realm of feudal chivalry derived from the romances he consumes. Don Quijote has a weaker sense of the anachronism he is committing than has the second innkeeper in Chapter 32, who believes just as firmly as the mad hidalgo in the literal truth of the chivalric romances, but who acknowledges that knight-errantry is no longer the custom ["ahora no se usa lo que se usaba en aquel tiempo" (324; 325)]. At times Don Quijote speaks of "reviving" ["resucitar" (186; 188)] chivalry and a lost golden age (Part One, Chapter 20); at the beginning of Part Two, on the other hand, he appears to believe that there are other knights-errant than he still wandering across Spain (Chapter 1). Through its hero who wants to live in the past, even or especially because it is an imaginary past, Cervantes's novel depicts the factual reality of the modern present.

Don Quijote's nostalgic, anarchic impulses—manifested above all in his refusal to pay money for his stays at inns and his claimed exemption from the king's laws that is symbolically enacted in his freeing of the galley slaves in Chapter 22—are what make visible the imprisoning bars of this reality, and Don Quijote himself is literally imprisoned in his cage and escorted home by the king's troopers at the end of Part One. (As we shall see in Chapter Three, it is a triumph of the novel and of its method of interlace to suggest that the inn itself is a kind of prison from which only money—i.e., paying one's bills—can allow one to escape.) What Don Quijote rides up against is not only the material solidity of windmills but the social arrangements of a moneyed economy and the nation-state.[24]

My examples suggest, furthermore, a progressive narrative unfolding in Part One that brings the novel from a nostalgic evocation of earlier social conditions and values (the knight and the monk as sacred vocations; the hand of the idealized lady) to the conditions and values of modernity that supersede them (the soldier, the judge, and the merchant as secular careers of worldly success; the hand of the lady that contains a packet of money). This progress is written large in Part One by the sequence that moves from its two main clusters of interlaced narratives, each organized around a separate chivalric-erotic fantasy of Don Quijote himself. These clusters will, respectively, be the focus of my next two chapters.

The first, which I want to label the "Dulcinea" cluster, comprises the remarkably closely interlaced stories of Cardenio, Luscinda, and Don Fernando and of the "Curioso impertinente," as well as the earlier pastoral story of Marcela and Grisóstomo; these stories of women variously idealized and victimized by the egotistic male imagination and the cult of male honor all comment on Don Quijote's apparently selfless worship of Dulcinea, his ideal lady who may or not exist. The second, the "Princess Micomicona" cluster, includes the Captive's Tale, the story of Don Luis and Clara, and the story of Leandra, and it comments on Don Quijote's project, which he outlines to Sancho in Chapter 21, of marrying the daughter of a king and ascending to the throne himself: his project of making himself emperor. This scheme seems about to be realized when Dorotea, disguised as the Princess Micomicona, promises to marry Don Quijote after he has defeated the giant who is oppressing her kingdom.

The fantasies involving Dulcinea and "Princess Micomicona" are both, to be sure, fantasies of self-aggrandizement and omnipotence—the peerlessness of Dulcinea makes her chosen knight (or the knight who chooses *her*) without peer, while the princess raises him to royalty—but the latter has an evident social correlative where the former does not. In the first "Dulcinea" narrative cluster, the lady is the object of intersubjective rivalry among men all conceived more or less as social equals—for Don Quijote, Dulcinea is the token by which he surpasses other, similar knights-errant—and these stories may thus look historically backward to what Jacob Burckhardt called the "medieval caste sense of honor" that preceded the more fluid and confused arrangements of rank and class that characterize the modern society of Burckhardt's Renaissance.[25] In the second "Micomicona" cluster, the lady is both the trophy and, in part, the cause of an advancement in worldly fortune, and these stories belong to a world of social ambition and mobility—and to the marriage-and-money plot of the novel, the new genre of this new, modern world.[26]

TABLE 1.1
Dulcinea vs. "Princess Micomicona"

Chapter		
12	D	(Marcela)
13	D	(Don Quijote describes Dulcinea; Marcela)
14	D	(Marcela)
16	M	(Don Quijote, Maritornes, and the Inn-Castle)
21	M	(Don Quijote's fantasy of the chivalric career)
23–24	D	(Cardenio's story)
25–26	D	(Don Quijote describes Dulcinea; Don Quijote's penance)
27	D	(Cardenio's story)
28	M	(Dorotea's story)
29–30	M	(Dorotea as Princess Micomicona)
33–34	D	("Curioso impertinente")
35	M	(Don Quijote and the wineskins)
35–36	D	("Curioso impertinente"; reunion of the lovers)
37–41	M	(Captive's Tale)
42	M	(The Judge)
43–44	M	(Luis and Clara)
47, 50	M	(Canon of Toledo and Don Quijote on social mobility)
51	M	(Leandra and Vicente de la Rosa)
51	D	(Eugenio and Anselmo as shepherd-suitors of Leandra)

It is possible to map these two clusters of stories—those organized around Don Quijote's ideal love for Dulcinea, those organized around his fantasy of a rise to power and riches and its supposed embodiment in "Princess Micomicona"—across the narrative of Part One and to see how they intertwine. The first cluster is marked D, the second M in Table 1.1.

If the two clusters of stories alternate in the first two-thirds of the narrative of Part One, this diagram suggests that from the Captive's Tale on, the second cluster of stories succeeds and very largely replaces the first. The novel and its stories, that is, come increasingly to recognize the importance of money and class mobility. They do so in ironic counterpoint to Don Quijote's own progress in the novel: his mobility as a knight-errant virtually ceases as the action stops at the inn and he is imprisoned in his cage in Chapter 46, five chapters after the Captive tells of his own liberation from captivity in Algiers. The larger narrative plan of Part One thus seems to follow a historical trajectory, traced in its stories of erotic intrigue, that moves from the idealized feudal past of Don Quijote's chivalric fantasies to the mentality and social arrangements of Cervantes's present-day Spain. Tales about lovers driven by old-fashioned notions of jealousy and honor are succeeded by others that bring us closer to the way that we live and love now, stories of modern desire.

It is not surprising that when Don Quijote is asked to choose between his two fantasies—as he is in Chapter 30, when Sancho urges him to marry Princess Micomicona immediately then and there (and keep Dulcinea as a mistress on the side), and still earlier in Chapter 16, when he imagines that the serving girl Maritornes is the princess of his dreams coming to a nocturnal assignation with him—he professes his unswerving devotion to Dulcinea. The ideal lady Dulcinea is not only a censoring device to keep real women at a distance for a character who we may begin to suspect has never had any sexual experience at all. The very disinterestedness of Don Quijote's love for Dulcinea and his simultaneous spurning of the wealth and power offered by the "princess"—his rejection of the poor-boy-makes-good, social-success story thinly veiled in chivalric garb—represent his spurning of the conditions of modernity. Don Quijote will not, finally, be in it for the money.

If Cervantes uses Don Quijote to criticize the mercenary motives and materialistic values of the modern world into which he is cast, he nonetheless skewers his hero's efforts to transcend that world: Don Quijote's attempt to return to the supposed ethos of an earlier time and to dedicate himself to his ideal lady. Cervantes does so not so much by bringing the knight into contact with the demands of a real, material existence; for, as we have just seen, Don Quijote can still choose in such a case to cling stubbornly to his ideals, choosing Dulcinea over Micomicona. Rather, Cervantes discredits Don Quijote's apparently selfless idealization of Dulcinea on its own terms by revealing just how selfish it actually is, how much this idolatrous cult of the lady feeds Don Quijote's male ego. Through the parallels among their interpolated stories, Cervantes criticizes Don Quijote as lover of Dulcinea by associating him with the monstrously self-centered lovers Cardenio, Grisóstomo, and the Anselmo of the "Curioso impertinente"—all madmen in their own way. Perhaps the most remarkable feature of this association is the way in which it conversely links these stories of male jealousy to the *premodern* mentality of Don Quijote's project. The code of male honor itself, so dear to the Spanish cultural and literary imagination, is viewed as a holdover from an aristocratic feudal past that is gradually being replaced in that imagination by the modern allure of wealth and the wordly career.

Part One of Cervantes's novel does not have much good to say for this new ethos that it represents in terms of marrying for money instead of for love. It may share, that is, many of its hero's apprehensions that the modern, moneyed world is bereft of heroism and human values. But, unlike Don Quijote, it has little use for the feudal values of the world that preceded it. Ten years later, as we shall see in Part Two of the novel, Cervantes and Don Quijote together begin to make peace with and discover positive worth in the conditions of modern society. Part One of *Don Quijote* is interested in depicting, as the very sequence of its episodes suggests—the succession of the "Dulcinea" by the "Princess Micomicona" cluster— how the atavistic values of an earlier social order come into conflict with and gradually yield to a modern social ethos, and how this shift is registered in a refocusing of human desire itself. It charts the emergence of modern times.

TWO

"DULCINEA"

W HAT MAN WOULD STAND idly by and watch the woman he loves
commit suicide when he thinks she is doing it for his sake? Just
try to find one who would not, *Don Quijote* responds. For
such men are the rule, not the exception, in the tales interpolated into the
early part of the narrative of *Don Quijote*, Part One. Cardenio watches
from behind a tapestry in the house of his beloved Luscinda, waiting for
her to retrieve the dagger she has promised to conceal in her bosom in
order to stab herself rather than wed his rival, Don Fernando; when she
fails to do so, he rushes away in a maddened rage (Chapter 27). Hidden
in the closet of his own house, Anselmo, the protagonist of the inset story
of the "Curioso impertinente," watches as his wife, Camila, citing the
example of Lucretia, stabs herself (although not fatally), and he goes away
with great satisfaction (Chapter 34). There is, of course, an ironic counterpoint in these two stories carefully juxtaposed by Cervantes's art of interlace: we subsequently learn that Luscinda intended to kill herself and left
a suicide note, but fainted before she had a chance to complete the deed
(286; 286); Camila is putting on a carefully prepared charade for the
husband she has, in fact, betrayed with his best friend, Lotario. But the
monstrous egotism of Cardenio and Anselmo, content to watch their ladies sacrifice themselves, remains the constant in both episodes—and their
respective rivals, Don Fernando and Lotario, behave hardly better.

Such male egotism, its relationship to codes of love and honor, and its
concomitant victimization of women are the focus of these stories that so
intricately mirror each other. It connects them, in turn, to the story of
Grisóstomo and Marcela—where it is the man who actually does commit
suicide, in an ultimate egotistical act, when his suit is rejected. Most important, it links all three of these interpolated stories to Don Quijote's
love for Dulcinea. Paradoxically, the mad hidalgo has a better understanding than these supposedly sane characters of how much his imaginary
lady is precisely that: a projection of his self-centered imagination.

In Chapter 25, Dulcinea momentarily appears to possess a real being,
when Don Quijote reveals to Sancho that she is none other than Aldonza
Lorenzo, native of El Toboso; we are told in Chapter 1 that Don Quijote
at some earlier time had loved her from afar. But no sooner has Dulcinea

materialized in Aldonza than Don Quijote turns her back into a figment of his literature-fed imagination. In an apparent dirty joke in Chapter 25, Don Quijote goes on to tell Sancho that "for what I want of Dulcinea of El Toboso, she is as good as the greatest princess in the land" (245; 249). But Don Quijote does not want Dulcinea, as the preceding anecdote he tells of the widow and the lay brother would suggest, for sexual satisfaction. Rather, he treats her as the poets he goes on to describe treat their mistresses, poets who for the most part invent the Petrarchan ladies they celebrate under pastoral names ("the Amaryllises, the Phyllises, the Silvias") in their verses—"las más se las fingen"—in order to be taken to be lovers and for men *who possess worth for being so* ["porque los tengan por enamorados y por hombres que tienen valor para serlo" (246; 246)].

Don Quijote creates the Dulcinea he loves in order to author and give value to his own self-image as lover.[1] He does so because, as he thinks to himself in Chapter 1 and then repeats in his conversation with Vivaldo in Chapter 13, there can be no knight without a lady to love, that such a knight would not be held to be a "legitimate knight but a bastard" ["no sería tenido por legítimo caballero, sino por bastardo" (133; 120)]. The lady is the attribute that legitimizes the true knight both in the eyes of others and, in the case of Dulcinea, in the eyes of the knight Don Quijote himself. And because Don Quijote aspires to be the greatest knight of all, Dulcinea must correspondingly be the greatest of ladies. He tells Vivaldo that "since she is my queen and mistress," her quality must be at least that of a princess, her beauty superhuman:

> for in her are realized all the impossible and chimerical attributes of beauty that poets assign to their ladies; that her hair is gold; her forehead the Elysian fields; her eyebrows rainbows, her eyes suns; her cheeks roses, her lips corals, pearls her teeth; alabaster her neck, marble her bosom, ivory her hands (134)

> pues en ella se vienen a hacer verdaderos todos los imposibles y quiméricos atributos de belleza que los poetas dan a sus damas: que sus cabellos son oro, su frente campos elíseos, sus cejas arcos de cielo, sus ojos soles, sus mejillas rosas, sus labios corales, perlas sus dientes, alabastro su cuello, mármol su pecho, marfil sus manos. (121)

Here, too, in this Petrarchan *blason* of the beauty of Dulcinea, her body itemized part by part, Don Quijote demonstrates a sophisticated awareness that his beloved is a construction of fantasy, an impossible and chimerical literary lady.[2] She is constructed the way she is, however, to be suitable for the perfect knight that Don Quijote himself wishes to be. The list of comparisons that eventually transforms Dulcinea into a series of precious gems and stones suggests that she is, like Petrarch's Laura, an idol, and when we worship idols, the things made of our own hands, we are, in effect, worshiping ourselves.

Don Quijote has fewer illusions on this score than do the male lovers—Cardenio, Don Fernando, Anselmo, Lotario, Grisóstomo—who surround him in the narrative of Part One of the novel. Cervantes makes obvious the egotism of his mad central character in order to comment on the folly of those lovers. He gets a certain amount of comic mileage out of the gap between the idealized image of Dulcinea and the coarse Aldonza Lorenzo whom Sancho describes in Chapter 25 and again in Chapter 31 (though in the second case Sancho reports a meeting that never took place, and his version of Dulcinea is thus as fictional as Don Quijote's own.)[3] But this gap may be no wider than that which exists between the image that Cardenio nurtures of Luscinda, that Anselmo nurtures of Camila, that Grisóstomo nurtures of Marcela—all images gratifying to their own self-love—and the real women involved. All three men, in fact, will turn those women into pastoral-Petrarchan poetic mistresses: Cardenio writes an accusatory sonnet to Luscinda, giving her the name of Phyllis (217); Anselmo encourages Lotario to write sonnets to Camila, addressing her as Chloris (348); Grisóstomo literally reenacts the role of the lovelorn pastoral swain. They do so, however, without Don Quijote's understanding that the unreal Dulcinea is a fantasy, part of a self-contained game that boosts his ego, and they accordingly victimize the real women on whom they project their own self-serving fantasies. Don Quijote's love for Dulcinea thus provides a model for understanding the selfishness of the romantic loves of these other male characters, and the relative harmlessness of the former—there is, in fact, no lady for Don Quijote to harm—contrasts with the destructive consequences for women in their stories.

But this model of understanding does not go in only one direction. With their exploration of male rivalry and jealousy, the mirroring love stories criticize, in return, the aggressively competitive dimension of Don Quijote's egotism and of the chivalric system he espouses. Cardenio, Anselmo, and Grisóstomo are obsessed as much with defeating their male rivals as with the women they profess to love. For Don Quijote, victory over one's rival is the whole point of chivalry. The self-aggrandizing honor to which Don Quijote the knight aspires turns all others into enemies to be triumphed over, and this structure is replicated and critically examined in the stories of love and honor that are juxtaposed to his career in the first half of Part One of the novel. In this specular relationship, to which I shall return at the end of this chapter, the competing lovers can be seen to be the counterpart of the knight and to perpetuate the emulative system of chivalry and its premodern ways of thinking into Cervantes's contemporary world and into its literary genres—the novella and the pastoral romance. They are themselves so many versions of the Don Quijote they laugh at as a walking anachronism.

Cardenio and Anselmo

The stories of two love triangles, the struggle of the novel's own characters Cardenio and Don Fernando over Luscinda (Chapters 23–24, 27–28, 36) and the struggle of Anselmo and Lotario over Camila inside the story of the "Curioso impertinente," the tale that is found in a traveler's trunk and read at the inn in Chapters 33–35, represent the clearest and most tightly structured instance of narrative interlace in *Don Quijote*. Nonetheless, the parallels between Cardenio's and Anselmo's stories have not been analyzed in depth by previous critical commentary.[4] The "Curioso impertinente" is placed inside the story of Cardenio, Don Fernando, and Luscinda, which is itself resolved in Chapter 36, right after the interpolated tale comes to an end. The thematic likenesses and oppositions between the two stories are initially clear. Both are stories of what René Girard, who offers some classic remarks on the "Curioso impertinente," calls "mimetic" or "triangular" desire.[5] They depict a man desiring a woman who is already desired by another man, desiring her, in fact, because of the other man's desire for her. To his surprise, Cardenio finds that his friend Don Fernando has secretly become his rival for Luscinda, and he mistakenly believes that Luscinda has also betrayed him and agreed to marry Don Fernando; eventually he realizes that Luscinda remained true to him and regains her in the comic ending of the story. The married Anselmo actually asks his bosom friend Lotario to court his wife, Camila, in order to test her, and he mistakenly believes that she has rejected Lotario's suit; eventually Anselmo learns the truth of his wife's adultery with his friend and dies of grief in the tragic resolution of the tale.[6] We can chart the parallels, the repetition of motifs, between the two stories, and, in doing so, give some idea of Cervantes's narrative artistry in setting them into place: see table 2.1.

Cervantes capitalizes upon the difference between the continuous third-person narration of the "Curioso impertinente" in linear, chronological succession and the fragmentary telling of the story of Cardenio and Luscinda, recounted initially through the letters and poems of Cardenio that Don Quijote and Sancho find in the Sierra Morena and then in first-person flashbacks by Cardenio and then Dorotea. We can usefully invoke Viktor Shklovsky's distinction between the *fabula*, the events of a story as they unfold in temporal succession, and *syuzhet*, the order in which they are presented to us by the ordering of the literary text, to understand this

TABLE 2.1
The Interlacing of the "Curioso impertinente"

Cardenio-Luscinda-Don Fernando				Curioso impertinente	
			322	The trunk is opened: *Life of Gonzalo de Cordoba* (33)	
223	Cardenio's Poem to Fíli		348	Lotario's poem to Clori	
217	(23)		348	(34)	
224	Cardenio's letter		370	Anselmo's letter	
218	(23)		370	(35)	
235	DQ interrupts		363	DQ interrupts	
231	(24)		363	(35)	
267	Don Fernando offers to broker marriage		326	Lotario brokers marriage	
265	(27)		327	(33)	
270	Luscinda's letter		344	Camilla's letter	
267	(27)		345	(34)	
271	Cardenio hides		355	Anselmo hides	
269	(27)		355	(34)	
272	Luscinda:"I do," faints		359	Camilla:stabs herself, faints	
270	(27)		360	(34)	
273	Cardenio leaves city for countryside		368	Anselmo leaves city for countryside	
271	(27)		369	(35)	
379	Luscinda in convent		368	Camilla in convent	
380	(36)		368	(35)	
Don Quijote interrupts Cardenio's story shortly after it begins.			370	Lotario dies in battle	
			371	between Lautrec and Gonzalo de Cordoba	
			Don Quijote interrupts *Curioso impertinente* shortly before it ends. (35)		

difference between the two narrative modes of the stories.[7] In the "Curioso impertinente," fabula and syuzhet correspond almost exactly. In the Cardenio-Luscinda story, the two are set at odds, as we can observe when we reverse our chart in table 2.2. The events of this latter story are narrated out of their chronological sequence, leaving gaps of information and loose ends that have to be filled in and pieced together by the reader—and by the characters themselves.

Through these contrasted modes of narration, one straightforward, the other fragmentary and scrambled, Cervantes appears to dramatize the difference between the neatness of the stories told by "literature" and the

TABLE 2.2

	Curioso impertinente		Cardenio-Luscinda-Don Fernando
326	Lotario brokers marriage	267	Don Fernando offers to broker
327		265	marriage (27)
344	Camila's letter	270	Luscinda's letter
345		267	(27)
348	Lotario's poem to Clori	223	Cardenio's poem to Fili
348		217	(23)
355	Anselmo hides	271	Cardenio hides
355		269	(27)
359	Camila: stabs herself, faints	272	Luscinda: "I do,"
360		270	(27)
		286	Luscinda did have dagger
		286	concealed in her dress (28)
368	Camila in convent	379	Luscinda in convent
368		380	(36)
369	Anselmo leaves city for countryside	273	Cardenio leaves city for countryside
369		271	(27)
370	Anselmo's letter	224	Cardenio's letter
370		218	(23)

confused and incomplete stories that human beings actually experience.[8] The "Curioso impertinente" is set off as a work of literary art completely separate from the lived experience of the characters of the novel: the tale is pulled out of the trunk of the inn and is probably a work, we later learn in Chapter 47, by the author of the story found beside it, "Rinconete y Cortadillo"—that is, it is a work by Cervantes himself.[9] It recounts events through a third-person narrator who enjoys not only omniscience, but also a perspective on past events that are completed by the deaths of its protagonists, Anselmo, Lotario, and Camila. By contrast, the tale of Cardenio and Luscinda is encountered as it is still groping toward its ultimate end of marriage, and is told through characters who are deluded or in incomplete possession of the facts.

Our own stories, Cervantes suggests, do not make sense to us, or we positively misunderstand them as we live them. That is why we turn to literature to grasp what is happening to us and to recognize why we act in the ways that we do: to see our stories in terms of other stories, to see our lives *as* stories in the first place. Perhaps paradoxically, the "literary" characters in the "Curioso impertinente" appear to possess more pyschological depth and complexity than the "real" characters of the novel, because the all-knowing narrator of the tale can describe the inner thoughts of Anselmo, Camila, and Lotario *and* because, as we shall see, these protagonists themselves come to moments of self-recognition that elude Cardenio, Luscinda, Dorotea, and Don Fernando. But, of course, the latter are no less literary characters—indeed, they are very much stereotypes of wronged and star-crossed lovers in the novella tradition. The power of Cervantes's juxtaposition of the two stories largely depends on our perceiving the difference between two kinds of the novella itself: between a conventional novella that is criticized because it simplifies and thereby mystifies human experience (Cardenio, Luscinda) and a superior Cervantine novella—a "novela ejemplar"—that, in the "Curioso impertinente," investigates and exposes human motives. As in the larger novel, Cervantes here conducts his quarrel with literature itself; the moral stakes of this quarrel, as is the case with his deluded would-be knight, consist in the opposition of egotism and self-knowledge.

The story of Cardenio and Luscinda that unfolds in scattered pieces in the novel begins with literal fragments found by Don Quijote and Sancho in Cardenio's abandoned saddlebag: the poem that Cardenio has written to Luscinda, addressed with the pastoral name of Phyllis ("Fili"), and a letter that he has also written to her, accusing her of ingratitude and falsehood for having chosen Don Fernando and Don Fernando's wealth and position over him. When Don Quijote reads the sonnet and letters of Cardenio, he drily comments that they tell him little more than that its author is some rejected lover ["algún desdeñado amante" (224; 218)]; and since the letters are unsigned, they are all the more generic. Cervantes points here to the purely conventional nature of Cardenio's laments: one rejected literary lover is like any other. Cardenio seems to have gone mad for love according to a preexisting script, just as the mad hidalgo himself tries to reenact the chivalric romances he has read: but Cardenio, unlike Don Quijote, does not appear to know that he is doing so.

The parallel in the "Curioso impertinente" further suggests the artificiality and falseness of this literary passion. Lotario, who has by now seduced Camila, is encouraged by the unsuspecting Anselmo to continue his courtship of his wife by writing sonnets to her, giving her the pastoral name of Chloris ["Clori"]. In a direct echo of Cardenio's sonnet ["Presto habré de morir, que es lo más cierto" (217)], Lotario writes that he will die of love ["Yo sé que muero; y si no soy creído, / es más cierto el morir . . . (349)] because of the disdain of a beloved whom he, in fact, possesses. Lotario's sonnet is not only a piece of Petrarchan convention; it is an out-and-out lie, and a twofold one at that: Anselmo spurs Lotario to write the sonnet as part of what he thinks is a make-believe courtship of his wife; Lotario and Camila know that the real joke of the sonnet is on

Anselmo. The sonnet in the interpolated tale brings out in retrospect the potential inauthenticity of Cardenio's sonnet, both of its literary posturing and of the self-pity that inspires it.

But it is the juxtaposition of Cardenio's letter with the letter that corresponds to it in the "Curioso impertinente" that indicts the forlorn lover in the Sierra Morena. Having discovered the truth about Camila's relationship with Lotario and finding himself abandoned, Anselmo, like Cardenio, heads out of the city for the countryside, and there he pens a letter that he does not live to complete or send and that, like Cardenio's letter to Luscinda, is found by others. Again the textual echoes are unmistakable. Cardenio writes of the news of his death reaching Luscinda before the words of his complaints ["antes volverán a tus oídos las nuevas de mi muerte que las razones de mis quejas" (224; 218)]. Anselmo also writes of the news of his death reaching Camila ["Si las nuevas de mi muerte llegaren a los oídos de Camila" (370; 370)]. But Anselmo does not complain of Camila. In his letter he pardons his wife and confesses that he was the maker of his own dishonor—"yo fui el fabricador de mi deshonra" (370; 370). This moment of lucid self-knowledge and self-condemnation, gained only at the moment of death, directly contrasts with Cardenio's letter, in which Cardenio writes that he does not so much pardon Luscinda as decline to "take the vengeance that I do not want" ["y yo no tome venganza de lo que no deseo" (224; 218)], and in which he casts blame on Luscinda and her womanly frailty, on Don Fernando and his wealth—on anyone and anything except himself. The contrast is only heightened by Cervantes's placement of Cardenio's letter at the *beginning* of the latter's story—before we meet Cardenio himself—and Anselmo's letter at the *end* of the "Curioso impertinente."

As these initial samples suggest, the effect of the interlacing with the "Curioso impertinente" is to demystify the story of Cardenio's betrayed love and abjection, to disclose the levels of self-dramatization and self-deception—and of self-love—in this suffering lover. Cardenio unwittingly creates a rival for himself when he sings Luscinda's praises to Don Fernando, shows her off to him, and—in another instance that suggests the way that reading and literature mediate desires—allows him to peruse one of his beloved's letters in which she begs Cardenio to ask her father for permission to marry her (234–35; 230). Anselmo, by contrast, actually seeks to make his friend Lotario into his rival, if only, so Anselmo thinks, in play. At some level, Anselmo wants Lotario to desire Camila, and he turns his wife into the prize of a game of male rivalry designed to gratify Anselmo's ego when Camila will choose him as winner over his best friend: what she appears to do when she plunges a dagger into her breast while the concealed Anselmo looks on and does nothing to stop her. But what Anselmo himself acknowledges from the outset to be a strange, unheard-of desire ["un deseo tan estraño y tan fuera del uso común" (328; 330)] is, we recognize as we look back at the parallel story, not so uncommon after all: it is shared, whether consciously or not, by Cardenio, who validates his love for Luscinda by making her desirable in the eyes of another man: he wants Don Fernando to approve his choice. Anselmo had originally sought the approval of his friend Lotario to marry Camila and made him his emissary to her father, in some ways already making him the mediator of his desire and the potential rival that he will subsequently ask Lotario explicitly to act out; when Don Fernando offers to broker Cardenio's marriage with Luscinda's father, Cardenio eagerly agrees.[10]

And Cardenio, it will turn out, is no less eager to play the game of male rivalry; for otherwise, why does he not step out from behind the tapestry to stop Don Fernando from marrying Luscinda? Cardenio subseqently accuses himself of cowardice for not stepping forward (272; 270), but that is itself a mystification of his motives. With the same impertinent curiosity that brought about Anselmo's downfall, he waits to see Luscinda choose him over Don Fernando, even if that means her killing herself as she has promised him. He is bitterly disappointed when she fails to do so.

Cardenio, Quijote, Amadis, Orlando

Yet Cardenio finds a way to gratify his ego nonetheless. He acknowledges that he lost the use of his reason after he heard Luscinda utter the fatal words of consent to marriage with Don Fernando ["Sí quiero"] just at the moment when he had instead expected her to draw her dagger to prove herself ["acreditarse"]. Mad or not, Cardenio takes a perverse satisfaction in avenging himself *on himself* in the wilderness of the Sierra Morena:

> so, instead of taking vengeance on my worse enemies (it would have been easy to do so, seeing that they were so ignorant of my presence,) I determined to take it on myself and execute on myself the penalty they so richly deserved, and even with greater severity than I should have used on them had I killed them on the spot, for death that is sudden ends all pain at once, whereas that which is long drawn out with tortures still slays but never brings life to an end. (273)

> y así, sin querer tomar venganza de mis mayores enemigos, que, por estar tan sin pensamiento mío, fuera fácil tomarla, quise tomarla de mi mano y ejecutar en mí la pena que ellos merecían, y aun quizá con más rigor del que con ellos se usara, si entonces les diera muerte, pues la que se recibe repentina, presto acaba la pena; mas la que se dilata con tormentos siempre mata, sin acabar la vida. (271)

Luscinda and Fernando are guilty and to blame, Cardenio says in this judicial conceit, but instead of punishing them, he will take on their punishment and in intensified form at that: a fate worse than death. Cardenio wallows and takes positive pleasure in his misery ["por mi gusto" (275; 273)]—and he willfully compounds it, as if by so doing he can aggrandize the wrong that has been done to him—and so aggrandize himself. If Luscinda would not kill herself for him, then he will show her up by his own self-destruction. He appears to forgo vengeance—now that it is too late—but, in fact, his suicidal course of action is an imaginary way of getting back at and shaming his enemies. By turning his impotent rage and spite against himself, however, Cardenio may merely demonstrate who has been the real object of his love all along.

Cardenio's going off to vindictive self-punishment and death in the mountains is contrasted, as we have seen, with the actions of Anselmo in the "Curioso impertinente," who, when he at last discovers Camila's unfaithfulness, leaves the city of Florence to die in the countryside, but who genuinely forgives his wife and acknowledges his own fault. But the self-punishing Cardenio also enters into a second pattern of interlace in *Don Quijote*; his story is juxtaposed with Don Quijote's own project, announced in Chapter 25, to undergo penance ["penitencia" (241; 237)] for the sake of Dulcinea in imitation of his literary models, Amadis and Orlando. Cardenio and Don Quijote memorably stare at each other, as if in a mirror, at the end of Chapter 23. If the contrast with Anselmo indicates Cardenio's lack of self-knowledge, the ensuing parallel that develops between the stricken, mad lover and the mad hidalgo who plays at being a stricken, mad lover suggests just how much gratification Cardenio can take in his abject suffering.

It is Cardenio himself who first describes his wandering in the Sierra Morena as a kind of penance imposed on him for his many sins ["cierta penitencia que por sus muchos pecados le había sido impuesta" (227; 222)] in a conversation that the old goatherd recounts to Don Quijote and Sancho in Chapter 23. This cue to the reader may also be a cue for Don Quijote himself to undertake two chapters later his penance for Dulcinea. Don Quijote is an equal opportunity imitator of others, of other characters he meets as well as of the chivalric heroes he encounters in his reading.[11] Earlier at the end of Chapter 12, he dreamed of Dulcinea in imitation of Grisóstomo and the other lovers of Marcela (128; 115). The love-madness Don Quijote stages in the Sierra Morena will, in fact, repeat several motifs of Cardenio's madness. The letter he writes for Sancho to carry to the ungrateful Dulcinea ["ingrata" (250; 247)] parallels the letter of Cardenio to the ungrateful Luscinda ["ingrata" (224; 218)] that is found in Cardenio's discarded saddlebag. Don Quijote, too, writes poetry to the absent Dulcinea (256; 252) as Cardenio writes poems to Luscinda

(223; 217); Don Quijote's stripping himself down ["Y desnudándose con toda la priesa los calzones, quedó en carnes y pañales" (253; 250)] in order to commit his "locuras" echoes the first appearance of the half-naked Cardenio ["iba desnudo . . . los muslos cubrían unos calzones, al parecer, de terciopelo leonado, mas tan hechos pedazos que por muchas partes se le descubrían las carnes" (225; 219–20)]; Don Quijote's somersaults (253–54; 250) are a comic version of the agile leaping from rock to rock that Cardenio performs in his madness (225, 229; 219, 224).

Cardenio, moreover, *already* imitates one of Don Quijote's dual *literary* models, the Orlando of the *Orlando furioso*: it is Orlando who goes mad and strips himself naked (OF23.133); the old goatherd tells how Cardenio attacks the shepherds in the Sierra Morena—and would have killed one ["le matara" 228; 223], had he not been restrained. Don Quijote later recounts how Orlando killed shepherds ["mató pastores" (242; 238); OF 24.4–6] in his raging madness. Most pertinently, Cardenio shares with Ariosto's hero the experience of betrayal in love: Luscinda, he thinks, has chosen Don Fernando over him as Orlando's beloved Angelica chose Medoro over the paladin. So Don Quijote, in choosing to imitate the jealous Orlando, may be imitating Cardenio at the same time.

But Don Quijote himself has a second model for his "penance" in the mountains: Amadis, the North Star among knights, whose example all those who follow chivalry should imitate. Cervantes's juxtaposition of Amadis and Orlando lies at the very center of his art and of his moral concerns. Amadis, so Don Quijote twice recounts, found himself disdained ["desdeñado" (241; 237, 255; 251)] by his lady, Oriana, and went off in book 2, chapter 48 of Rodríguez de Montalvo's *Amadís de Gaula* to do penance ["hacer penitencia" (241; 237)] in a hermitage on the Poor Rock ("Peña Pobre") under the assumed name of Beltenebros. As any seventeenth-century reader would have known, however, Amadis does not seek penance because he feels himself wronged by Oriana; quite the opposite: he has caused Oriana (mistakenly) to think that he has wronged her, betraying their love with another lady, the child princess Briolanja (2.40). Oriana has sent Amadis a letter (2.44) forbidding him to come into her presence, but it is Amadis's sense of having caused injury and displeasure to the woman he loves that sends him into his penitential sojourn with the hermit.[12]

When his squire Gandalin tries to console Amadis by pointing out that Oriana has been mistaken about his supposed infidelity and that he needs only to disabuse her, Amadis turns on him:

> My lady Oriana never erred in anything. And if I die it is with reason, not because I deserve it, but because thereby I carry out her wish and command. And if I did not know that you said it to comfort me, I would cut your head off.

Oriana, mi señora, nunca erró en cosa ninguna. Y si yo muero es con razón, no porque lo yo merezca, mas porque con ello cumplo su volontad y mando. Y si yo no entendiesse que por me conortar me lo has dicho, yo te tajaría la cabeça.[13] (2.48; 546)

Although Amadis may exculpate himself, he will not have his lady blamed; she remains perfect, and if he has caused her pain, even unintentionally, he must punish himself. This selfless, chivalric devotion of Amadis makes him a North Star indeed. He stands at one pole among the various peniten- tial and mad lovers of this episode: at one end of a spectrum of possible attitudes to the beloved lady which has the vindictively mad Orlando at its opposite extreme.

Amadis ← Don Quijote ↔ Cardenio → Orlando

The characters in the middle of this spectrum, Don Quijote and Cardenio, are shown choosing between these two models, between the penance of Amadis and the madness of Orlando. At the end of Chapter 25, Don Quijote has comically imitated Orlando by turning somersaults and exposing the lower parts of his body to Sancho, who rides away to avoid the distressing sight. At the beginning of Chapter 26, however, Don Qui- jote sits down to consider his options in soliloquy. Orlando, he acknowl- edges, had a cause to go mad, when confronted with the evidence that Angelica had slept with the lowborn Moor Medoro:

If he believed that this was true and that his lady had done him wrong, it is not to be wondered that he went mad. But how can I imitate him in his mad- ness without a similar cause? For I dare swear that my Dulcinea of El Toboso has never in her life seen a Moor in Moorish dress and that she is today as her mother brought her into the world, and I should do her a grave injury were I to imagine otherwise and go crazy after the manner of Orlando the Furious. On the other hand, I know that Amadis of Gaul, without ever losing his wits or committing crazy actions, won an unparalleled reputation as a lover, for as history relates, when he found himself slighted by his lady, Oriana, who had ordered him not to appear in her presence until such was her pleasure, he simply retired to the Peña Pobre in the company of a hermit, and there he wept to his heart's content until Heaven came to his aid in the midst of his greatest tribulation. Now if this is true—and it is—why do I now take the trouble to strip myself stark naked, give pain to these trees that have done me no harm, and trouble the clear water of these streams that must give me drink when I am thirsty? Long live the memory of Amadis, and let him be the model, as far as may be, of Don Quixote of La Mancha, of whom it shall be said what was said of that other one: that if he did not achieve great things, he died attempting them. If I am not rejected and scorned by Dulcinea of El Toboso, let it suffice, as I have said, that I am absent from her. (254–55)

y si él entendió que esto era verdad y que su dama le había cometido desaguisado, no hizo mucho en volverse loco; pero yo, ¿como puedo imitalle en las locuras, si no le imito en la ocasión dellas? Porque mi Dulcinea del Toboso osaré yo jurar que no ha visto en todos los días de su vida moro alguno, ansí como él es, en su mismo traje, y que se está hoy como la madre que la parió; y haríale agravio manifiesto si, imaginando otra cosa della, me volviese loco de aquel género de locura de Roldán el furioso. Por otra parte, veo que Amadís de Gaula, sin perder el juicio y sin hacer locuras, alcanzó tanta fama de enamorado como el que más; porque lo que hizo, según su historia, no fue más de que, por verse desdenado de su señora Oriana, que le había mandado que no pareciese ante su presencia hasta que fuese su voluntad, de que se retiró a la Peña Pobre en compañía de un ermitaño, y allí se hartó de llorar y de encomendarse a Dios, hasta que el cielo le acorrió, en medio de su mayor cuita y necesidad. Y si eso es verdad, como lo es, ¿para qué quiero yo tomar trabajo agora de desnudarme del todo, ni dar pesadumbre a estos árboles, que no me han hecho mal alguno? Ni tengo para qué enturbiar el agua clara destos arroyos, los cuales me han de dar de beber cuando tenga gana. Viva la memoria de Amadís, y sea imitado de don Quijote de la Mancha en todo lo que pudiere; del cual se dirá lo que del otro se dijo: que si no acabó grandes cosas, murió por acometellas; y si yo no soy desechado ni desdeñado de Dulcinea del Toboso, bástame, como ya he dicho, estar ausente della. (251)

In this richly humorous but ethically decisive moment, the madman Don Quijote resolves not to go mad for love, to choose Amadis rather than Orlando as his model.

His arguments contain a comic dash of pragmatic considerations. Does he really want to strip naked like Orlando—so far he has only gone halfway—and muddy the waters of the stream from which he needs to drink? These thoughts recall his initial resolution in the preceding chapter to imitate the penance of Amadis, because it is easier ["más fácil" (241; 237)] to imitate his hero in this than in killing monsters and routing armies. There is an element of rueful prudence—and Cervantine concern for novelistic verisimilitude—in Don Quijote's thinking, a regard for life and limb that may be the result of the various beatings he has suffered in earlier chapters at the hands of the Yanguesans, the shepherds, the galley convicts, and Cardenio himself.

But the mad Don Quijote also makes sane calculations about what the choice between Amadis and Orlando would mean about the lady he worships.[14] That Dulcinea is only an imaginary lady is both beside the point and the very point itself. One's lady is what one chooses to believe about her. At the beginning of Chapter 25 Don Quijote has defended the sexual reputation of another imaginary lady, the fictional Queen Madásima of the *Amadís*—this is what earns him his drubbing from Cardenio, who is, to the contrary, now suspicious of all women, real and imaginary. Don Quijote tells Sancho, "Every knight errant . . . is bound to stand up against everyone, sane or mad, in defense of the honor of women, whoever they may be" ["Contra cuerdos y contra locos, está obligado cualquier caballero andante a volver por la honra de la mujeres, cualesquiera que sean" (239; 235)]. He is so bound all the more when the woman in question is his own lady, and Don Quijote now will not do Dulcinea the injury of *imagining* that she has wronged him with another, just as Amadis will think no wrong of Oriana. The woman in this scenario can never be to blame: Don Quijote acknowledges that Dulcinea has not scorned him and that his melancholy and penance are justified only by his absence from her. Like Dulcinea herself, it is all in his head.

Cardenio, too, is suspended between the alternatives of penance and madness, but without the benefit of Don Quijote's lucid awareness that he is choosing between the literary types of Amadis and Orlando, and without Don Quijote's awareness, too, of the ethical import of that choice. Cervantes adds a layer of human complexity to the character by first allowing Cardenio momentarily to blame himself for his behavior at the wedding in Luscinda's house: "In short, since I was such a craven coward and idiot, are you surprised that I now die of shame and, repentance, and insanity?" ["En fin, pues fui entonces cobarde y necio, no es mucho que muera ahora corrido, arrepentido y loco" (272; 270)]. If Cardenio's determination to punish himself is mostly vindictive spite turned in upon itself, it may still contain an element of genuine penance and self-loathing: an inkling of his own responsibility for his misfortune that his pride is unwilling fully to acknowledge, perhaps an inkling, too, of a moral cowardice more serious than the physical cowardice he attributes to himself, a cowardice perpetuated by his running away to sulk in the Sierra Morena.

But Cardenio's narrative ultimately lets him off the hook and puts the blame squarely on his lady. Here, too, there is some ambivalence: Cardenio goes back on forth on the question of Luscinda's guilt, first cursing ["desaté la lengua en tantas maldiciones de Luscinda"], then exculpating her ["la desculpaba"], before settling on his final verdict ["En fin, me resolví"]: "faint love, foolishness, social ambitions, and desire for grandeur" ["poco amor, poco juicio, mucha ambición y deseos de grandezas" (273–74; 271–72)] caused her to betray him. Cardenio's uncomfortable intimations that he is himself, like Anselmo in the "Curioso impertinente," the fabricator of his own dishonor, are submerged and forgotten when he turns to the much more ego-gratifying game of casting blame on Luscinda and judging her degree of fault. Cardenio chooses to be a wronged lover, like Orlando, rather than the defender of a lady who can do no wrong, like Amadis—and like Don Quijote, who makes the opposite choice from Cardenio's and elects to believe the best of his Dulcinea. Cardenio may punish himself, but he is miles away from the selfless penance of Amadis, who rues his having caused distress, however inadvertently, to Oriana; the embittered Cardenio rather falls into Orlando's madness. By comparison the mad Don Quijote is the saner lover.

Yet the comparison of the two madmen punishing themselves for love in the Sierra Morena also brings out the shared motive of self-aggrandizement that makes them alike and, in this respect, true mirrors of each other. Don Quijote's amatory egotism may not depend, as does Cardenio's, on the vilification of the beloved lady, who, in Don Quijote's case, is imaginary anyway; but it is egotism nonetheless, all the more so *because* his lady is purely imaginary. So we have seen in his exposition to Sancho in Chapter 25 of just what he wants of Dulcinea. Earlier in the same chapter he spells out to Sancho the explicit reason for his undergoing penitence for Dulcinea's sake—it will make him famous:

> I intend to carry out an adventure that will win me everlasting fame and renown over the whole face of the earth. And it shall be such that I shall set the seal on all that can make a knight-errant perfect and famous. (240)

> he de ganar perpetuo nombre y fama en todo lo descubierto de la tierra; y será tal, que he de echar con ella el sello a todo aquello que puede hacer perfecto y famoso un andante caballero. (236)

Don Quijote's penance will make him as excellent and acclaimed a knight as the Amadis and Orlando he sets out to imitate; he will himself be the stuff of the literature that he has so much difficulty distinguishing from real-life experience. (And the author Cervantes may stake his claim here to overgo Montalvo and Ariosto.) Don Quijote loves in Dulcinea the image of himself as great lover and knight: it is intense self-love.

Cardenio's narrative ends on a similar note, as he clings to his suffering and refuses consolation. From being just another rejected lover, as his found letter had suggested him to be to Don Quijote, Cardenio transforms himself by his story into a unique case:

> I wish to have no health without Luscinda, and since it pleases her to be another's when she is, or ought to be, mine, let me devote myself to misery, though I might have been the devotee of happiness. By her fickleness she sought to make my perdition irrevocable, and I shall gratify her wishes by

my own destruction. And future generations shall learn that I alone lacked what other wretches possess in abundance, for they may derive consolation from the certainty that no relief is possible, whereas in me this is the cause of greater anguish and evil, for I do not believe that they will even cease with death itself. (275–76)

Yo no quiero salud sin Luscinda; y pues ella gustó de ser ajena, siendo, o debiendo ser, mía, guste yo de ser de la desventura, pudiendo haber sido de la buena dicha. Ella quiso, con su mudanza, hacer estable mi perdición; yo querré, con procurar perderme, hacer contenta su voluntad, y será ejemplo a los por venir de que a mí solo faltó lo que a todos los desdichados sobra, a los cuales suele ser consuelo la imposibilidad de tenerle, y en mí es causa de mayores sentimientos y males, porque aun pienso que no se han de acabar con la muerte. (273)

No one, Cardenio concludes, has or will ever suffer as he has; his story, he tells the Curate and Barber is one to be celebrated—"celebrarse" (275; 273)—and reserved for posterity. Cardenio's pride has been wounded, and he seeks both to lick his wounds and to deepen them. He claims to carry out Luscinda's wishes, faithful to her to the end—and here, too, there is an ironic echo of the penitent Amadis banished by the "voluntad" of Oriana—but only to spite and revenge himself upon her. The oscillation between humiliation and pride-in-his-humilation defines the spiral of his love-madness.

As should be clear by now, Cardenio is not the simple sentimentalized figure of the weak and wronged lover that he may at first appear to be and for which he has often been taken by critics and readers.[15] In Cardenio, in fact, Cervantes, the inventor of so many elements of the subsequent history of the novel, creates the hero of hurt pride and involuted ressentiment who will later populate the pages of Dostoevsky in figures like the Underground Man and Nastasya Fillipovna: the hero who holds on obsessively to his or her humiliation and victimization as a source of identity and as a form of self-love.[16] What is important to insist upon is the continuity of Cardenio's character before and after his fall into madness; his love story is a movement from one form of blinded egotism, his rivalry with Don Fernando, to another, his luxuriating in his sense of injury. Despite his claims to the contrary, the lady in question, Luscinda, appears hardly more real to Cardenio than Dulcinea is to Don Quijote. She is easily enough sacrificed and removed from the story in which the self-dramatizing Cardenio alone takes center stage: his is a first-person narrative with a vengeance. At the wedding scene, this devoted lover positively demands to see accomplished the sacrifice ["sacrificio" (271; 268)] that Luscinda has offered to make of herself.

Camila and Marcela: What Is the Woman to Do?

What course of action is the desired woman allowed in a world in which rivalry between men and the honor code it creates reduce her to an extension of the male ego? So Lotario tells Anselmo early on in the "Curioso impertinente," when he reminds him that husband and wife are one flesh, and that the head of this corporate body feels the pain felt in the foot (336; 338), an image that in itself tells the story of the woman's subordination. The interpolated tale, in fact, rehearses several clichés of misogyny: Lotario further describes women to Anselmo as Aristotle's "imperfect creature" ["animal imperfecto" (334; 335)], and the tale's narrator comments that women naturally have a quicker wit than men—"naturalmente tiene la mujer ingenio presto" (354; 354)—and hence a greater capacity for trickery, though they fail when it comes to reasoning. Such sentiments chime with Cardenio's earlier denunciation of Luscinda in his letter to her; her beauty made him think she was an angel, but her deeds proved her to be a woman ["por ella entendía que eras ángel, y por ellas conozco que eres mujer" (224; 218)]. It is a world, moreover, as the case of Cardenio attests, where men are quick to shift blame from themselves to the women they profess to love. How can women answer these charges?

Don Quijote presents two instances of women who attempt to take control of their situations, particularly to defend themselves from the accusations men level against them: the adulterous Camila of the "Curioso impertinente" and Marcela, the chaste shepherdess who in an earlier episode is denounced for having caused the death of Grisóstomo when she spurned his unwanted suit to her. The carefully constructed contrast between the two women is instructive in its ironies. Marcela truthfully declares her independence from men and their love, but she is not listened to; Camila professes devotion not only to her husband Anselmo but also to the dictates of honor that demand that she take blame on herself, and she clears herself of suspicion. The novel mounts a defense of women that one might call protofeminist not only by allowing women to speak and act in their defense, but also by insisting upon what it is that men want to hear and see.[17] Camila gives her audience of one just what it wants. But she is lying.

Camila offers herself up as a sacrifice—"sacrificio" (359; 359)—to the wounded honor of her husband. The echo of Luscinda's earlier words is clear, and in the wonderful play of Cervantine interlace and perspective, the character inside the interpolated tale that is being read to Cardenio at the inn seems—like the reader of the novel—to have read *his* story and now reproduces it for the benefit of the husband she is, in fact, deceiving.

By a kind of recursive, meta-literary logic, Camila's performance questions whether the story of the "real characters" Cardenio and Luscinda is not also overly stagy, whether we should believe that any woman would—or ought to—kill herself out of devotion to her lover, whether, in fact, this type of story is not itself a fantasy gratifying to the male ego that Cervantes has served up only to criticize precisely here through his interpolated tale. Here, too, the "Curioso impertinente" presents itself as more realistic and psychologically revealing—a better kind of fiction—than the supposedly real narrative of the novel that surrounds it.

The meta-literary implications of the scene are, moreover, redoubled by the theatrical form in which Camila presents to Anselmo what the tale will call the "tragedy representing the death of his honor" ["la tragedia de la muerte de su honra" (361; 362)]; Cervantes indicts a whole corpus of honor plays that, so it is implied, present similar fantasies to his contemporary theatergoing audiences. Yes, she will kill herself, Camila declares before Anselmo, who she knows is standing concealed behind some tapestries in his own house watching the playlet she has authored. Not only that, she will kill Lotario as well, the best friend of her husband whose advances toward her she pretends to repulse here, but to whom she has long since surrendered herself in adultery. And, in fact, Camila does neither: she makes a feint at stabbing Lotario, then gives herself a nonfatal wound, and finally, superb actress that she is, she pretends to swoon.[18] In her apparent suicide attempt, Camila seems to have done what Luscinda, in the eyes of Cardenio, promised and then treacherously failed to do at her wedding to Don Fernando. Like Cardenio, Anselmo does not rush out from his hiding place to stop Camila from carrying out her stated intention to kill Lotario and to make a sacrifice of herself; he is enjoying the show too much, a show designed for his eyes only, and he wants to watch it to its conclusion.[19]

Camila is playacting, and everything she says and does in this scene before the hidden Anselmo has to be put within quotation marks.[20] One effect is a corrosive irony that casts doubts upon the classical models of female chastity and marital devotion she resembles or invokes: Penelope (356; 356), Lucretia (356; 357), and Portia (360; 361). Were these exemplary women also just actresses who knew how to put up a good front for their husbands? Far from defending women, the guilty Camila may incriminate them along with herself. Her playlet confirms misogynist stereotypes about the duplicity and histrionic nature of her sex, especially at the moment when, after she has recovered from her feigned swoon, Camila joins her maid, Leonela, in declaring that she cannot tell a lie, even if her life depended on it: "que no me atreveré a forjar ni sustentar una mentira, si me fuese en ello la vida" (363; 361).

But the ironies of the scene also move in a different direction that implicates the men of the tale. For if Camila falsely presents herself as a willing sacrificial victim to male honor and rivalry, she is, in fact, a real victim and more of one than she knows. She has not only been put in the position of having to defend herself by her lover Lotario's jealous suspicions that she has taken still a third man to her bed. Camila is unaware that Lotario himself was egged on by Anselmo to test her fidelity by pretending to seduce her, and that this trusted best friend went beyond his commission when he seduced her in fact. She is unaware, that is, of the extent to which Lotario's love for her is itself a double lie, both to her and to Anselmo, and a lie of which her own husband is the ultimate inventor—the maker of his own dishonor, as Anselmo will finally acknowledge in the letter he writes but does not live to send to her. Camila playacts before the hidden Anselmo, but she is also an unwitting actress in a play that is not of her devising and whose author remains hidden from her to the very end.

There is thus a moment of particular irony and poignancy during Camila's performance when she declares to Leonela that she must know what Lotario saw in her to make him bold enough to reveal his evil desires to her and to betray Anselmo—"de darle atrevimiento a descubrirme un tan mal deseo" (355; 355)—a question she answers to Lotario himself:

> It must have been some frivolity in me; I will not call it immodesty, for it did not spring from deliberate design but from one of those indiscretions into which women unconsciously fall when they think that reserve is unnecessary. . . . As I know that no one can persevere in his wooing unless he is sustained by some hope, I shall, take the blame for your insolence, for without doubt it is my carelessness that has made you persist in your suit so long. I shall, therefore, punish myself and inflict the penalty of your guilt upon myself. (358–59)

> que debe de haber sido alguna desenvoltura mía, que no quiero llamarla deshonestidad, pues no habrá procedido de deliberada determinación, sino de algún descuido de los que las mujeres que piensan que no tienen de quien recatarse suelen hacer inadvertidamente. . . . Pero, por parecerme que alguno no puede perseverar en el intento amoroso luengo tiempo, si no es sustentado de alguna esperanza, quiero atribuirme a mí la culpa de tu impertinencia, pues, sin duda, algún descuido mío ha sustentado tanto tiempo tu cuidado; y así, quiero castigarme y darme la pena que tu culpa merece. (359)

Camila reproaches herself for having given encouragement, however unintentionally, to Lotario, some hope that made him continue to press his suit to her. It must somehow have been my fault, she proclaims in this scene she has scripted. But, in doing so, she mimics in a complicated way—and the tale verbally echoes—what had been her *real*, initial reaction to the advances of Lotario.

Lotario had himself predicted what this reaction *ought* to be when he tried to discourage Anselmo from pursuing his project to test his wife:

> once Camila sees me wooing her, she will immmediately imagine that I have detected a touch of frivolity in her that has encouraged me to reveal my lustful desires. When she considers herself dishonored, her disgrace is bound to reflect on you as a part of her. (334)

> viendo Camila que yo la solicito, ha de pensar que yo he visto en ella alguna liviandad que me dio atrevimiento a descubrirle mi mal deseo, y teniéndose por deshonrada, te toca a ti, como a cosa suya, su mesma deshonra. (337)

Camila, says Lotario, will consider herself responsible for his attempts to seduce her; as the first cause of her husband's dishonor, she will hold herself already dishonored. Now this is not quite what happens. After sending a letter to her absent husband complaining of his friend's behavior, and receiving a response that she was not to stop seeing Lotario in their house, Camila

> was sorry she had written as she had to her husband, and she worried that he might imagine that Lotario had seen some frivolity in her that encouraged him to fail in the respect he owed her. (345)

> y ya le pesaba de haber escrito lo que escribió a su esposo, temerosa de que no pensase que Lotario había visto en ella alguna desenvoltura que le hubiese movido a no guardalle el decoro que debía. (345–46)

Contrary to Lotario's prediction, in this first instance Camila knows herself to be innocent. But she also understands what her husband may think and how she is trapped by the laws of honor that Lotario has earlier set forth. As a woman she will be blamed for the actions of the man; as a woman, moreover, she is supposed to blame herself. Where there is smoke, the logic of honor would have it, there must be fire: some "desenvoltura" on her part, a letting down of her guard, has urged Lotario on.

The second time around, as she recites her part before Anselmo, Camila puts to use this knowledge of the dictates of honor: she professes herself ready to obey them and to inculpate and punish herself for a fault that she must undoubtedly have committed even if she was unaware of it. She now fulfills Lotario's prediction to the letter, as the verbal parallels in the text spell out. The irony against Camila is obvious, since she has by now not simply encouraged Lotario's advances by some inadvertent and innocent behavior, but has given in to them as a willing adulteress.

But the irony against the men of the story and against their code of honor that victimizes women is more sweeping. Without her knowledge, Camila's speech points to the central mystification of romantic desire that the "Curioso impertinente" sets out to unmask. The woman asks what it is that she has done to arouse the desire of the man when the answer, unknown to her, is that the man was set on by another man, her husband, to seduce her. Anselmo may, in fact, be less interested in Camila's chastity, or finally in Camila herself, than he is in seeing her prefer him over the friend whom he has made to assume the role of rival: a setup that suggests an unspoken competition and intersubjective struggle beneath the surface of this intimate friendship. And when Lotario begins to seek Camila for himself, he does so by making "comparisons between himself and Anselmo" ["hacía discursos y comparaciones entre él y Anselmo" (342; 344)]: both men use the woman to measure and test themselves against each other. Cervantes carefully loads Camila's words; when she declares to Lotario her willingness to take on the blame for his insolence—"quiero atribuirme a mí la culpa de tu *impertinencia*"—her words apply not only to Lotario but, once again in a way that she cannot know, to the watching Anselmo as well, the "impertinente" of the tale. It is the "impertinencia" of Anselmo that is responsible for that of Lotario: male pride and rivalry have created a game of desire in which Camila is little more than a pawn and in which her actions and desire count hardly at all. Nonetheless, the rules of honor demand that Camila as the woman blame and punish herself—and so offer a kind of cover for the actions of the men who need not confront their own motives. It is no wonder that Anselmo cannot get enough of her act.

The would-be shepherdess Marcela need not blame herself, for she is already almost universally condemned by the men who surround her in the novel's first major inset episode in Chapters 12–14.[21] Pedro the goatherd introduces her story by calling her a "she-devil" ["endiablada moza" (123; 110)]; a companion of the curious traveler Vivaldo refers to her as the "homicidal shepherdess" ["la pastora homicida" (129; 116)]; Ambrosio, the friend of the poet Grisóstomo who appears to have killed himself for her sake, denounces her as "that mortal enemy of the human race" ["aquella enemiga del linaje humano" (135; 123)]; all of her many lovers, who, like Grisóstomo, have dressed up as shepherds and gone out to woo her in vain, decry her as "cruel and ungrateful" ["cruel y desagradecida" (127; 114)]. Above all, it is the verses of the dead Grisóstomo, rescued from the fire to which Grisóstomo had himself consigned them, that, so their rescuer Vivaldo says, keep the cruelty of Marcela alive as an example for future times—"de ejemplo, en los tiempos que están por venir" (136; 124).

Cardenio, we have seen, will speak later on in the novel of his own misfortunes in love as an example for future times—"ejemplo a los por venir"—and his subsequent story is interlaced with that of Grisóstomo just as is Don Quijote's love for Dulcinea, which the rueful knight describes at length to Vivaldo in Chapter 13, a passage sandwiched between the two main parts of the story of Marcela and Grisóstomo in Chapters 12 and 14. As another character who seeks to live life as literature, although in the genre of the pastoral novel rather than chivalric romance, Grisóstomo is one of the novel's obvious foils for Don Quijote.[22] The parallel is already made explicit at the end of Chapter 12, where Don Quijote spends "all the rest of the night thinking of his lady, Dulcinea, in imitation of Marcela's lovers" ["y todo lo más de la noche se la pasó en memorias de su señora Dulcinea, a imitación de los amantes de Marcela" (128; 115)]. But in the three-way mirroring relationship of Grisóstomo, Cardenio, and Don Quijote, it is the first two who most clearly resemble one another: wallowing in abjection, they are much madder and more self-destructive in their loves than is the crazy knight.

"Yo no quiero salud sin Luscinda," Cardenio will tell the Curate and Barber: it is not only the recovery of his sanity but his eternal salvation he refuses without the Luscinda he thinks has rejected him, and a few sentences earlier he has implored the mercy of heaven on his soul (275; 273). For Cardenio recognizes that his descents into madness are leading to a kind of suicide, the fate of Grisóstomo, who is interred in the fields as if he were a Moor (110; 123)—it appears that Grisóstomo has killed himself for love of his Marcela and has been denied Christian burial.[23] He is instead buried on the spot where he first saw Marcela—just as Petrarch, in one of the most famous poems of the *Canzoniere* (127), fantasizes of being buried by the clear, cool, sweet waters where he first met Laura and where he imagines her visiting his grave and shedding a tear when it will be too late. In his erotic idolatry, inspired by literature, Grisóstomo has courted damnation.

In similar anticipation of Cardenio, Grisóstomo, in the last poem he wrote before his death, professes that by killing himself, he will take on the punishment due to the woman who has spurned him—at the same time that he makes clear that it is precisely *she* who is to blame for his misery and death. He will, he writes, remain true to his fantasy—"mi fantasía" (139; 127)—and so he will pretend that the fault lies in himself and in a personified Love:

> I'll swear that she, my constant enemy,
> As fair a soul as body does possess,
> That her heedlessness is born from my fault,
> For only by the ills he sends upon us
> Can Love his empire in just peace preserve. (139)

Diré que la enemiga siempre mía
hermosa el alma como el cuerpo tiene,
y que su olvido de mi culpa nace,
y que en fe de los males que nos hace
amor su imperio en justa paz mantiene. (127)

All is fair in love, Grisóstomo protests, and I have nothing to complain of—but he defines this protestation as willing make-believe and barely disguises his resentment at Marcela. Just as Cardenio will claim to gratify the wishes of Luscinda—"hacer contenta su voluntad"—by seeking his own perdition, Grisóstomo's poem goes on to assert that his death will give Marcela what she desires:

If, haply, one day you discover
That I'm so worthy of your sympathy
As to dim the blue heaven of your eyes
When you hear of my death, shed no tears,
For I refuse to let you in any way repay me for the prize
I give you of my soul; but rather may you gaily laugh,
Proclaiming that my death did make you glad.
Yet, why am I so foolish as to teach
You, knowing that your glory will be made manifest
In hastening my early end? (140)

si, por dicha, conoces que merezco
que el cielo claro de tus bellos ojos
en mi muerte se turbe, no lo hagas;
que no quiero que en nada satisfagas,
al darte de mi alma los despojos.
Antes, con risa en la ocasión funesta
descubre que el fin mío fue tu fiesta;
mas gran simpleza es avisarte desto,
pues sé que está tu gloria conocida
en que mi vida   llegue al fin tan presto. (128)

Grisóstomo forbids Marcela to mourn for him; he pointedly does not follow Petrarch's model and imagine her one day having pity on him. Such is his supposed devotion to Marcela that he does not allow her in any way to atone for the suffering and death that he takes entirely upon himself. It is my show alone, this Petrarchan lover protests, and I get all the credit for it, a sardonic enough comment on a whole poetic tradition that can transform the poetry of love into a quest for the poet's own fame.[24]

But Grisóstomo does not entirely succeed in turning his aggression against Marcela solely against himself, nor does he really want to do so. For this masochistic egotism of the spurned lover, in fact, presumes an equally self-centered sadism on the part of the lady: Grisóstomo attributes to Marcela a positive pleasure in learning of his demise. You'll be glad when I'm gone, he says, because I will be a trophy—"despojos"—that will spread the fame of your beauty's conquests. This, too, is the purpose of the poem itself, written, so Grisóstomo claims at its beginning, because the cruel Marcela bids him to publish wide and far the power of her hard-heartedness: " Ya que quieres, cruel, que se publique / de lengua en lengua y de una en otra gente / del áspero rigor tuyo la fuerza" (137; 125). Far from exculpating Marcela, Grisóstomo projects upon her both his own ambition for poetic fame and his own pride, hurt as it may be. His suicide is a public act of revenge on her that will show her true nature to the world, just as he intends his poem both to carry out her command *and* to spite her—"por gusto mío   sale y tu despecho" (138; 126). Was there ever a lady so cruel?

Marcela breaks into the funeral of Grisóstomo to speak for herself— "por mí misma" (141; 130)—and to ask why she should be given the blame for the sufferings of Grisóstomo: "¡mirad ahora si será razón que de su pena se me dé a mí la culpa!" (143; 132). Her self-defense will be pointedly inverted in Camila's subsequent (false) claim that she wishes to suffer herself for the guilt of Lotario: "quiero castigarme y darme la pena que tu culpa merece" (359; 359). Alongside these passages that verbally echo each other, we should hear a third: Cardenio's resolution to take on the punishment deserved by Luscinda and Don Fernando: "ejecutar en mí la pena que ellos merecían" (273; 271)—the same logic, we have just seen, that leads Grisóstomo to suicide. Marcela refuses to adapt Camila's pretense, so gratifying to male egos, that as a woman she must somehow be to blame for exciting the desire of men and therefore will punish herself. She likewise refuses to accept responsibility for Grisóstomo's self-punishment.[25] Unlike Camila, she will not be a victim of male folly, nor offer an alibi for it.

Marcela succinctly gives her reasons: men may claim that her beauty makes them helplessly—"sin ser poderosos a otra cosa" (142; 130)—love her and that she is therefore obliged to return their love. This cannot be true because (*a*) all beauties would then equally inspire love, and (*b*) she would then be obliged to love an ugly man who loves her. Furthermore, she has made it clear to all men who court her that she intends to marry no man and to live a life of solitude and freedom.[26] Desires, she says, are sustained by hope—"los deseos se sustentan con esperanza" (143; 131)— and she gave none to Grisóstomo or any other man; therefore no one should call her cruel or homicidal ["pero no me llame cruel ni homicida" (143; 132)]. In her playlet Camila will similarly assert that amorous intent cannot last without hope—"si no es sustentado de alguna esperanza" (359; 359)—and concludes that she must have inadvertently given Lotario encouragement: she pronounces a guilty verdict upon herself. The contrast could not be more sharply drawn.

Marcela's decision to free herself entirely from erotic desire and the bonds of marriage is an extreme reaction to her situation, but the comparison to Camila, victim of both lover and husband, makes her choices seem stark indeed in the world of *Don Quijote*. Her alternative is to make herself complicit with the fantasies of male love and honor or, as is really the case with Camila, to pretend to do so: Marcela could choose, then, either literal self-sacrifice or the duplicity that men are all too willing to attribute to women.

Because Marcela's behavior is extreme, it is not above question, and some critics of the novel have been rather hard on her.[27] Her adaptation of the guise of shepherdess suggests that she might be, in her way, as deluded a reader of pastoral novels as Grisóstomo; she may be taken in by descriptions of the pastoral Golden Age such as the one evoked by no less impressionable a reader than Don Quijote himself in Chapter 11: "Maidens and innocence went about, as I have said, alone wherever they pleased without fear or danger from the unbridled freedom and lustful desires of others" ["Las doncellas y la honestidad andaban, como tengo dicho, por dondequiera, sola y señora, sin temor que la ajena desenvoltura y lascivo intento le menoscabasen" (119; 105–6)]. Marcela may see in the pastoral a realm freed from desire just as much as Grisóstomo sees it as a place for his Petrarchan conceits. The idea of pastoral innocence will subsequently be belied by Cervantes's interlaced narrative when Dorotea recounts how her experience disguised as a shepherd led to her near rape (288; 288). Marcela's avoidance of marriage may be linked to a fear of repeating the fate of her mother, who died giving birth to her (125; 112). Women who desired to leave the world had the option of becoming nuns rather than shepherdesses, and in their respective stories both Luscinda and Camila take refuge in convents. The idea has already been introduced at the end of the goatherd Antonio's love song, written by his uncle, the parish priest, in Chapter 11; if his beloved Olalla will not marry him, Antonio says, he will become a capuchin (122; 109). And, as is frequently noted by critics, the story of Marcela is followed by the horse Rocinante's pursuit of the Galician mares, who receive him with their hooves and their teeth (147; 136), a low-comic deflation which reminds us of the sexual instincts that underlie the pastoral posturings of the episode, instincts that may be more difficult to escape from than Marcela thinks.[28] It should be noted, however, that the implied butt of this juxtaposition seems to be the male lover—and we remember how ugly a suitor Rocinante is in equine terms—rather than the woman who wants to be free of him.

To criticize Marcela and her motives is, in fact, to put oneself in the position of the men who accuse her, those who persist in thinking that the woman really means yes when she says no. There is at least one male observer, the traveler Vivaldo, who remains skeptical: after reading Grisóstomo's poem, he comments to Ambrosio that the dead shepherd's jealousy does not seem to accord with the good fame of Marcela's morals. Ambrosio explains his friend's despair:

> To satisfy your doubts, sir, I must tell you that when the unfortunate man wrote this song, he was absent from Marcela, from whom he had voluntarily withdrawn to see if absence would have its usual effect upon him. And as there is nothing that does not vex the absent lover and no fear that does not haunt him, so Grisóstomo was tormented by imaginary jealousies and suspicions as frightening as if they were real. So Marcela's goodness, therefore, is as genuine as fame proclaims it, and but for cruelty, a little haughtiness, and much disdain, envy itself cannot justly find fault in her. (141)

> Para que, señor, os satisfagáis desa duda, es bien que sepáis que cuando este desdichado esribió esta canción estaba ausente de Marcela, de quien él se había ausentado por su voluntad, por ver si usaba con él la ausencia de sus ordinarios fueros; y como al enamorado ausente no hay cosa que no le fatigue ni temor que no le dé alcance, así le fatigaban a Grisóstomo los celos imaginados y las sospechas temidas como si fueran verdaderas. Y con esto queda en su punto la verdad que la fama pregona de la bondad de Marcela; la cual, fuera de ser cruel, y un poco arrogante, y un mucho desdeñosa, la mesma envidia ni debe ni puede ponerle falta alguna. (129)

Ambrosio cannot resist renewing his charges against Marcela at the end of this admission of her goodness, that is, of her sexual probity. But this admission effectively shifts blame back on Grisóstomo and on the male jealousy and competition that have surrounded Marcela. For we realize that Grisóstomo died not because of Marcela's spurning him but *because he feared someone else had obtained her.*

It is important to insist upon this point. Grisóstomo is clearly guilty of making a Petrarchan, erotic idol of Marcela, of making her into a projection of his own ego. In doing so, he is connected to Don Quijote, who in Chapter 13 described Dulcinea in his Petrarchan *blason* to the same Vivaldo. Vivaldo, in turn, had questioned the practice of knights in the chivalric romances of commending themselves in battle to their ladies and not to God: it is a pagan practice, Vivaldo says—"que huele algo a gentilidad" (132; 119)—and his words echo the objection of the village curates to Grisóstomo's funeral rites, devoted to his cult of Marcela, which, the goatherd Pedro agrees, seem to belong to paganism ["parecen de gentiles" (123; 110)]. But if Grisóstomo has substituted Marcela for his God—and the implication is that Don Quijote is doing much the same with Dulcinea—it is not such spiritually dangerous idolatry that finally drives him to the true act of damnation in suicide; it is jealousy.

Like the other suitors of Marcela described by Pedro in Chapter 12, Grisóstomo is obsessed by the question of who will be the lucky man— "el dichoso" (128; 115)—who will win the lottery for her hand. In her defense, Marcela argues that she cannot make anyone jealous since she loves no one at all; by the same token, her rejections of her suitors should not be taken for the disdain of which Ambrosio accuses her—"que los desengaños no se han de tomar en cuenta de desdenes" (143; 132)—since disdain would imply that she treats others any differently. But the very thought of a successful rival torments Grisóstomo, a jealousy that is purely imaginary, for he has absented himself from the real woman Marcela.

In the subsequent rewriting of the Marcela episode in the story of Leandra in Chapter 51, Grisóstomo's absence becomes universalized, for it is only in Leandra's absence, *after* her father has locked her away from sight, that her suitors populate the hills in pastoral dress and both disparage and adore Leandra. The madness goes so far, comments one of Leandra's two original lovers, Eugenio, that some complain of her disdain without ever having spoken to her: "se estiende a tanto la locura, que hay quien se queje de desdén sin haberla jamás hablado" (506; 509). From the original rivalry for Leandra's hand between Eugenio and his "competidor" (503; 506), Anselmo, the number of suitors explodes in imitation—"a imitación nuestra" (506; 509)—a textbook case of Girard's concept of mimetic desire that glosses in retrospect not only the the conduct of the shepherd suitors of Marcela, but of Cardenio and Don Fernando, Anselmo and Lotario: jealous men more concerned about copying and competing with one another than about the woman whom they seek as the prize of their victory over their rivals, a woman who, otherwise, might as well be out of the picture. In his absence from Marcela, Grisóstomo anticipates the behavior of Cardenio, who runs away from Luscinda and Don Fernando into the Sierra Morena, and in the same Sierra Morena Don Quijote explicitly recalls Ambrosio's words and Grisóstomo's example when he tells Sancho that his mere absence from Dulcinea is reason enough for him to go mad (242; 238).

The interlaced stories create mirroring relationships among (1) Cardenio's going mad because of a jealousy that is mistaken and imagined over a real woman and real rival, (2) Grisóstomo's suicide because of an imaginary jealousy that nonetheless has the force of reality for him over an absent woman and a nonexistent rival, and (3) Don Quijote's proposal to play the role of a madman on account of an imaginary jealousy that he knows to be imaginary over his imaginary lady, Dulcinea. In all three cases, the beloved woman is reduced to a figment of the male imagination, an imagination obsessed with the phantom of a successful rival. Yet we remember that Don Quijote finally refuses to imagine himself jealous and to think ill of a Dulcinea who has not disdained him—"yo no soy desechado ni desdeñado de Dulcinea del Toboso" (255; 251)—and he elects to separate absence from jealousy; he adapts the penitence of Amadis rather than go mad like Orlando. This choice, too, is reproduced in the Leandra story, where of the two rivals Anselmo only complains of absence—"sólo se queja de ausencia" (506; 510)—while the narrator, Eugenio, takes the easy way out. He thinks ill not just of Leandra but of all women:

> I follow an easier and, in my opinion, a wiser path, which is to curse the fickleness of women, their inconstancy, their double-dealing, their broken promises, their broken faith, and last of all the lack of judgment they show in their choice of objects for their desires and affections. (506)

> Yo sigo otro camino más fácil, y a mi parecer el más acertado, que es decir mal de la ligereza de las mujeres, de su inconstancia, de su doble trato, de sus promesas muertas, de su fe rompida, y, finalmente del poco discurso que tienen en saber colocar sus pensamientos e intenciones que tienen. (510)

When in doubt, blame the woman, especially when she is absent from the scene and cannot speak for herself.[29] This sweeping denunciation not just of the woman but of womankind suggests just what is at stake in Marcela's talking back to her accusers near the beginning of *Don Quijote*: she is defending her entire sex, and, in anticipation, other women characters of the novel, both the virtuous Luscinda and the more blameworthy Camila. The causes of a larger, cultural misogyny, *Don Quijote* repeatedly suggests, are to be found not in the behavior of women, but in the conduct of men. And that conduct is hard to change. For unlike Camila, the witting and unwitting accomplice of male jealousy, Marcela tells men what they do *not* want to hear—and they simply ignore her. She says no, but she must mean yes.

The ironic conclusion of the Marcela episode can be briefly told. The dying Grisóstomo himself, like the dying Anselmo of the "Curioso impertinente," may have come to a moment of self-knowledge: he asks that his poems be burned and that he and his story of misfortune be buried in eternal oblivion—"eterno olvido" (135; 123). But Vivaldo, with perhaps the tacit consent of Ambrosio, has rescued a few verses from the flames, and these keep alive Grisótomo's defamation of Marcela and her cruelty as an example for posterity. This moment parallels the earlier episode of the burning of Don Quijote's library in Chapter 6, where the Curate and the Barber save a few volumes from the general auto-da-fé of books and thus keep alive the chivalric romance and its poisons against which, the Prologue to Part One declares, Cervantes's novel is one long invective (46; 24). Neither habits of mind nor the literature that perpetuates them are so easy to destroy and lay to rest. Furthermore, Ambrosio promises to erect a tombstone and epitaph that will eternize the harshness and ingratitude of Marcela: "Murió a manos del rigor / de una esquiva hermosa ingrata" (145; 133). As Alban Forcione comments, "We are left with a strong sense of the solipsistic nature of Grisóstomo's love, the emptiness of Petrarchan love poetry, which commemorates self-generated idols and which, in the fragment that escapes the flames, like the mendacious stone text sealing off the corpse, survives to perpetuate a delusion."[30]

Marcela's words, meanwhile, fall largely on deaf ears:

And some (those wounded by the powerful shafts from the radiance of her lovely eyes) made as though they would follow her, not profiting from the frank warning they had heard. (111)

Y algunos dieron muestras—de aquellos que de la poderosa flecha de los rayos de sus bellos ojos estaban heridos—de quererla seguir, sin aprovecharse del manifiesto desengaño que habían oído. (132)

But she is defended by Don Quijote, who forbids these new lovers to pursue Marcela and who declares that she bears little or no blame for Grisóstomo's death—"poca o ninguna culpa" (144; 133). He seems to speak both for himself and for the novel *Don Quijote*, which has, in the speech of Marcela and in the whole episode, done its best to demystify—as a "manifiesto desengaño"—the processes of male desire. Such desire does not arise spontaneously, as Petrarchan and other Renaissance physiological explanations of love would have it, from the beautiful eyes of the woman, but is mediated by a web of male vanity and rivalry. Nonetheless, the mystification persists, and Marcela only seems to acquire new suitors from the assembled shepherds. The men do not want to listen, and the novel seems to project their attitude on its own (male) readers. It is one of the ironies built into the structure of *Don Quijote* that Marcela's protest on her behalf and on behalf of her sex will literally be left behind as the narrative moves on to other stories of jealous men and the victimized women they profess to love.

Happy Ending and Mystification

Marcela has the novel's first word on desire, but she does not have the last. The ending of the story of Cardenio, Don Fernando, and Luscinda that brings this complex of interlaced stories and episodes to its conclusion in Chapter 36 suggests just how little the illusions about love have been dispelled. The denouement that restores the lovers to one another and to a happy ending of marriage takes place in two stages. To the inn, where Cardenio and Dorotea have just listened to a reading of the "Curioso impertinente," Don Fernando brings Luscinda, whom he and a band of friends and retainers have abducted from the convent where she sought asylum. Masks and veils fall away, and the four characters recognize one another. Dorotea eventually persuades and shames Don Fernando into honoring the promise of marriage he had made to her, but not before Luscinda has first called on him to kill her:

> to turn your love to fury, your affection to hatred, and to put an end to my life, for I shall consider it well lost provided I die before the eyes of my good husband. Perhaps my death will convince him that I kept my faith to the last act of my life. (374)

> volváis, ya que no podáis hacer otra cosa, el amor en rabia, la voluntad en despecho, y acabadme con él la vida; que como yo la rinda delante de mi buen esposo, la daré por bien empleada: quizá con mi muerte quedará satisfecho de la fe que le mantuve hasta el último trance de la vida. (374)

Luscinda offers herself up as victim once again, and we subsequently learn at the chapter's end that Don Fernando did indeed try to kill her when, after Luscinda fainted at their wedding, he found her suicide note that declared her already to be the wife of Cardenio (379; 380): on that occasion Don Fernando was no less ready to see her die for his honor than was Cardenio. And now, with her true husband once more looking on, Luscinda repeats her willingness to die for the satisfaction of Cardenio. Between these two offers, in Chapters 27 and 36, that Luscinda makes to sacrifice herself, Cervantes has interlaced the "Curioso impertinente," where in Chapter 34 the adulteress Camila has faked her suicide in order to trick the watching Anselmo, and by now Luscinda's words, however sincere, sound stagily melodramatic and inauthentic—not least because Luscinda seems to be deluded when she acquiesces to act the role of victim in a scenario of desire that has less to do with her, the woman in question, than with the jealous rivalry of the two men.

That this rivalry is and has been the true cause that generates the action of the story becomes clear in the second stage of its denouement. As the relenting Don Fernando takes up and recognizes the kneeling Dorotea as his true wife, he releases Luscinda, who has once again fainted. Cardenio steps forward from where he could not be recognized to take her into his arms. Cervantes appears to contradict himself—the text has earlier said that Don Fernando has seen and recognized Cardenio (374; 374)—in order to create a second scene of recognition, one with possibly murderous consequences:

> What a strange spectacle for Don Fernando and for the onlookers! They were dumbfounded at such an unforeseen incident. Dorotea thought that Don Fer-

nando changed color and made a move to take revenge on Cardenio; she saw
his hand reach for his sword. (376)

Estraño espectáculo fue éste para don Fernando y para todo los circunstantes,
admirándose de tan no visto suceso. Parecióle a Dorotea que don Fernando
había perdido la color del rostro y que hacía ademán de querer vengarse de
Cardenio, porque le vio encaminar la mano a ponella en la espada; (377)

Don Fernando may have renounced Luscinda in order to marry Dorotea,
but that does not mean that he is willing to concede her to his rival. (We
remember, too, from Dorotea's earlier narrative, that it was the news that
her parents were planning to betroth her to another that caused Don Fernando to force his way into her bedchamber and to "marry" her; see 281;
281.) Don Fernando rather takes Cardenio's public claiming of Luscinda
as an affront to his honor that he is prepared to avenge. The actions of
the two male lovers have all along been motivated by their desire to best
each other. Their desire for the woman has been conditioned by the fact
that the other desires her, by the fear that the other may possess her. And
they are prepared to fight over her. Cardenio is as resolved to defend
himself and to attack—"defenderse y ofender" (377; 378)—as is Don
Fernando.

Nonetheless, the men never acknowledge their rivalry: there is no true
recognition in this double recognition scene. Dorotea and the rest of the
onlookers, especially the Curate, restrain Don Fernando, who undergoes
a kind of conversion, both as a Christian and a nobleman—"de caballero
y cristiano" (377; 378)—and he gives his consent to Cardenio and Luscinda's marriage. But when it comes to explaining his conduct to Dorotea,
Don Fernando resorts to a time-honored plea:

turn and look at the eyes of the now happy Luscinda. There you will find the
excuse for all my errors. (378)

volved y mirad los ojos de la ya contenta Luscinda, y en ellos hallaréis dis-
culpa de todos mis yerros; (379)

How could I help myself, Don Fernando asks, when Luscinda was so
beautiful? Her overpowering eyes that took away his will are like those
of Marcela, which supposedly attract new suitors even as Marcela's
words aim to discourage them by telling them the truth about their desire
for her. Don Fernando protests that it was the loveliness of Luscinda, the
force of her sexual attractiveness, that made him love her—rather than
his jealousy of Cardenio. With this shifting of blame back on the woman,
even in the form of a gallant compliment, and with Luscinda's own offer
to sacrifice herself, the story of the four lovers doubly concludes on a note
of bad faith.

Unlike the tragic outcomes of the episode of Grisóstomo and Marcela and of the tale of the "Curioso impertinente," this story reaches a happy ending, but at the price of mystification.[31] It lacks the "desengaño" provided by Marcela and the self-recognition finally attained by Anselmo. Cardenio and Don Fernando remain blind to the self-centered nature of their love; Luscinda is still ready to collude with the ego-gratifying fantasies of the men by victimizing herself. Their story itself, that is, when observed from the meta-literary perspective that *Don Quijote* repeatedly encourages, is the kind of stereotyped novella that is born from and then in turn feeds a self-serving male imagination, the bad fiction that Cervantes aims to drive out with the good, demystifying fiction of *Don Quijote* and of the good novella, the "Curioso impertinente," in particular. But Cervantes acknowledges the difficulty of his task. At the end of Chapter 35, the Curate closes the "Curioso impertinente" and judges it to lack literary truth; such a story could not happen between a husband and wife, says the Curate, who, of course, has no personal experience of wedded life. He does concede that the story might be plausible were it about a lover and his lady—"un galán y una dama" (371; 371)—and thereby suggests to the reader its possible relevance to the story of Cardenio with which it is interlaced. Upon the heels of this critical dismissal of the interpolated tale, Don Fernando and Luscinda appear immediately next upon the scene in Chapter 36. The star-crossed lovers are reunited and happily paired off, and fiction-as-usual is allowed to have the final say.

Love and Chivalry

Cervantes depicts a markedly old-fashioned love in the "Dulcinea" complex of episodes and tales, the stories that mirror and comment upon Don Quijote's love for Dulcinea. It lacks the modern component, an accompanying concern for riches and status, that distinguishes the second complex of love stories of Part One of *Don Quijote* that we shall examine in the next chapter. The men who compete for the women they love—Grisóstomo, Cardenio and Don Fernando, Anselmo and Lotario—are all gentlemen and compete for them as equals, even when, in the case of Cardenio and the second son of a duke, Don Fernando, they belong to different ranks within the aristocracy: Cardenio tells Dorotea that he will use his license as a nobleman—"la libertad que me concede el ser caballero" (290; 291)—to challenge Don Fernando for her sake. These lovers do not seek to best one another by their claims to social position, a position that they take more or less for granted. They love their ladies without the ulterior motive of marrying for wealth and rank, and they assume, in turn, that they are loved for themselves when they are preferred to their rivals—or rather they gain their sense of self from defeating those rivals in love.[32] Without a social and economic arena in which to displace competition, erotic desire, in fact, becomes, as we have seen, a contest of jealousy, the beloved woman a battleground over which male egos war for ascendancy. It is, as we have noticed, a fine irony of the novel that Don Quijote first flirts with and then rejects the idea of being madly jealous about his imaginary lady Dulcinea: he may be saner in this respect than the jealous lovers who surround him. But then, unlike them, Don Quijote has another arena in which he can feed his pride by conquering others. He has chivalry.

The satisfaction sought by the jealous lovers is, in fact, closely analogous, perhaps identical to the pleasure that Don Quijote expects from the chivalric life. He explains to Sancho in Chapter 18 just what an "honorable thing it is to follow this profession. Now tell me: what greater contentment can the world offer, or what pleasure can equal that of winning a battle and triumphing over one's enemy. Undoubtedly none" ["cuán honrosa cosa es andar en este ejercicio. Si no, dime: ¿qué mayor contento puede haber en el mundo, o qué gusto puede igualarse al de vencer una batalla y al de triunfar de su enemigo? Ninguno, sin duda alguna" (169; 160)]. The passage is meant to be juxtaposed with Sancho's earlier declaration in Chapter 15 that he is a man of peace who forgives the wrongs done to him: "And from this time on, I pardon, in the name of God, whatever insults have been or shall be offered against me, whether by high or low, rich or poor, noble or commoner, without any exception whatsoever" ["desde aquí para delante de Dios, perdono cuantos agravios me han hecho y han de hacer, ora me los haya hecho o haga, o haya de hacer, persona alta o baja, rico o pobre, hidalgo o pechero, sin eceptar estado ni condición alguna" (148; 138)]. The contexts that unite the two passages are Don Quijote's being bested by the lower-class Yanguesan carriers and by the city artisans who blanket Sancho at the inn—the latter have journeyed from Segovia, Córdoba, and Seville—and his subsequently reminding Sancho that the rules of chivalry "do not allow a knight to take up arms against one who is not one" ["no consienten que caballero ponga mano contra quien no lo sea" (168; 159: compare 148; 137]. For Don Quijote the highest reward of knighthood is to triumph over a knight similar to oneself and of one's own social status in the aristocratic fantasyland of chivalry. The response of the peasant Sancho, while it may smack of cowardice, is resolutely Christian, and it pointedly levels the ranks of society in the forgiveness that Sancho extends to all.

The contrasting assertions of knight and squire make clear just how incompatible with Christianity are Don Quijote's dreams of chivalry with their insistence on conquering, rather than forgiving, one's enemy, with their social exclusiveness. They are the dreams of pride, which the novel ironically punctures when it depicts Don Quijote helpless before lower-class adversaries in a society whose new mobility and fluidity seems to be depicted in these itinerant workers traveling across Spain. Nonetheless, it is pride in what seems to be its distilled form—divorced from social distinctions and purely the product of rivalry with "equals" to whom one proves oneself not equal but superior—that marks the similarity between Don Quijote's chivalry and the behavior of the jealous lovers of Part One.[33] And like his long outmoded chivalry, their love, driven by competition and a cult of honor, looks back to an earlier social formation.

In the *The Autumn of the Middle Ages*, Johan Huizinga distinguishes a premodern, feudal mentality from the thought of a later society changed by the circulation of money:

> Pride and greed can be placed beside one another as the sins of the old and the new times. Pride is the sin of the feudal and hierarchic period during which possessions and wealth circulate very little. A sense of power is not primarily tied to wealth, it is rather more personal, and power, in order to make itself known, has to manifest itself through imposing displays.[34]

Huizinga describes the late-medieval society that is the subject of his classic study as already moving to the "new times": greed is ubiquitously denounced, but it is a greed still married to aristocratic pride, fond of lavish pomp and finery. Such splendor and pageantry dominates the pages of the chivalric romances of Don Quijote's reading and, as we shall see, shapes his own ideas about power and wealth. For our present purposes, Huizinga suggests how the type of self-aggrandizement sought in *Don Quijote* by overcoming one's rivals, whether in the contest of love or in chivalric battle, is a carryover from a feudal past into the society that has superseded it.

Don Quijote's project to revive chivalry is obviously anachronistic and absurd, but so, Cervantes's novel intimates, is an erotic desire that turns the beloved woman into the imaginative extension of male jealousy and honor—and it depicts such love as a displaced version of Don Quijote's chivalry. We are inclined to see erotic jealousy as a constant part of the human condition, but we may no longer wish to celebrate it, in the concept of honor, as culturally sanctioned behavior. It is the achievement of *Don Quijote*, and part of its critique of Spain's national obsession with honor, to argue that such jealousy can be situated, in its purest, most exacerbated form, in the particular historical circumstances, and as part of the class ideology, of aristocratic feudalism. As a thing of the past, this form of desire, which ultimately reduces to pride, should be as outmoded as chivalry itself in a newly modern society. At least there should no longer be a place for a literature that uncritically perpetuates the code of honor and valorizes such jealousy—for a literature that does not, as *Don Qui-*

jote does, expose its egotistical motives and the ways that it victimizes women. *Don Quijote* thus provides its own historical explanation for why it should inaugurate the demystification of romantic desire that Girard has argued is a defining feature of the new genre of the novel: it is because it enjoys the perspective of history itself that, from the vantage point of a changing social order, makes such desire appear to be the vestige of a premodern mentality.

But what kind of desire, then, has come to replace or modify this old-fashioned, prideful love? The episodes and tales that fill up the rest of Part One of *Don Quijote* are increasingly dominated by money and by the idea of the worldly career—of marrying for wealth and status. Modern desire, in Huizinga's terms, has shifted from pride to greed. It is not necessarily an improvement.

THREE

"PRINCESS MICOMICONA"

T HE LURE OF RICHES plays an important role in the pair of stories interpolated into the final section of the *Orlando furioso* that were among Cervantes's models for his tale of the "Curioso imperti-nente." With the help of the enchantress Melissa, the disguised Mantuan host corrupts his own wife by offering her rubies, diamonds, and emeralds (43.35–38). The wife of the Ferrarese judge Anselmo is won over when her lover offers her a magic dog that excretes coins, pearls, and gems (43.114–15); Anselmo himself sells his body in return for a fabulously costly palace that is similarly the product of magic (43.132–39). Riches are the new enchantment in Ariosto's own modern world of the early-sixteenth century, a world toward which the *Furioso* begins to gesture more insistently as its action winds down and traverses the poet's Po val-ley geography. Avarice, concludes the knight Rinaldo, the audience of both tales, has caused many women to betray their husbands, just as it has caused many men to betray their lords and friends: gold conquers all (43.48–49).[1]

The Anselmo of the "Curioso impertinente," named after Ariosto's character, gives Lotario two thousand gold escudos and money to buy jewelry of equal worth (339; 341) to help him to seduce Camila, whose chastity is itself described as a gem or treasure (333; 335, 341; 343) and who will receive her lover in the recess of Anselmo's house where he keeps his jewels—"alhajas" (352; 353). After he has, in fact, seduced Camila, Lotario returns the money to his friend, assuring him that "Camila's in-tegrity will not surrender to such base things as gifts and promises" ["la entereza de Camila no se rinde a cosas tan bajas como son dádivas ni promesas" (346; 347)]. What Lotario says is true, even if the irony is clear, for he has not needed Anselmo's money to make Camila love him. Cervantes thus marks the distance of his tale from those of Ariosto: this is not a story about the corrupting force of riches that tempt one into the arms of a lover, and that can turn women, and even some men, into sexual commodities to be bought and sold.

Money is precisely beside the point in the "Curioso impertinente," as it is also in the story of Cardenio, whose letter to Luscinda accuses her of having spurned him for Don Fernando's greater wealth and rank, "for one who possesses more, but is not worthier than I am" ["por quien tiene más, no por quien vale más que yo" (224; 218)], and who later says that it was her "social ambitions and desire for grandeur" ["mucha ambición y deseos de grandeza" (274; 272)] that caused her to love his rival instead of him. But, in fact, Luscinda does *not* succumb to the prospect of social elevation and material wealth; whatever he may think, Cardenio's story is not about that at all.[2] In yet another case, the shepherdess Marcela is rich, as she reminds her suitors when she proclaims her self-sufficiency (143–44; 132). We are told that she is courted equally for her beauty and for her great wealth—"así por ella como por sus muchas riquezas" (126; 113). Nevertheless desire for that wealth seems to play no role at all in Grisóstomo's jealous passion for her.

In the complex of love stories that we have just looked at in the preceding chapter, those which are clustered around Don Quijote's love for Dulcinea, Cervantes introduces the possibility of mercenary and social motives—only pointedly to discount them. He would have us focus instead on how erotic desire in these stories is driven by rivalry between men, like Cardenio, who think of themselves as being as worthy as any other, social rank notwithstanding—and who wish, in fact, to be acknowledged as worthier by the beloved woman who chooses them over their competitors. In its material disinterestedness, this love is akin to Don Quijote's yearning for Dulcinea; in its impetus of emulous pride, it is the counterpart of his chivalry: in both respects, it is a premodern love.

The motives of riches and of a rise in social status do, however, inform the second cluster of interlaced love stories of Part One of *Don Quijote*, the "Princess Micomicona" stories that now overtake and seem to replace the "Dulcinea" cluster in the second half of the narrative. The greatest of these, the story of Captain Viedma, the captive in Algiers, and of Zoraida, the beautiful and fabulously rich Arab woman who rescues him, succeeds in the narrative in Chapters 37–42 immediately after the reconciliation of the four young lovers at the inn, and is then followed by the little love intrigue of Clara and the high-titled Don Luis in Chapters 43–44. The story of Leandra in Chapter 51, of a woman pursued by one of her "lovers" exclusively for her money, provides a debased parody of the Captive's Tale itself and comments on the whole complex of stories of love and social ascent. (In the return to pastoral guise and lamentation of Leandra's other lovers, it also comments, as we have seen, upon the Marcela story and the first complex of stories of love and male jealousy, and it thus lends the structure of a ring composition to the entire group of interpolated episodes and stories of Part One.)

The idea of marrying for money and status has already been introduced earlier into the novel by Don Quijote's own fantasy about being loved by royalty—a fantasy that is distinct from, and in potential conflict with, his other erotic fantasy, his love for Dulcinea. It is an imaginative scenario that Don Quijote expounds at length in Chapter 21 in the miniature chivalric romance that he tells to Sancho and that explains how a knight rises to become king—through marriage to a princess—and is then in a position to reward his squire's service. This fantasy will then be seemingly actualized in Chapters 29–30 by the Curate and the Barber, who, in order to lure Don Quijote out of the Sierra Morena, enlist Dorotea to pose as Princess Micomicona. This princess from far-off Guinea promises to marry Don Quijote and bestow her African kingdom on him once he has conquered the giant Pandafilando (304; 305); Don Quijote will think he has done just that when he destroys the winesacks in his sleepwalking delirium in Chapter 35, interrupting the telling of the "Curioso impertinente."

Dorotea is a hinge figure in the novel who stands between the two narrative complexes. As the woman whom Don Fernando has seduced and pledged to marry, she belongs to the Cardenio, Luscinda, and Don Fernando story, and it is her prior claim on Don Fernando that allows that story to reach its happy ending. But Dorotea's own story, which she tells in Chapter 28, of a rich farmer's daughter who would rise through marriage to Don Fernando into the ranks of the nobility, belongs to the plots of social mobility. Moreover, her story of social ascent bears an inverse relationship to the role she plays as Micomicona, the princess who offers to raise Don Quijote to royalty. Pandafilando, the giant who supposedly oppresses Micomicona by seeking her hand by force in an "unequal marriage" ["desigual casamiento" (302; 303)] is, at one level, a kind of mythic substitute for Don Fernando, whom she warned against "unequal marriages" ["desiguales casamientos" (283; 283)] in her own life-history, and Sancho Panza will himself perceive as much at the opening of Chapter 37, when the lovers are reunited and the giant turns in his eyes into Don Fernando (380; 381). In terms of social ambition, however, the aspiring giant mirrors not so much Don Fernando as the lowborn, social-climbing Dorotea herself.

In a moment of meta-literary commentary on the theme, the debate between the Canon of Toledo and Don Quijote on the value of chivalric romance in Chapters 47–50 repeatedly raises the issue of social mobility, and links this issue to the generic capaciousness and mixture of *Don Quijote*. The prose epic that the socially conservative Canon designs for the values of an exclusive, aristocratic audience is only one generic option among many that Cervantes's book entertains as it juxtaposes and combines earlier literary forms. Defined in contrast to the Canon's norms, the form of *Don Quijote* is shaped by the newfound fluidity of the social world it depicts. Generic and social boundaries become permeable in the new, open genre—the novel—that Cervantes is in the process of creating for his modern times.

We shall see that all of these stories of love and marriage that are tied to wealth and status are carefully interlaced in the novel: they repeat narrative elements and verbally echo and reflect upon one another, just as did the complex of stories about love and male rivalry examined in the previous chapter. As was the case in those "Dulcinea" stories, the motives of love in the stories of the "Princess Micomicona" cluster reflect upon the motives of Don Quijote's chivalry, epitomized in his two erotic fantasies. Chivalry and love as rivalry—that highest pleasure Don Quijote describes of triumphing over one's enemy—give way to chivalry and love as career: the way to get rich and rise in status, to become the emperor that Don Quijote has promised himself. The disclosure that such mercenary and social aims have infiltrated into the profession of knighthood suggests that the romances of chivalry may have all along contained disguised versions of the modern success story of worldly advancement. It further comments, in the Captive's Tale, on the modern counterpart of chivalry: the vocation of the professional soldier in which the author Cervantes had a biographical stake. Don Quijote's early coupling of the knight with the monk had argued that the knight's prowess made him the minister of God on earth (131; 118), and Spain's sixteenth-century struggle with the Ottoman Turks was carried out in the crusading spirit held over from the Christian reconquest of the Iberian peninsula. But *Don Quijote* questions how much of that spirit still remains, and what can be left of heroism, as well as of love, in a world in which money dominates and transforms all human activity. Is chivalry, then, dead?

Zoraida and the Princess

The Captive's Tale represents, in the scheme of *Don Quijote*, the irruption of the historically real and of an authentically heroic and even providential narrative into the novel's fictional world and the mock-heroics of its crazy knight.[3] The narrator and hero of the tale, Captain Viedma, takes the entire Chapter 39 to describe his action in the Spanish-Turkish theater of war of the early 1570s, action in which Cervantes, too, had taken part as a soldier. The captain served beside Diego de Urbina, as did Cervantes (395; 398); the captain fought and was captured at Lepanto, where Cervantes's left hand was shattered; the captain was a captive in Algiers, where Cervantes spent five years in captivity before he was ransomed. Captain Viedma even mentions the stalwart behavior of the historical Cervantes, a "so-and-so de Saavedra" ["tal de Saavedra" (404; 407)] who was a prisoner alongside him in Algiers.[4] The parallels between character and author almost amount to a disguised autobiography, not so very different from the kind of screen story that Dorotea tells of Princess Micomicona and the giant Pandafilando in order to give fantastic form to her true-life relationship with Don Fernando.[5]

Within the novel, the Captive's Tale is "authenticated" when the captain mentions a fellow captive, one Don Pedro de Aguilar, only to find one of Don Pedro's brothers among those listening to his story, ready to confirm his words and to recite two of Don Pedro's sonnets on the fall of the fortress of the Goleta when the Turks recaptured Tunis in 1574. The Captive's story thus belongs to history and the world of modern military heroism: Don Quijote may fantasize about fighting huge Muslim armies when he attacks the sheep in Chapter 18; Captain Viedma has fought real Turks. His career reminds us of Spain's great crusade only a few decades in the past—though inasmuch as his story does not end with the great victory at Lepanto, but with the missed opportunity at Navarino (397; 399), the disaster of the Goleta, and finally captivity in Algiers, it hints at the decline and exhaustion of the nation's military glory.[6]

And yet the story is aligned with fiction in the novel. Don Fernando judges it as a literary critic in Chapter 42: "Indeed, captain, the way in which you have told your strange adventure has been as fascinating as the strangeness and novelty of the events themselves. The story is an unusual one and full of astonishing incidents that hold the listener in suspense" ["Por cierto, señor capitán, el modo con que habéis contado este estraño suceso ha sido tal, que iguala a la novedad y estrañeza del mesmo caso. Todo es peregrino, y raro, y lleno de accidentes que maravillan y suspenden a quien los oye" (431; 433)].[7] We may conclude that truth may be not only stranger than fiction but can even make a better story. Shortly afterward, as the Curate intercedes between Captain Viedma and his brother the Judge, he remarks of the Captain's story of the career choices he and his two brothers made—among the army, law, and commerce in the New World—that "I should have set it down for an old wive's tale told over the fire in winter" ["lo tuviera por conseja de aquellas que las viejas cuentan el invierno al fuego" (434; 436)]. And indeed the motif of three brothers setting out to make their fortunes in the world is a common fairy-tale formula. As is so often the case in *Don Quijote*, it seems that we cannot escape the realm of fiction or at least of thinking about human experience in the terms already provided by fiction.

The Curate's response, however, becomes clearer when we come to the main part of the Captive's Tale, where the beautiful Algerian young woman, Zoraida—inspired by her memories of her Christian nurse who told her of the Virgin Mary—wants to convert to the true religion and chooses Captain Viedma from among the captives she spots from the window of the house of her father, the rich Agi Morato; she asks Viedma to take her away from Algiers. He alone, she says, seems to be a "caballero" (408; 410)—a gentleman might be the best translation, but also, in the context of this particular novel, a knight. In Zoraida's eyes, the captive is a knight in shining armor who will carry her away—"llevarme" (410; 412)—from her own captivity in Islamic error and bring her to Christianity. And she promises to marry him. It is a story as fantastic as any fairy tale or any chivalric romance.

In fact, it is a story right out of the chivalric romances, one that governs Don Quijote's own fantasies during his two stays at the second inn, which he takes for a castle, and one that the Curate and Barber exploit when they dress Dorotea up as Princess Micomicona. Early in the novel, in Chapter 16, he mistakes Maritornes, the ugly Asturian wench who is no better than she should be and who is groping her way in the dark for a nighttime assignation with her muleteer lover, for the princess of the castle. "He fancied that he was now in a famous castle (for, as we have said, all the inns where he lodged seemed to him to be castles) and that the landlord's daughter (daughter of the lord of the castle) captivated by his gallant presence had fallen in love with him and had promised to lie with him that night for a good space of time without her parents being any the wiser" ["y fue que él se imaginó haber llegado a un famoso castillo—que, como se ha dicho, castillos eran a su parecer todas las ventas donde alojaba—, y que la hija del ventero lo era del señor del castillo, la cual, vencida de su gentileza, se había enamorado dél y prometido que aquella noche, a furto de sus padres, vendría a yacer con él una buena pieza" (157; 147)].

Don Quijote includes this stock scenario in the miniature romance that he subsequently tells to Sancho Panza in Chapter 21, one more interpolated tale placed in the larger narrative of the novel.[8] The knight-errant, Don Quijote says, will be given the most lavish welcome by the king or lord of the city at which he arrives. This idea of aristocratic hospitality—especially measured against the commercial hospitality of inns—becomes an organizing thread of Cervantes's interlace, both here and in Part Two, where the castle of the Duke and Duchess takes the place of the inn of Part One. Don Quijote goes on to recount that the knight-guest "will find [the queen of the palace] with her daughter who is sure to be one of the loveliest and most accomplished damsels to be found anywhere in the wide world, however hard you search. After this she will gaze into the knight's eyes and he into hers, and each will appear to the other somewhat more divine than human; and without knowing the why and wherefore, they will be imprisoned and entangled in the intricate net of love." And later, as the knight takes his leave of the princess at night "through the railings of a garden that adjoins her sleeping chamber. . . . He will sigh, she will swoon; the lady-in-waiting will fetch water and be greatly distressed because morning is nearly there, and she will fear for her lady's honor if they be discovered. At last the princess will come to herself and give her white hands through the railings to the knight, who will kiss them a thousand times and bathe them with his tears. . . . From there he withdraws to his chamber, flings himself upon the bed, but cannot sleep for the agony of parting" ["adonde el caballero la hallará con la infanta, su hija, que ha de ser una de las más fermosas y acabadas doncellas que en gran parte de lo descubierto de la tierra a duras penas se pueda hallar. Succederá tras esto, luego en continente, que ella ponga los ojos en el caballero, y él en los della, y cada uno parezca a otro cosa más divina que humana, y, sin saber cómo ni cómo no, han de quedar presos y enlazados en la intricable red amorosa . . . por las rejas de un jardín, que cae en el aposento donde ella duerme. . . . Sospirará él, desmayaráse ella, traerá agua la doncella, acuitaráse mucho, porque viene la mañana, y no querría que fuesen descubiertos, por la honra de su señora. Finalmente, la infanta volverá en sí, y dará sus blancas manos por la reja al caballero, el cual se las besará mil y mil veces, y se las bañará en lágrimas. . . . Vase desde allí a su aposento, échase sobre su lecho, no puede dormir del dolor de la partida" (204–5; 197–98)].

Don Quijote's evocation of this stereotypical scene of chivalric romance is funny both for the way it falls into the high-flown, if totally clichéd, rhetoric of the romances—that intricate net of love—and for its reduction of the scene to summary. Cervantes rhetorically underscores the formulaic nature of the romances first by polysyndeton, the repeated "ands," subsequently by asyndeton, no "ands" at all. One action becomes interchangeable with the next; none seems to have more importance than the other, because all conform to time-honored—and by now threadbare—conventions. The use of the future tense throughout much of Don Quijote's account also reinforces our sense of the predictability of the chivalric romance, one much like the other.[9]

Don Quijote may dwell somewhat longer on the love that springs up spontaneously between the knight and princess, and thereby offers an insight both into what the romances have to offer him, the aging bachelor, and what, Cervantes appears to suggest, they offered to sixteenth-century readers. Yet the same technique—the knight will sigh, the princess will swoon, the lady-in-waiting will fetch water to revive her—indicates the mechanical conventionality of such amorous fictions. In spite of the witty injection of a Cervantine realistic detail in the figure of the water-fetching damsel (one can't just leave the princess lying there in a swoon), the eroticism of Don Quijote's scenario is quickly reduced to the white hand of the otherwise barred and inaccessible princess, a fetish that suggests the substitution of such romance fictions themselves for erotic fulfillment. The knight as well as Don Quijote and other consumers of romance fantasy are left to their restless beds.[10]

That white hand of the princess at the railings of her garden clearly reappears in the Captive's Tale in Chapter 40, when Zoraida's "very white hand" ["una muy blanca mano" (405; 407)] opens the window of her father's house, a window that in Moorish fashion is not a window but one of a series of loopholes—"agujeros" (405; 407)—and lets down a cane with a handkerchief full of coins. Zoraida is being cast—in a supposedly true story of the exotic East—as a romance princess who falls in love with the visiting knight: even if Captain Viedma is not enjoying hospitality, but rather captivity, in Algiers. Cervantes, in fact, knew that the scenario that Don Quijote describes to Sancho had a variant version in which the Christian knight ventures into pagandom, is imprisoned by trickery when his religious identity is known, and is subsequently rescued by a Saracen princess who has fallen in love with him.[11]

Lest we miss the connection he is drawing, Cervantes immediately follows the Captive's Tale with the episode in Chapter 43 where the innkeeper's daughter and Maritornes play a practical joke on Don Quijote, calling to him from a hole—"agujero" (443; 444)—in the loft of the inn and asking for one of *his* "beautiful hands" ["hermosas manos" (444; 446)], which they truss up, leaving him helplessly and ridiculously standing in his saddle:[12]

> They beckoned him from the hole which he imagined to be a window, and even with gilded bars suitable to such a castle which he conceived that inn to be. At once he believed in his strange fancy that again, as once before, the beautiful damsel, daughter of the lord of the castle, conquered by love of him, had come to tempt him. (443)

> Le llamaban del agujero que a él le pareció la ventana, y aun con rejas doradas, come conviene que las tengan tan ricos castillos como él se imaginaba que era aquella venta; y luego en el instante se le representó en su loca imaginación que otra vez, como la pasada, la doncella fermosa, hija de la señora de aquel castillo, vencida de su amor, tornaba a solicitarle; (445)

This time it is the innkeeper's daughter herself who plays the role of princess for Don Quijote, while he addresses Maritornes as the duenna, or lady-in-waiting.

We might be tempted to read these artfully interlaced passages in a manner something like this: on the one hand, if you want to find true heroism and chivalry in the contemporary world, a true princess and her knight of the kind that Don Quijote dreams of through his reading of the chivalric romances, look to Zoraida and her captain in the real history of Spain and its epic crusade against Islam, although there is also a sense that this history may now be over and in the past. If, however, like Don Quijote himself, you look for these chivalric scenarios in everyday life, you will not find a castle, but an inn, not a princess but the innkeeper's daughter or her even more lowly maidservant, not a king or chatelain, but an innkeeper who will demand to be paid.

Yet it becomes apparent that this division into three domains—Don Quijote's fantasy, epic national history, and the disenchanted world in which Don Quijote finds himself—will not entirely hold up. For the realism of the world of the inn, or what we would call the novelistic world, encroaches upon and infects the other domains as well. The informing principle of this world is money: the first innkeeper whom Don Quijote meets in Chapter 3 and who dubs him knight impresses upon him the need to carry money on his quest. Since he nevertheless mistakes the second inn where he stays in Chapter 16 for a castle, complete with obliging castellan's daughter, Don Quijote is dismayed to discover that it is, in fact, an inn and to be asked to pay for the hospitality he has received:

> I cannot break the rule of the order of knights-errant, of whom I know for certain (since I have never read anything to the contrary) that they never paid for lodging or anything else in the inns where they stayed. For the good entertainment that is given them is fair reward in consequence of the sufferings they endure, seeking adventures both day and night. (165)

> Yo no puedo contravenir a la orden de los caballeros andantes, de los cuales sé cierto, sin que hasta ahora haya leído cosa en contrario, que jamás pagaron posada ni otra cosa en venta donde estuviesen, porque se les debe de fuero y de derecho cualquier buen acogimiento que se les hiciere, en pago del insufrible trabajo que padecen buscando las aventuras de noche y de día. (156)

Don Quijote's refusal to pay up on this occasion earns Sancho Panza his memorable tossing in the blanket. The squire evokes this episode in retrospect in Chapter 52 at the end of Part One, but he also, in what is virtually the last word in the novel, regards freeloading as one of the special charms of knight-errantry—and by implication a worthwhile trade-off for its hardships: "when all's said and done, it's a fine thing to be gadding about spying for chances, crossing mountains, exploring woods, climbing rocks, visiting castles, lodging in inns at our own sweet will, with devil a maravedi to pay" ["pero, con todo eso, es linda cosa esperar los sucesos atravesando montes, escudriñando selvas, pisando peñas, visitando castillos, alojando en ventas a toda discreción, sin pagar ofrecido sea al diablo el maravedí" (514; 517)]. Both hidalgo and squire, though to be sure in different ways, regard free hospitality as the recompense due to them for their knightly calling: it is the novel's principal emblem of how Don Quijote's re-creation of a chivalric past attempts to escape from a modern world of money.[13]

In Chapter 46, however, Don Quijote would not be able to leave the inn at all if Don Fernando and the Curate did not pay his bills in order to secure his release. The point is driven home in a minor, otherwise irrelevant incident interlaced into the narrative two chapters earlier. Two nameless guests "tried to slip away without paying what they owed. But the landlord, who paid more attention to his own than to other people's business, laid hold of them as they were going out the door and demanded his money" ["habían intentado a irse sin pagar lo que debían; mas el ventero, que atendía más a su negocio que a los ajenos, les asió al salir de la puerta, y pidió su paga" (451; 454)]. It is money—particularly the money required in exchange for hospitality—that measures the distance between the heroic, aristocratic world of Don Quijote's fantasy and the modern, material world in which he finds himself a prisoner: he escapes the inn only to be placed in his "enchanted" cage.

And it is money that the white hand of Zoraida, the "princess" of the Captive's Tale, is letting down from her window to Captain Viedma and his fellow prisoners: a handkerchief filled with gold coins. I have already described in Chapter 1 how the novel prepares for this movement from Don Quijote's fantasy princess to the exotic Zoraida in its juxtaposition of two scenes in the story of Cardenio and Luscinda: Luscinda offering her white hands for Cardenio to kiss at the railings of her window; Luscinda offering a handkerchief filled with gold coins to an unknown Christian (268–69; 266–67). The money, which Zoraida is stealing from her father, is to be used to ransom Captain Viedma and to purchase a boat for their flight from Algiers. It is like settling your bill, as Don Fernando must do for Don Quijote, before you can leave an inn. Through his juxtaposition of episodes, Cervantes suggests the kind of grim analogy between hospitality and being a prisoner of war that led American captives to nickname their Vietnamese jail the "Hanoi Hilton." The analogy fit that much closer in the sixteenth and seventeenth centuries when the taking and ransoming of prisoners, by both sides, had become an established feature of the Christian-Muslim conflict in the Mediterranean—and had developed into a major business.[14]

Buying one's way out of captivity is hardly heroic. Captain Viedma's subsequent stealing Zoraida and her father's money may be hardly more so: "Christians, Christians, thieves, thieves!" [¡"Cristianos, cristianos! ¡Ladrones, ladrones!" (420; 422)], the old man cries before he, too, is carried off—"llevar cautivo" (421; 423)—a potential hostage, as he supposes, for ransom (422; 424). Zoraida, indeed, seems to turn here into Captain Viedma's ticket not only to freedom but to wealth, a means for him to rise in the world in his chosen career as soldier, as his brothers, the judge and the merchant, have risen in their professions.[15] For all of its elements of derring-do and marvelous divine intervention, the Captive's

Tale risks falling into a sordid story of fortune hunting and extortion. Implicit here is a retrospective critique of the impure motives of Spain's crusading mission in her great century, a mission that could too easily lose sight of its spiritual goals in favor of material ones—transforming Christians into thieves—and that could end up exchanging money for human lives and liberty, as Cervantes, five years a captive in Algiers, knew all too well.[16]

These motives cast a new light, in turn, on the model chivalric romance that Don Quijote tells Sancho back in Chapter 21, a romance that is also an outline of a knightly career. Let us pick it up where we left off, with the knight, who spent a sleepless night agonizing on his bed, going off to make his way in the world:

> he fights in the war, he defeats the king's enemies; he captures many cities, triumphs in many battles; returns to court and sees his lady in the usual place; it is agreed that as a reward for his services he shall ask her father for her hand in marriage, but the king will not consent because he does not know who he is. In spite of that, either by abducting her or in some other way, he marries the princess and her father in the end considers it a most fortunate arrangement, for it transpires that the knight is the son of a valiant king, of what kingdom I do not know. (205–6)

> pelea en la guerra, vence al enemigo del rey, gana muchas ciudades, triunfa de muchas batallas, vuelve a la corte, ve a su señora por donde suele, conciértase que la pida a su padre por mujer, en pago de sus servicios. No se la quiere dar el rey, porque no sabe quién es; pero con todo esto, o robada, o de otra cualquier suerte que sea, la infanta viene a ser su esposa, y su padre lo viene a tener a gran ventura, porque se vino a averiguar que el tal caballero es hijo de un valeroso rey de no sé qué reino. (199)

The knight has earned his princess, but obtaining her is another matter. In the face of parental resistance, he can carry the princess off and so force the hand of the king, her father, who will have to accept him as son-in-law or face her disgrace. Eventually the knight will become king himself, and then he can reward his squire with an island, as Don Quijote has promised Sancho from the beginning of their partnership. But Don Quijote ponders the problem of whether he himself is of royal blood: the princess, he says,

> will have to love me so much that she will take me as her lord and husband in spite of her father, even though she knows for certain that I am the son of a water carrier. And if she does not, then it is a question of abducting her and carrying her off wherever I please, for time or death will put an end to her parents' displeasure. (207)

me ha de querer de manera que, a pesar de su padre, aunque claramente sepa
que soy hijo de un azacán, me ha de admitir por señor y por esposo; y si no,
aquí entra el roballa y llevalla donde más gusto me diere; que el tiempo o la
muerte ha de acabar el enojo de sus padres. (200; my emphasis)

And Sancho Panza agrees that "there is nothing to do but, as your worship
says, to carry her off" ["no hay sino, como vuestra merced dice, roballa
y trasponella" (207; 200]. And he will similarly urge his master to marry
his princess when she materializes in Dorotea/"Princess Micomicona,"
telling him to seize the good luck that Fortune is offering him (305; 306).

Here, too, the ideal chivalric romance that Don Quijote expects for
himself offers a parallel and blueprint for the Captive's Tale and for the
stealing of Zoraida from her unhappy father. But there is no religious
motive or alibi at all in Don Quijote's story, which for all that it may take
place in a never-never land of chivalry in which money plays no apparent
part, may be a thinly disguised version of the economic success story of
the poor boy who makes good and marries into wealth and social position.
The romances of chivalry whose escapist fictions seem ridiculously far
removed from the novelistic world of *Don Quijote* may thus be the unacknowledged product of that world and its values after all. And so, finally,
may be Don Quijote's own fantasies that he models on those fictions.

In the process of Don Quijote's telling his story of the princess to Sancho, the intricate net of love has been left behind. If the princess refuses
to love me because of my low birth—and we should note how slyly Cervantes has made Don Quijote switch from a third person narration of the
story to place himself inside his fantasy—I shall have to carry her off, he
says. The princess is turned from the object of romantic love that she has
earlier played into a prize to be seized by the fortune hunter, an object
now of potential rape. This is the case of the farmer's daughter Leandra
in the debased version of the Captive's Tale told in Chapter 51 that completes the pattern of interlace charted in Table 3.1. The charlatan soldier
Vicente de la Rosa poses as a captain and a veteran of the Turkish wars
like Captain Viedma, and wins the heart of Leandra, who sees him from
the window of her house, as Zoraida had spotted the Captive. Vicente
carries off—"la llevó"—and abandons Leandra, robbing her of the jewels
and money that she has stolen from her rich father, but, to everyone's
surprise and perhaps incredulity, allows her to keep her virginity, her
jewel—"joya" (505; 508)—above price.[17] Vicente's motive here is completely mercenary and has nothing to do with erotic desire; once one has
the princess's money, she is not needed at all.

The Captive's Tale, we shall see, ends on the opposite note: it discards
the money rather than Zoraida. It does not finally succumb to the temptation to treat the woman as merely the means to wealth, and it depicts

TABLE 3.1
The Interlacing of the Captive's Tale

Don Quijote's Fantasy	Captive's Tale	Don Quijote at Inn	Leandra
	Zoraida sees Viedma from window		Leandra sees Vicente from window
White hand of princess at railing	Zoraida's white hand at loophole	Don Quijote's hand at loophole	
	Zoraida steals from father		Leandra steals from father
	Viedma pays ransom	Fernando and Curate pay Don Quijote's bill; innkeeper detains non-paying guests	
Knight carries off princess	Viedma carries off Zoraida		Vicente carries off Leandra
	Corsairs leave Zoraida with her jewel		Vicente leaves Leandra with her jewel

the survival of spiritual values and human love in the face of mercenary considerations. But just how far those considerations have infiltrated and become confused with Captain Viedma's nobler thoughts is disclosed in his account of Zoraida in all the glory of her beauty—and her jewels:

> It would be beyond my power now to describe Zoraida's great beauty, her gentleness, and the rich brilliant attire in which she appeared before me. I shall only say that more pearls hung from her fair neck, her ears, and her hair than she had hairs on her head. On her ankles, which, as is the Moorish custom, were bare, she wore *carcajes* (for so the Moors call the rings and bracelets for the feet) of the purest gold, set with many diamonds, which, she told me afterward, her father valued at ten thousand doubloons; those she wore on her wrists were worth just as much. . . . Zoraida's father had the reputation of possessing a great many of the purest [pearls] in Algiers, and of possessing also more than two hundred thousand Spanish crowns. She who was the mistress of all this is now mine only. . . . All I can say is that Zoraida was then surpassingly bejeweled and surpassingly beautiful, or at least, she seemed more so to me than anything I had ever seen. When, in addition, I considered all that I owed her, I felt that some goddess from Heaven had descended on earth to bring me happiness and salvation. (415)

Demasiada cosa sería decir yo agora la mucha hermosura, la gentileza, el gallardo y rico adorno con que mi querida Zoraida se mostró a mis ojos: sólo diré que más perlas pendían de su hermosísimo cuello, orejas y cabellos que cabellos tenía en la cabeza. En las gargantas de los sus pies, que descubiertas, a su usanza, traía, traía dos carcajes (que así se llamaban las manillas o ajorcas de los pies en morisco) de purísimo oro, con tantos diamantes engastados, que ella me dijo después que su padre los estimaba en diez mil doblas, y las que traía en las muñecas de las manos valían otro tanto . . . el padre de Zoraida tenía fama de tener muchas y de las mejores [perlas] que en Argel había, y de tener asimismo más de docientos mil escudos españoles, de todo lo cual era señora esta que ahora lo es mia. . . . Digo, en fin, que entonces llegó en todo estremo aderezada y en todo estremo hermosa, o, a lo menos, a mí me pareció serlo la más que hasta entonces había visto; y con esto, viendo las obligaciones en que me había puesto, me parecía que tenía delante de mí una deidad del cielo, venida a la tierra para mi gusto y para mi remedio. (417)

The passage is meant to be contrasted with Cardenio's earlier description of Luscinda at her wedding to Don Fernando, where the glittering jewels that bedecked all her bridal attire were surpassed by Luscinda's own beautiful golden hair—"las vislumbres que las piedras y joyas del tocado y de todo el vestido hacían, a todo lo cual se aventajaba la belleza singular de sus hermosos y rubios cabellos" (271; 269). Cardenio's Petrarchan conceit—suitable to this forlorn lover—is reversed in the Captive's extraordinary vision of Zoraida, whose hairs are outnumbered by her pearls. As the cause of her desirability, the beauty of the woman cannot quite compete with the dazzling richness of her jewelry, which Captain Viedma is able to translate into its monetary equivalent.

Cervantes shows how money itself can be fantastic—the fabulous wealth of the East—and furnish the matter for a modern-day adventure story as marvelous as those of Don Quijote's romances: Zoraida is as rich as any princess in those romances. Moreover, he suggests how, to a captive in Algiers, the money that comes to ransom him seems to be a miracle, in this case the intervention of the Virgin Mary who has inspired Zoraida and whose name she takes: God himself can work through cash.[18] But for a moment Zoraida seems to *be* her wealth in the eyes of Captain Viedma, and the Captive's Tale works to separate her from it both in this passage and in its subsequent narrative. The Captain is already looking back here, with some nostalgia, on the riches that Zoraida used to command, all that she has had to give up to become his "señora." She needs to be distinguished from her jewels so that her true beauty, both physical and spiritual—her human worth—can be recognized for what it is.

In its attitude toward wealth, the Captive's Tale is usefully compared to a work by Cervantes's greatest contemporary writer that tells a strikingly similar story of a young woman of alien faith who is abducted from her father's house and who steals his property in order to convert to Christianity and marry: the Jessica-Lorenzo subplot in *The Merchant of Venice*. Monetary issues are *never* set aside in Shakespeare's play, perhaps because it is about Jews, not Muslims; perhaps, too, because it is a comedy. Jessica and Lorenzo lose the riches she has carried away in a casket from Shylock's house, but only because they have squandered them away in high living before they wash up at Portia's Belmont in Act 3 (3.4.5f.). They stand in need of the half of Shylock's remaining wealth that is legally extorted from him in the courtroom drama of the following act (4.1.379–89)—"manna in the way / Of starvéd people," Lorenzo calls it—in a play in which "conversion" refers to the transfer of property in marriage: "Myself and what is mine, to you and yours / Is now converted," Portia tells her new husband, the self-avowed fortune hunter Bassanio (3.2.166–67).[19] Shylock, who in the trial scene reminds the Venetians that they own slaves and that he does not insist that they set them free (4.1.90–98) is, of course, no better—"My daughter! O my ducats! O my daughter!" (2.8.15), he is reported to cry, and subsequently he himself wishes to see Jessica "dead at my foot, and the jewels in her ear! Would she were hears'd at my foot and the ducats in her coffin!" (3.1.88–91). Shylock does not distinguish the corpse of his daughter from his gems and coins, and the deadening effects of money could not be clearer.

By contrast in the Captive's Tale, it is Zoraida's father—the Muslim enemy—who first draws the line between his daughter and money. After he curses the hour when she was born and, like Shylock, calls for her destruction, Agi Morato has a change of heart and movingly begs his beloved Zoraida to return to him: "I forgive all you have done. Let those men have the money, for it is theirs now, and come back to comfort your father" ["todo te lo perdono; entrega a esos hombres ese dinero, que ya es suyo, y vuelve a consolar a este triste padre tuyo" (425; 427)]. The ties of love, he protests, are greater than those of material possession: he wants the daughter, not the ducats. To separate Zoraida from the loot, however, it finally takes the arrival of French corsairs—fellow Christian thieves—at which the Renegade who has masterminded the captives' escape secretly throws the coffer of her stolen riches into the sea.[20] The French rob Zoraida of her remaining jewelry, including those fabulous "carcajes" at her ankles, but, anticipating the behavior of Vicente de la Rosa in the Leandra story, they do not rob her of her virginity, her most precious jewel—"la joya que más valía" (427; 429). Nor are the French, presumably Huguenots since they have sailed from La Rochelle, completely heartless, for their French captain, satisfied with his haul, helps to land the captives back in Spain, and even gives Zoraida a token amount of money.[21] But, unlike Shakespeare's Lorenzo and Jessica, ready to live off of Shylock's money and perhaps run through it a second time, the Captive and Zoraida are virtually penniless. Instead, they have freedom, conversion, and each other. Cervantes tells the same story as Shakespeare, but at the end without the money, and that makes all the difference, for his version allows a final triumph of human and religious values—on all sides, moreover, of its different religious divides.

For a brief moment, when Zoraida first appeared to him in all her glory, it had seemed that Captain Viedma could have had it all: not only deliverance and a beautiful bride, but wealth beyond his dreams. It would have provided a different goal to his tale and changed its meaning, turning it into a story of worldly success like those of his judge and merchant brothers, a story aligned, too, with Don Quijote's fantasy of marrying a princess and becoming king or emperor. But the Captain returns to Spain in poverty. Zoraida's riches have been jettisoned, literally thrown overboard and out of the tale, in order to focus attention on the jewel and treasure that is not so much Zoraida's virginity as her soul, and it is her baptism, still to be accomplished, that now becomes the goal and final meaning of the tale.

The Captain's own deliverance from Algiers becomes in this light a figure for the Christian deliverance that is the greater event of the story: the salvation of Zoraida's soul and her own escape, as the Captain tells her father, "out of darkness into light, out of death into life, out of suffering into glory" ["de las tinieblas a la luz, de la muerte a la vida y de la pena a la gloria" (423; 425)].[22] The marvels of Zoraida's wealth give way to the possibly miraculous, Marian dimension of the tale: to the Captain his "señora" is like a deity descended from heaven "para mi remedio," and we are reminded both here and subsequently in his story of "Nuestra Señora de los remedios."[23] Zoraida has come down in the world, but her own descent from riches is a descent into humility like that of the Queen of Heaven herself, both when Mary condescends and intercedes now for men and women, and when humble herself, she became the vessel for the still greater humbling of God, who came to earth to ransom humanity— the event that is recalled when Captain Viedma first appears in *Don Quijote*, leading Zoraida seated on a donkey, only to find no room at the inn (384; 386).[24] The ensuing story of Leandra may suggest a different, purely human interpretation of the Captive's Tale by which we are to see Zoraida's actions as the behavior of a flighty young woman, and Zoraida's father blames her for immodesty and for having been spoiled by her wealth (425; 427). But Zoraida insists that she has been prompted by forces beyond her will (425; 427), and it is hard to dispel the feeling of sublimity that the tale evokes, or the opinion expressed by the uncle of one of the returning companions of Captain Viedma that their deliverance has indeed been miraculous—"milagrosa libertad" (429; 431).

The Captive's Tale thus raises and ultimately disavows the notion that mercenary motives have infiltrated into and all but destroyed human love and heroism, particularly the national heroism of Spain for which Captain Viedma's career may stand as an epitome. The tale suggests that such heroism could itself be made captive to money, turning the war against Islam into mere piracy and the back-and-forth trading of human lives. But as it divests itself of Zoraida's riches and makes her conversion its final objective, the Captive's story regains heroic stature and reinvokes the crusading mission of Spanish arms. By the same token, the tale has depicted the Captain's desire diverted from Zoraida's beauty to her wealth, the two becoming one and the same in his imagining of her, and suggests how money and worldly interests enter the chemistry of love; at the tale's end, the Captain has Zoraida alone to love. The jettisoning of Zoraida's jewels and gold may thus be read as a narrative trick by which Cervantes is able to back away from and repudiate the troubling intimations of the story—and to substitute a Christian resolution in their place. The money that has been the means of action and desire in the story is not allowed to be their end.

Modern Marriage

Captain Viedma does not marry for money, however tempted he may have been to do so; Don Quijote merely fantasizes about it. Other characters of *Don Quijote* do marry up in the world. The Captive's Tale is contrasted in the chapters that immediately follow it with the goings-on of his brother's side of the family. Virtually the first thing we learn about Judge Juan Pérez de Viedma is that he had married well: he had become very rich when his wife died in childbirth, leaving him her dowry with her newborn daughter (436; 435). This story of social ascent climaxes in the next generation of the Viedma family, for the daughter, Clara, in one more interpolated episode of Part One, is sought in marriage by the higher-ranking Don Luis in Chapters 43–44. Money brought into the family from one advantageous alliance has led to a second advantageous alliance: the Viedmas have reached the high nobility.[25]

It is appropriately to Dorotea that Clara confides her fear that the father of Don Luis is so grand and rich that he will not think her worthy of being his son's servant, much less his wife—"criada de su hijo, cuanto más esposa" (442; 444). For Clara's dilemma strongly parallels Dorotea's own story: she had told Don Fernando how angry *his* father would be at finding him married to the peasant daughter of one his own vassals—"casado con una villana, vasalla suya" (283; 283). Peasant Dorotea may be, but she sees herself as rising socially even before Don Fernando courts her. Her family, she recounts, are of the sort of in-between rank of people "who by their wealth and handsome ways of living are by degrees acquiring the name of hidalgos, even of gentlemen" ["que su riqueza y magnífico trato les va poco a poco adquiriendo nombre de hidalgos, y aun de caballeros" (280; 279)]. And Dorotea is already the lady of the manor, that is, she is the "señora" or accountant of her parents' farm: "tenía yo la cuenta, y era mayordoma y señora" (280; 279). (We may think ahead to Zoraida, who is the "señora" of her own father's vast wealth.) Cervantes deliberately quibbles and plays with perspective to suggest the gap between the middling sort "mayordoma" that Dorotea is and the noblewoman she aspires to be. Dorotea's economic skills of calculation— "la razón y cuenta" (280; 279)—mark, in fact, her belonging to a modern class, moneyed but without defined status, and they help to explain her pluckiness and ingenuity that has impressed critics of the novel.[26]

This calculation also colors her relationship with her seducer, Don Fernando, who suddenly appears in her bedroom in the dark of night. When her "razones" against their marriage fail to impress him, she describes Don Fernando as "like a man so eager to clinch a bargain that he brushes aside all the troublesome conditions he is bound to pay" ["como el que no piensa pagar, que, al concertar de la barata, no repara en inconvenientes" (283; 283)]. Dorotea drives a hard bargain, the exchange of her body for Don Fernando's promise to marry her. But it is Dorotea's calculation with herself—"a esta razón"—that is most striking:

> I did give brief thought to the matter, saying to myself: "I shall not, after all, be the first whose marriage has raised her from low to high state, nor will Don Fernando be the first whom beauty or blind love (which is more probable) has prompted to choose a bride of humble station. As I am doing nothing that has not been done before, I should be wise to accept this honor that Fortune offers me, for even if his desire only lasts until he has had his way, I shall be his wife in the eyes of God. (283)

> Yo, a esta razón, hice un breve discurso conmigo, y me dije a mí mesma: "Sí, que no seré yo la primera que por vía de matrimonio haya subido de humilde a grande estado, ni será don Fernando el primero a quien hermosura, o ciega afición, que es lo más cierto, haya hecho tomar compañía desigual a su grandeza. Pues si no hago ni mundo ni uso nuevo, bien es acudir a esta honra que la suerte me ofrece, puesto que en éste no dure más la voluntad que me muestra de cuanto dure el cumplimiento de su deseo; que, en fin, para con Dios seré su esposa." (283)

Dorotea rationalizes her acquiescence to her lover's desires, and in so doing she blurs the meaning of the scene. Is Dorotea describing her near rape by Don Fernando or her entrapment of him into an unequal match?

A few chapters later, the situation will be inverted, when Dorotea will play the role of Princess Micomicona, supposedly willing to confer her wealth and rank on Don Quijote. Sancho tells his master to marry Micomicona-Dorotea and asks him whether he thinks Fortune offers such opportunities every day: "¿Piensa que le ha de ofrecer la fortuna tras cada cantillo semejante ventura como la que ahora se le ofrece?" (305; 306). He goes on to suggest that Don Quijote can keep Dulcinea, his true love, as a mistress on the side. Don Quijote refuses marriage on these terms, but Dorotea herself knew well enough to seize the prize that fortune— "la suerte"—offered her in Don Fernando, even if that meant a loveless marriage: Don Fernando may no longer desire her, but it will be too late for him—and for her as well. Her rational calculation already makes clear that for her, marriage is foremost a matter of worldly position, rather than of love. When Dorotea is not in disguise feeding Don Quijote's fantasies of fortune hunting and social climbing, she is participating in and actually carrying out her own. She is a thoroughly modern young woman.

Unattractive as Dorotea may appear at this moment, she is generally treated with sympathy by Cervantes, in part because she is placed in a genuine dilemma by Don Fernando's forcing himself upon her, but also because she subsequently becomes the agent who tames Don Fernando's aristocratic pride and violence.[27] He will indeed be reformed under her influence, the epitome of noble generosity who pays Don Quijote's bills and becomes the protector of the love of Don Luis and Clara. As the aristocrat made a better man by the love of a good woman of lower social standing, Don Fernando will have a long line of successors in the future of the novel. Stephen Gilman compares the calculating Dorotea to Becky Sharp, but she is more like Pamela, Elizabeth Bennet, and Jane Eyre.[28]

Don Quijote reverses genders when it depicts successful social advancement through marriage: Don Quijote himself may aspire to wed his princess, to carry her away by force if necessary, but it is the women, Dorotea and Clara, who marry up. The novel may make a concession to social reality, where the marriage of daughters of the middle class into the nobility was more normal and socially approved than of its sons: daughters who brought with them the wealth to replenish aristocratic fortunes.[29] This kind of exchange of money for noble rank does, in fact, take place in *Don Quijote*—both Dorotea and Clara are rich and therefore eligible for the greatness thrust upon them. Dorotea cattily observes that her rival Luscinda may come from "a very noble parentage, though not so rich that her dowry could justify so great a match" ["de muy principales padres, aunque no tan rica, que por la dote pudiera aspirar a tan noble casamiento" (285; 285)]: the implication is that Dorotea may have a larger dowry herself to bestow on Don Fernando, and we are once again privy to her modern way of looking at things.

Nevertheless, Don Fernando and Don Luis do not appear to need the money, and their loves appear as disinterested infatuation, what Dorotea calls, with characteristic self-deprecation, "blind love." We may feel that Cervantes's fiction is perpetuating a conservative social myth—that the nobleman stoops to marry beneath him on account of love—while it quietly allows us to read another story about the movement of money going on behind the scenes.[30] Social advancement through marriage may be conceded to women like Dorotea because it may be their only means to rise in the world, while there is something shameful and, as the Captive's Tale suggests, unheroic in a man's wedding for wealth and position— something shameful, too, for the woman of higher status, who both dishonors her family and seems to reveal sexual immodesty and forwardness in choosing to love a social inferior.[31] *Don Quijote* establishes a pattern for the classic history of the novel that will generally be more tolerant of women who marry into a higher condition than to similarly aspiring men: the latter may be thwarted and punished (think, in different ways, of Julien Sorel, Alexei Karenin, Clyde Griffiths, Maestro Don Gesualdo—or, to take a satirical version contemporary to Cervantes, the rise of the pauper Lazarillo de Tormes into prosperity through his marriage with the mistress of his lordship the archpriest). Whether successful or failed, however, the attempt to rise in the world—which the advantageous marriage either enables or confirms—becomes the abiding subject of the novel. In the "Princess Micomicona" story Cervantes has hit upon a staple plot of the new genre he is inventing in *Don Quijote*. It succeeds the "Dulcinea" story of idolatrous male jealousy, which his novel simultaneously portrays as its holdover from an earlier era, as the love story of modern fiction.

Social Mobility, Generic Mix

With the "Princess Micomicona" plot and the marriage-and-money stories clustered around it, *Don Quijote* seems to have entered fully upon the terrain and preoccupations of the modern novel, the measure of a historical shift from a stratified feudal society to the more open social world of a nascent capitalism. What are the *formal* effects of this social openness on the genre that Cervantes is inventing to portray it? Cervantes suggests some answers when he pauses to reflect on the generic nature of *Don Quijote* in the discussions about literary matters that the Canon of Toledo has with the Curate and Don Quijote in Chapters 47–50. A bitter critic of chivalric romances, the Canon has nonetheless undertaken to write one of his own according to the best neo-Aristotelian rules: he hopes to write an epic in prose—"la épica también puede escrebirse en prosa como en verso" (479; 483). As critics have pointed out, the literary model that the Canon upholds contrasts not only with the fantastic romances, but with the fiction of Cervantes's novel.[32] What has been less noticed is how the Canon's conversations are framed and determined by questions of class mobility.

The Canon significantly begins by rejecting the "Princess Micomicona" story itself, the plot of marrying for wealth and status that organizes this section of *Don Quijote*. In the passage below from Chapter 47, in which the Canon lists a series of absurdities in the chivalric romances that offend against literary verisimilitude, we should note how Cervantes craftily injects the tale of the marriageable princess:

> But what beauty or what structural harmony can there possibly be in a book or story where a youth of sixteen gives one slash of his sword at a giant as tall as a steeple and slices him in two halves as tidily as if he was made of almond paste? And when they wish to describe a battle, they tell us that there are a million fighting men on the enemy's side, and if the hero of the book is to face them, they compel us to believe, in spite of our protests, that such and such a knight obtained the victory by the valor of his doughty arm alone. *Then, what shall we say of the ease with which a hereditary queen- or empress-to-be sinks into the arms of an unknown knight?* How could any mind that is not wholly barbarous and unlettered be entertained by reading that a massive tower filled with knights sails over the sea like a ship with favoring breezes . . . ? (477–78, my emphasis)

> Pues ¿qué hermosura puede haber, o qué proporción de partes con el todo, y del todo con las partes, en un libro o fábula donde un mozo de diez y seis años da una cuchillada a un gigante como una torre, y le divide en dos mitades, como si fuera de alfeñique, y que cuando nos quieren pintar una batalla, después de haber dicho que hay de la parte de los enemigos un millón de competientes, como sea contra ellos el señor del libro, forzosamente, mal que nos pese, habemos de entender que el tal caballero alcanzó la vitoria por solo el valor de su fuerte brazo? *Pues ¿qué diremos de la facilidad con que una reina o emperatriz heredera se conduce en los brazos de un andante y no conocido caballero?* ¿Qué ingenio, si no es del todo bárbaro e inculto, podrá contentarse leyendo que una gran torre llena de caballeros va por la mar adelante, como nave con próspero viento . . . ? (481, my emphasis)

As he protests against improbable fictions, the Canon makes no distinction between violations of physical nature and violations of social decorum, and thereby suggests that in his mind social hierarchy is itself naturalized. His ideas of literary verisimilitude—of what makes a plausible fiction—are conditioned by fixed notions of class and status. The princess in question is a *hereditary* one. High rank is something one is born with, not something to which one can rise, and we are reminded of Don Quijote's comic worries in Chapter 21 about whether his lack of royal lineage will cause his princess to reject him. The Canon's social conservatism is clear enough. When he goes on to describe the ideal chivalric romance that he has been trying to write to replace the bad ones full of their improbabilities, he concludes in a final phrase that it should represent "the goodness and loyalty of vassals, the greatness and generosity of noblemen" ["representando bondad y lealtad de vasallos, grandezas y mercedes de señores" (479; 483)]. The faithful subordinate and the generous superior, each knowing his place and duties: this is the static, stratified social order that the Canon presupposes and that his vision of literature, focused on epic, the highest of genres, would maintain and reproduce.[33]

The Canon's precepts are returned to him with an ironic twist, however, at the end of his conversations. In Chapter 50 Don Quijote tells him that his own chivalric career is precisely motivated by his aim to demonstrate noble generosity—"la virtud de liberalidad"—and to reward the loyal service of Sancho Panza. For that reason he returns to his hopes that fortune will soon offer him the chance that will make him an emperor— "querría que la fortuna me ofreciese presto alguna ocasión donde me hiciese emperador" (498; 502)—a rise in social status that will enable him to raise Sancho, in turn, to the rank of count.

Such offers of Fortune, we know by now, consist primarily of marriage partners, of nubile princesses ready for the taking. And that princess seems to appear once more in the little chivalric episode—the story of the knight's adventure in an enchanted realm beneath a burning lake—that Don Quijote has just recounted to the Canon in order to demonstrate the pleasure that can be derived from reading the romances.[34] She is the damsel, much more beautiful than the others—"mucho más hermosa doncella que ninguna de las primeras" (498; 501)—who appears to the knight at the story's end. Before she comes on the scene, however, the knight has already been given the royal treatment by a whole bevy of damsels:

> [They] bathe him in luke-warm water and then anoint him all over with sweet-smelling ointments and put on him a shirt of finest samite, all fragrant and perfumed, while another damsel hastens to throw over his shoulders a mantle that they say is worth at least the price of a city, and even more. (497)

> bañarle con templadas aguas, y luego untarle todo con olorosos ungüentos, y vestirle una camisa de cendal delgadísimo, todo olorosa y perfumada, y acudir otra doncella y echarle un mantón sobre los hombros, que, por lo menos menos, dicen que suele valer una ciudad, y aún más. (501)

We should recognize in the knight's lavish entertainment in the enchanted palace—the bathing and scenting of his body by the maidens, the rich clothing he is given, the sumptuous feast with its musical accompaniment that he will go on to enjoy—one more version, in ever more fantastic form, of the aristocratic hospitality that Don Quijote had described in the model chivalric romance he tells to Sancho in Chapter 21: the "rich mantle of scarlet" ["un rico manto de escarlata" (204; 197)] awarded to the knightly guest in the earlier passage now becomes a mantle beyond price. Details of both chapters will be picked up and imitated by those attentive readers, the Duke and Duchess, when they host Don Quijote in Part Two. Don Quijote's evocation of this scene suggests, however, other motives for the chivalric career than the desire to exhibit liberality to his faithful servant. The pleasures of the romances, pleasures that appeal to the five senses and that seem all the more attainable here—all the knight has to do is jump into the burning lake, perhaps a figure for passing through the looking glass of literature itself—are for Don Quijote the imagined luxury of aristocratic life. Wealth on constant display is enchanting, the underwater Elysium a consumer's paradise. Never mind Sancho and his earldom: Don Quijote hungers to meet his princess and to rise to this high life for himself, and, in this respect his desires may be more modern than he knows. This frame to the Canon's literary discussions permits us to infer that the different social visions of the Canon and of Don Quijote condition their respective aesthetic ideas. The traditional, unchanging social hierarchy that the Canon takes for granted underlies his neoclassical epic norms, while Don Quijote's wild dreams of social mobility allow for the free flight of romance fantasy, pure wish-fulfillment.

But epic is distinguished here not only from romance, but from novel: we should also infer that *real* mobility in a society made newly fluid by the force of money separates *Don Quijote* itself from the aesthetic strictures of the Canon. The Canon, indeed, is deterred from writing his prose epic by one aspect of this newly mobile society, the emergence of a literary marketplace. In Chapter 48 he says that he put his project aside when he considered the contemporary state of the public theater, in which plays, the Curate goes on to note, have become a "marketable commodity" ["mercadería vendible" (483; 487)]. The taste of a mass, rather than elite, audience—taste that may include an appetite for stories of social advancement between classes—has produced a drama that does not observe the rules of Aristotle and his Renaissance commentators.[35]

The Curate agrees in deploring the plays of his time. In addition to violating the classical unities of time and place, he complains, they also offend against social decorum:

> What could be more ridiculous than to portray a valiant old man, and a young coward, an eloquent lackey, a statesmanlike page, a king as a porter, and a princess as a kitchen maid? (482)

Y ¿qué mayor que pintarnos un viejo valiente y un mozo cobarde, un lacayo
rectórico, un paje consejero, un rey ganapán y una princesa fregona? (486)

These characters do not act their age, nor do they act their station in life:
servants speak too well and wisely; royalty behave like servants. Cervantes once again chooses his examples pointedly, and this polemic against
the commercial theater, and against the plays of Lope de Vega in particular, turns back to comment on his own novel—a book that is itself
"found" in the marketplace of Toledo in Chapter 9.

At around fifty years of age, Don Quijote is himself a valiant old man,
or at least, says his niece in Chapter 6 of Part Two, he is an old man who
thinks himself valiant—"se dé a entender que es valiente, siendo viejo"
(567; 579–80). Sancho Panza is an eloquent servant, so much so that in
the preceding Chapter 5 of Part Two, the narrator questions whether the
conversation that he shares with Teresa Panza is not apocryphal because
of its style (557; 570): a conversation that is precisely about social advancement and the making of their daughter either into a duchess or princess. The princess–scullery maid should makes us think of the earlier episode of Chapter 16 in which Don Quijote's imagined princess was, in
fact, the inn's servant wench Maritornes: a Maritornes who, moreover,
fancies herself of noble birth—"presumía muy de hidalga" (155; 146)—
forced by circumstances to serve at the inn, much like Costanza, the heroine of Cervantes's novella, *La ilustre fregona*, written either shortly before
or after Part One of *Don Quijote*. (Meanwhile, his love for Clara has
made Don Luis, the highest ranking character of Part One, disguise himself in Chapter 43 as a lowly muleteer—a "mozo de mulas" (439; 441)—
which puts him in the same profession and social level as Maritornes's real
lover, the "harriero" in Chapter 16.)[36] We may think, too, of "Princess
Micomicona"/Dorotea revealed to Sancho only a few chapters back in
Chapter 46 as something worse than a kitchen maid: the word "puta"
that escapes his lips causes Don Quijote to banish his squire from his
sight for "being the enemy of the decorum owed to royal personages"
["enemigo del decoro que se debe a las reales personas" (467; 470)].

What the Curate criticizes as a lack of social decorum in the theater is
virtually the condition of Cervantes's novel, in which the central hero's
taking up of a new chivalric role and a career that leads, through the
obliging princess, to nothing less than emperorship is the fantasy reflection of the modern society and characters that surround him—a world in
which it is, in fact, possible to rise and free oneself from the identity of
caste. The three Viedma brothers seek success in "Iglesia, o mar, o casa
real." Dorotea becomes, if not a princess like the "Micomicona" she pretends to be, the wife of a duke's son, and Clara may become a duchess.
The lowliest character of all, Andrés, leaves a peasant existence that seems

hardly better than servitude, and heads in Chapter 31 for Seville (318; 319), where he will either be swallowed into the picaresque urban under-world described by Cervantes in "Rinconete y Cortadillo" or from where he will find his fortune, like two of the Viedma brothers, in the New World—the Judge is also traveling to Seville in order to embark for Mex-ico (437; 439).[37] In this world on the move, classes mingle and distinctions between high and low—the stuff of decorum—begin to blur.

Genre distinctions also begin to blur in this novelistic world: they are not the same as social distinctions, but they are evidently closely related. The Canon wants to write a prose epic. While he allows for the new Renaissance aesthetic goal of Ariostesque variety, and intends to include lyric, tragic, and comic elements inside his work, he nonetheless subordi-nates them in Chapter 47 to the epic goal of modeling idealized and exem-plary military—read aristocratic—heroes: the valorous captain, the Chris-tian knight, the valorous prince himself, summed up in the "varón ilustre" (479; 482–83). He assimilates such characters in Chapter 49 with biblical and classical heroes as well as with the heroes of Spain's national history, such as Gonzalo Fernández, the Great Captain, and Diego García de Pa-redes (491; 494). As he takes social hierarchy for granted, the Canon also accepts a traditional notion of the hierarchy of literary genres ranked according to the dignity of their subject and the class of their protagonists. Epic occupies the top rung of this generic ladder, and in his literary aspira-tions the Canon aims nowhere if not high.[38]

Don Quijote is less socially exclusive when it comes to questions of genre, and perhaps less inclined to identify high-mindedness with high rank. The novel offers an emblem of its capaciousness and of a variety much more far reaching than that entertained by the Canon in the trunk of literary matter found at the inn in Chapter 32. Inside the trunk the Curate finds the very work that the Canon will later recommend to Don Quijote, the *Historia del Gran Capitán Gonzalo Hernández de Córdoba, con la vida de Diego García de Paredes*, but he finds it alongside two chivalric romances, *Don Cirongilio de Tracia* and *Felixmarte de Hircania*, the preferred reading of the Innkeeper. The Curate distinguishes the rela-tion of the deeds of Spain's great military leader, Gonzalo de Córdoba, in the Italian wars at the beginning of the sixteenth century as true history— "historia verdadera" (322; 323)—and the contrast with the fantastic der-ring-do of the chivalric heroes initially suggests the distinction between historical fact and fictional impossibility, support for the Canon's later criticism of the romances. But, as the title suggests, the *Historia* is a double work, and it also contains the exploits of Gonzalo's lieutenant, García de Paredes, exploits such as stopping a mill wheel with one finger, told by none other than Diego García himself, as the Curate says, "with the mod-esty of a knight and of his own self-chronicler" ["con la modestia de caballero y de coronista propio" (322; 323)]. Cervantes winks at us and through this last phrase suggests that García Paredes was a braggart, whether the Curate and Canon realize it or not, and that "history" is open to self-interested embroidery that makes it hardly less fantastic than the chivalric fictions to which the Canon wishes to oppose it. It is, in fact, Vicente de la Rosa, the boasting, charlatan soldier of the Leandra story in Chapter 51, who will claim to have engaged in more single combats in the Turkish wars than García de Paredes (504; 507).

To these initial offerings of the trunk, Don Quijote's romances on the one hand, the Canon's history on the other, the trunk yields two more works, the *Novela del Curioso impertinente*, taken out and read by the Curate in Chapters 33–35, and the *Novela de Rinconete y Cortadillo*, whose presence in the trunk is revealed in Chapter 47 (473; 477) and which appears also to have been written by the author of the "Curioso impertinente"—that is to say, both novellas are by Cervantes, the author of "Rinconete y Cortadillo," a picaresque story of two young Sevillian thieves. The play of fiction and history is continued at the end of the "Curioso impertinente" in Chapter 35 when it is learned that its protagonist, Lotario, has died in a battle between the French commander Lautrec and "the Great Captain, Gonzalo Hernández de Córdoba" (370; 371), a sudden framing of the story within history that lends it an apparently factual basis. Cervantes may be suggesting that the realism of his Italian novella and his Spanish picaresque tale occupies a kind of generic middle ground between chivalric extravagance and historical "truth," a truth already made suspect by the modest chronicle of García de Paredes.

It would be mistaken, however, merely to see Cervantes carving out in *Don Quijote* a place for modern realistic fiction between fantasy and history and opposed to both. The trunk and its entire, varied contents stand for the larger novel *Don Quijote*, which will include not only the heroic, historical matter (the Great Captain) singled out by the Canon, but other genres as well.[39] In fact, each of the works the trunk contains has its corresponding generic feature or plot episode inside the novel, mapped out in table 3.2.

The two books of chivalry, of course, correspond to all of the parodic romance elements of the novel, either contained in or reflected by the fantasies that Don Quijote has derived from his reading, some from these very books. Specifically, the exploits that the innkeeper attributes to Felixmarte, slicing five giants in two with a backhand cut—"de un revés"— and routing an immense army as if they had been sheep (322–23; 324), remind us of Don Quijote's assault on the Innkeeper's wineskins, which he takes for a giant in Chapter 35, and which he subsequently claims to have despatched "de un revés" (380; 382), and his attacking the sheep, which he takes to be an army in Chapter 18; Don Cirongilio's adventures

TABLE 3.2
The Trunk at the Inn

Trunk	Novel
Don Felixmarte	Don Quijote and the Winesacks
	Don Quijote and the Sheep
Don Cirongilio	Don Quijote's Fantasy of the Lake
The Great Captain Gonzalo Hernández de Córdoba	Captain Viedma and the Captive's Tale
Diego García de Paredes	Vicente de la Rosa
Curioso impertinente	Cardenio-Don Fernando-Luscinda
Rinconete y Cortadillo	Ginés de Pasamonte; the Inn and the Road

in the enchanted underwater realm (323; 324) will be expanded into Don Quijote's description of the paradise beneath the burning lake in Chapter 50. The true history of the Great Captain has its counterpart in the Captive's Tale, a true story—"discurso verdadero" (392; 394)—told by *Captain* Viedma about the real military theater of the wars against the Turks; the Great Captain has his debased version in the boasting Diego García de Paredes, just as Captain Viedma's story is parodied by the swaggering Vicente de la Rosa with whom, we have just observed, Diego García is assimilated. The tale of the "Curioso impertinente" is interlaced—as Chapter Two demonstrated—with the novella narrative of Cardenio, Don Fernando, and Luscinda. "Rinconete y Cortadillo" finds its match in the picaresque structure and setting of *Don Quijote*, in the wandering of its hero through the impoverished world of the road and the inn, in his encounters with the pícaro author Ginés de Pasamonte.

All of these genres of the trunk, then—epic history, make-believe history, romance, novella, picaresque adventure—are contained together and, more importantly, combine and coalesce in the portmanteau novel that Cervantes assembles. The effect is what Mikhail Bakhtin called "novelization." Inside the emergent novel, he wrote, traditional genres become "permeated with laughter, irony, humor, elements of self-parody and finally—this is the most important thing—the novel inserts into those other genres an indeterminacy, a certain semantic openendedness, a living contact with unfinished, still evolving contemporary reality."[40] Two modern expositors of Bakhtin helpfully comment: "At times, [genres] may be forced to compete with rival genres as the best way to visualize a given aspect of life. No longer sensed as indisputably correct within its sphere, a genre may instead be perceived as one participant in an ongoing dialogue about its characteristic type."[41] Thus genres are tested as they jostle for space and present different versions of lived experience within a novel-istic framework, a contestation that accounts in no small part, too, for the "perspectivism"—the call to look at the same phenomenon from different angles and different systems of value that Leo Spitzer analyzed in *Don Quijote*.[42] With such a mixture of genres there arises the typically modern sensibility of the novel: a perception of the impurity of human experience itself, which cannot be contained within the categories, conventions, and decorum of any single genre.

This modern sensibility depends upon modern circumstances. For what Bakhtin calls "an evolving contemporary reality," we may read in *Don Quijote* a new world of money and social openness that challenges an older, closed aristocratic order and that order's idealized self-image held up by the conservative literary theory of the Canon of Toledo.[43] The social mobility that destabilizes class hierarchy finds its literary reflection in *Don Quijote* in the blurring of generic contours and of distinctions between high and low narrative forms. The Captive's Tale is a case in point. The story of the valorous Captain Viedma is the closest equivalent in the novel to the kind of epic subject matter that the Canon has in mind, yet his tale shares features of chivalric romance (the white-handed princess who falls in love with the visiting knight) on the one hand, of the picaresque (paying the innkeeper) on the other. The affinity to the picaresque goes further: the liberation of Captain Viedma, the former gal-ley slave, is juxtaposed and contrasted with Don Quijote's liberation of the convicts on their way to the galleys in Chapter 22. The Captain's true first-person narrative that, so he tells the listeners at the inn, may surpass lying fictions—"un discurso verdadero a quien podría ser que no llegasen los mentirosos" (392; 394)—seems to be linked generically not only to the "historia verdadera" of the Great Captain, but to the life-"history" ["historia" (214; 208)] penned by one of those rescued convicts, the pica-resque author Ginés de Pasamonte, who assures us that it deals with truths more delightful than lies—"verdades tan lindas y tan donosas que no pueden haber mentiras que se le igualen" (215; 208). Like his brothers, the Captain sets out in his story to find his place in the world, and his social indeterminacy—he is at once a heroic, if impoverished career sol-dier, a gentleman/knight (the "caballero" described by Zoraida), and a miserable slave—places him in more than one genre at once. At the same time the agent of social fluidity—money—can simultaneously raise his tale to the fantastic stuff of romance (the fabulous wealth that turns Zora-ida into a princess) or lower it to the quotidian realism of the picaresque (the negotiations for buying his way out of captivity.) In the Captain's story genres compete and are superimposed one on the other to become something new: they are "novelized." The same can be said of *Don Qui-jote* as a whole.

When the Canon of Toledo rejects the "Princess Micomicona" story, the marriage of high and low, he rejects the conditions of the genre of the novel: both its new subject matter, the desire for worldly advancement promoted by a fluid, moneyed society, and its innovative form: the absorption and mixture of earlier genres. In fact, the literary discussions inaugurated by the Canon permit us to see how modern subject and modern form are connnected in *Don Quijote*. The novel's depiction of a social world that is more mobile and heterogenous than the Canon wishes to recognize is accomplished not through a single, highest epic genre, but through the juxtaposition and combination of multiple genres that the Canon wishes to keep hierarchically distinct. The varied contents of the trunk at the inn are matched as an emblem of the larger novel by the inn itself, which houses under one roof characters and their stories ranging up and down the social and generic spectrum from Don Luis to Maritornes. The inn is a place of mobility and transition: it is a traveler's trunk that we are talking about. It is also a place of money, where one pays as one goes. It attests to the openness and provisionality of the new genre that Cervantes is inventing for modern times. To keep up with a society that from now on will always be in flux, the novel commits itself to a future of continuing formal evolution.

A final comment on "novelization" returns us to where these analyses of Part One began: to narrative interlace. Cervantes uses the technique of interlace that he inherited from chivalric romance to structure the book and establish thematic connections among its episodes. The juxtaposition of different stories that turn out to be so many variants of a single plot produces the "Dulcinea" and "Princess Micomicona" narrative clusters. But Cervantes's interlace does double duty: it also juxtaposes the different genres in which the parallel stories are told. The romance and picaresque elements in the Captive's Tale become visible because of the resemblances of Zoraida at her window to Don Quijote's fantasy princess at the garden railing on the one hand, to the Innkeeper's daughter at the loophole in the loft on the other. Interlace is thus a formal instrument of "novelization": hitherto separate genres become parodic of each other or reveal secret affinities—they begin to look alike. Interlace not only unifies *Don Quijote* thematically; it also contributes to the novel's generic and stylistic unity by dissolving the boundaries of the earlier genres contained in its hybrid fiction. As it moves among genres in the novel, the formal effect of interlace is the counterpart of the social mobility portrayed in its fictional world: it acts much like money itself, making different classes rub shoulders and breaking down distinctions among them. Cervantes adds into the mix that other universal solvent of genres—prose—and the novel is born.

Coda: "Nuestra Señora"

Don Quijote's final and crowning act in Part One is his most outrageous. He assaults a group of disciplinants carrying an image of the Virgin Mary in Chapter 52. He concludes that she is a noble lady being carried off against her will—"contra su voluntad" (510; 514)—and seeks to rescue her. Sancho tries to warn him and, in doing so, spells out the meaning of Don Quijote's act: "What devils in your heart are driving you on to attack our Catholic faith?" ["¿Qué demonios lleva en el pecho, que le incitan a ir contra nuestra fe católica?" (510; 513)]. It is Don Quijote's third attack on ecclesiastical figures: in Chapter 8, he attacks two Benedictine friars; in Chapter 19 he breaks the leg of a licentiate accompanying a funeral procession and acknowleges that he has incurred excommunication. Don Quijote does not pay heed to Sancho's words, and would not have turned back "though the king himself had commanded it" ["si el rey se lo mandara" (510; 513)]. He opposes himself both to church and state, and the episode underscores just how anarchic and antisocial his behavior really is in Part One. Don Quijote's attack is interlaced with his promise earlier in the same chapter to rescue Leandra, whose beauty has been described as like that of a "wonder-working image" ["imagen de milagros" (502; 506)], from the convent where her father has placed her against her will—"contra su voluntad" (507; 511). Once Don Quijote is released from his own captivity in his cage, he is intent on freeing others. But his deluded attempt to play the role of redeemer—we are reminded, too, of his freeing of the galley slaves—here brings him into conflict not only with the authorities, but with the true source of human redemption.

One of the disciplinants, a peasant—"villano" (511; 514)—knocks Don Quijote senseless in one last example of the knight being bettered by the lower social orders. As he comes to, Don Quijote invokes the name of his lady: "He who lives absent from thee, sweet Dulcinea, endures far greater sufferings than these" ["El que de vos vive ausente, dulcísima Dulcinea, a mayores miserias que éstas está sujeto" (512; 515)]. These flowery words—one notes the alliteration and repetition—are virtually the last he speaks in the book, Don Quijote's valediction.

The irony is clear, even heavy-handed. Beside the image of "Nuestra Señora," Don Quijote calls upon the lady he calls "mi señora," the mistress of his soul—"señora de mi alma" (104; 88). The episode culminates a chain of symbolic arguments that runs through Part One of *Don Quijote* and begins when Don Quijote commends himself to Dulcinea before plunging into battle in Chapters 3 and 8 (71, 104–105; 51, 88).[44] The traveler Vivaldo questions this practice of knights-errant in Chapter 13: "never at the instant of attack do they remember to commend their souls to God, as every Christian in such danger is obliged to do. Instead they commend themselves to their mistresses with as much fervor and devotion as if they were their god, a practice that seems to me to smack somewhat of heathenism" ["nunca en aquel instante de acometella se acuerdan de encomendarse a Dios, como cada cristiano está obligado a hacer en peligros semejantes; antes se encomiendan a sus damas, con tanta gana y devoción como si ellas fueran su Dios: cosa que me parece que huele algo a gentilidad" (132; 119)]. Don Quijote argues the point, but he is prudent enough to remember to recommend himself to Dulcinea and also "by the way"—"y de camino" (194; 187)—to God before facing the perils of the fulling mills in Chapter 20.

A more specific parallel and opposition between Dulcinea and the Virgin Mary is suggested by Ginés de Pasamonte in Chapter 22, who proposes that instead of going to El Toboso with chains around their necks— like captives newly redeemed from Algiers—he and his fellow galley slaves rescued by Don Quijote should say a certain number of Ave Marias and Credos (218; 213). Don Quijote remonstrates, but again seems to adapt the idea of the other character when he does penance for Dulcinea's sake in the Sierra Morena by reciting "a million Ave Marias" ["un millón de avemarías" (255; 252)], a penance that is contrasted with the real religious penitence of the self-mortifying disciplinants at the book's end.[45]

The Virgin Mary enters the fiction of Part One as a spiritual presence hovering over the Captive's Tale. Don Quijote's attack on the disciplinants scrambles the motifs of the Captive's story and is a final thread in the novel's pattern of interlace. When she first appears at the inn in Chapter 37, the converted Zoraida insists on the change of her name to Maria, and by the end of Captain Viedma's tale she seems to stand in place of the heavenly patroness who has inspired her, like those "imágenes" (430; 432) she sees in the churches of Spain and immediately recognizes as being like the Virgin. Don Quijote fails to "rescue" a similar image of the Virgin from whom the disciplinants seek miraculous intervention. Zoraida has, in fact, worked the wonder of ransoming the Captive—the "file of our chains" ["la lima de nuestras cadenas" (423; 425)], he calls her—and he has rescued her, in turn, from the captivity of Islam. Don Quijote's liberation from his cage in Chapter 49 is itself faintly reminiscent of this Marian deliverance: "I still put my faith in God and in His Blessed Mother" ["Aún espero en Dios y en su bendita Madre" (489; 493)], he declares to Rocinante—his only mention of the Virgin Mary in Part One. Though Captain Viedma will subsequently marry Zoraida, he now accompanies her "as a father and squire, not as her husband" ["de padre y escudero, y no de esposo" (430; 432)], and as she now plays the role of Mary to his Joseph, Zoraida points to a love that transcends worldly, even erotic considerations. In his final gesture in the novel, Don Quijote substitutes for the image of the Virgin the lady of his own idolatrous imagination, in effect opposing to divine love his love for Dulcinea.

Cervantes introduces "Nuestra Señora" as a shadowy third term into Part One of *Don Quijote*, a third object of love alongside both "Dulcinea" and "Princess Micomicona." In doing so, I want to suggest, he distinguishes his novel's criticism of the new world of money from that of his character Don Quijote, who both rejects that world and attempts to transcend it. Here, too, *Don Quijote* makes a decisive contrast between Don Quijote's chivalry and the story of the modern Christian soldier, Captain Viedma.

By the end of Part One, the "Micomicona" cluster of stories has largely succeeded the "Dulcinea" cluster: the shift in love fantasies from woman as object of male rivalry to woman as means to wealth and status marks a shift in historical mentalities conditioned respectively by an older aristocratic caste ethos and by the calculations of a modern, mobile society. In the latter, Cervantes appears to have understood the enabling circumstances for the new literary form that would become the modern novel— for the novel's mixture of genres, for its realism anchored in the presence and power of money. But Cervantes does not therefore approve in Part One of the modern world of money: he is hardly less critical of its replacement of human values than he is of the earlier world of jealous pride and honor.

The Captive's Tale, we have seen, is the principal modern enactment of the "Princess Micomicona" story of worldly advancement. But the Tale falls short of that story's goal and shifts goals entirely. It requires the relinquishment of money—the wealth of Zoraida that the Renegade throws overboard—in order to restore a heroic and religious meaning to its ending. The gallant Captain Viedma, who goes East to crusade against the Turks, is clearly a more heroic figure—the eldest and truest son of his father, the former soldier—than his two brothers, who make their fortunes sailing West to the literal and figurative gold mines of the New World; it is the Captain whom the fiction rewards by allowing him to return to and remain in Spain. Modern chivalry may not be dead after all, but it can only be preserved by separating itself from the mercenary projects and motives of modernity. Once Zoraida's wealth is gone, she ceases to be the princess of the get-rich-quick fantasy, and the Captive's love for her is itself redeemed, made akin to devotion to the Virgin.

Don Quijote, too, chooses chivalry over money; he rejects wealth and power when it seems that Fortune is offering them to him in the person of "Princess Micomicona." As much as Don Quijote may fantasize about the princess who will lead him to the luxury life of the rich, in Chapter 30 he turns down "Micomicona"'s offer of her person and kingdom in order to remain true to Dulcinea (305; 306).[46] He does so much to the dismay of

Sancho Panza, who despairs of receiving his island and the black African subjects whom he intends in Chapter 29 to sell off into slavery in order to finance the purchase of an earldom back in Spain (295; 296)—the novel's most pessimistic vision of how economic opportunities, especially those recently created by a transatlantic economy, have made for a new social mobility.[47] In order to separate Don Quijote from "Princess Micomicona" and to allow the real-life Dorotea to go off with Don Fernando, the Curate and Barber cage Don Quijote by "enchantment" in Chapter 46, but console him with the prophecy that he will one day marry Dulcinea—and that Sancho will receive his wages, if not the island. But Don Quijote had, in fact, already long before made his choice for Dulcinea.

It is a choice only partly made for the right reasons. Don Quijote may renounce marrying "Micomicona" for her money, though he reassures the unhappy Sancho in Chapter 31 that he can strike a deal that will give him part of her kingdom without the necessity of marrying her (314; 315). His love for Dulcinea, he goes on to explain in the same passage, is a selfless one that does not seek any benefit in return:

> "Do you not see, Sancho, that all this redounds to her greater aggrandizement? You should know that according to our code of chivalry it is a great honor for a lady to have many knights-errant serving her, with no greater aim in life than that of serving her for what she is and without expectations of any rewards for their many, good desires than that she should be content to accept them as her knights."
>
> "That's the sort of love," said Sancho, "I've heard them preach about, and they add we ought to love Our Lord for Himself alone, without being driven to it by hope of glory or the fear of punishment; but speaking for myself, I'm all for serving Him for what He can do for me." (315)

> ¿Tú no ves, Sancho, que eso todo redunda en su mayor ensalzamiento? Porque has de saber que en este nuestro estilo de caballería es gran honra tener una dama muchos caballeros andantes que la sirvan, sin que se estiendan más sus pensamientos que a servilla por sólo ser ella quien es, sin esperar otro premio de sus muchos y buenos deseos sino que ella se contente de acetarlos por sus caballeros.
>
> —Con esa manera de amor—dijo Sancho—he oído yo predicar que se ha de amar a Nuestro Señor, por sí solo, sin que nos mueva esperanza de gloria o temor de pena. Aunque yo le querría amar y servir por lo que pudiese. (316)

The comic pragmatism with which Sancho ends his rejoinder slightly blunts the critical force of its Christianity; while Sancho may not love God as selflessly as he should, it is his master who is misguided and who has made a god out of his lady. Don Quijote's disclaiming of interested, mercenary motives for his love may be creditable in itself, but it substitutes a false transcendence of the world for a true one.

The mad hidalgo ultimately renounces the modern desire for wealth and status barely disguised in his dreams of the princess. His choice is emblematic of his refusal of the modern world itself, however he may secretly be tempted by it. But Don Quijote's response to the real, modern present is to retreat into a fantasy past and into a premodern love—his idolatrous cult of Dulcinea—that, as we have seen in Chapter Two, Cervantes's novel shows to be anything but selfless: it is rather fueled by pride. The aggrandizement—"ensalzamiento"—of his lady that Don Quijote describes is in fact the self-aggrandizement of the man who has imagined her, who worships himself in the idol he has made. Where the Captive finds Zoraida's wealth replaced by a miracle of the Virgin Mary, Don Quijote lets "Princess Micomicona" go for the sake of Dulcinea—but Dulcinea is a kind of anti-Mary.[48]

Part One of Don Quijote thus ends with an impasse. It brings its reader along with its hero face-to-face with a modern world in which the desire for money threatens to infect love and the sum of human relations love represents. But the proper response to this world, Cervantes makes clear in this final episode, is not to turn back the clock to an earlier historical formation in which love, represented in Don Quijote's love for Dulcinea and in the various stories that reflect upon it, reduces to egotism and aristocratic rivalry. There can be no going back. In Part Two of Don Quijote Cervantes finds an accommodation with modernity: he suggests how money can enable the charitable and peaceable ethos of a middling social class, and he contrasts this Christian ethos to the further disadvantage of older, aristocratic modes of behavior. At the same time, Don Quijote himself changes into a saner, more conciliatory and generous character. A new attitude toward money and its potentially beneficent uses will distinguish both the hero and the fiction of the second installment of Don Quijote.

DON QUIJOTE, PART TWO

FOUR

THE GENTLER, WISER DON QUIJOTE

CERVANTES REWRITES AND TURNS inside out the opposition between Dulcinea and "Princess Micomicona" that structures Part One of *Don Quijote* in the celebrated episode of the Cave of Montesinos in Part Two. In doing so, he registers a reorientation of his novel in its second installment. In Chapter 23, Don Quijote recounts his experience, a vision or dream vision, in the underground cavern. There he beheld heroes and heroines from his chivalric books and ballads dwelling in a state of enchantment that seems not so much suspended animation as living death. The lady Belerma carries the mummified, dried-up heart of the knight Durandarte; she herself has passed menopause, has few teeth in her head, circles under her eyes, and a sickly complexion. Don Quijote is informed that the hair and nails of the enchanted continue to grow: they are like corpses. Don Quijote's guide, the similarly enchanted Montesinos, compares the lady Belerma to Dulcinea of El Toboso, only to be brought up short by the ingenious hidalgo, who tells him that all comparisons are hateful: "The peerless Dulcinea is what she is, and Doña Belerma is what she is and has been, and there let the matter rest" ["La sin par Dulcinea del Toboso es quien es, y la señora Belerma es quien es, y quien ha sido, y quédese aquí" (691; 708)]. Shortly thereafter Don Quijote finds his own Dulcinea herself and two companions, leaping and frisking like she-goats—"iban saltando y brincando como cabras" (692; 709)—in the cave of enchantment. She appears to him as she had earlier done in Chapter 10, when Sancho Panza passed off a snub-nosed peasant girl as his master's beloved lady; by the pretended conditions of her enchantment only Don Quijote cannot see her in her proper form. This Dulcinea runs away from her devoted knight, swifter than an arrow, but one of her attendant damsels approaches Don Quijote to ask him for a loan of six reals on the good security of a new petticoat, promising him a prompt repayment. Don Quijote is amazed to learn from the sage Montesinos that "what is called want is the fashion all over the world" ["esta que llaman necesidad adondequiera se usa" (694; 711)]. Alas, he has only four reals to offer, and he wishes, in order to be able to relieve her need that he were a "Fúcar," a member of the family of great sixteenth-century banker-princes, the Fuggers of Augsburg. The damsel takes the deficient

TABLE 4.1
Dulcinea Compared

	Chivalric Past	Modern Times
Part One	Dulcinea	Micomicona/Bestows money
Montesinos (Part Two)	Belerma	Dulcinea/In need of money

sum, and perhaps registers her disappointment by cutting a caper—"ca-briola" (695; 712)—instead of curtsying in farewell, a final comic punctuation point to the episode.

Like other literary descents into the underworld, this episode seems to enter into the mind of the hero. It has been hailed as the pyschologically densest moment in Cervantes's novel.[1] When Don Quijote is extracted from the cave at the end of Chapter 23, he is asleep, and we are encouraged to think of his vision of its contents as a dream. If so, it is an anxiety dream that reveals the dread of the aging and impoverished Don Quijote. He is doubly alienated, both from a chivalric past revealed to be moribund and from a money-ridden modern world with which he is unable to cope. The noble Belerma is a zombie; his idealized Dulcinea is ugly and common—and perhaps something worse if we understand the loan for the petticoat to stand in for another kind of money-for-sex transaction.[2]

The comparison that the episode proposes between the lady Belerma and Dulcinea strikingly inverts the contrast in Part One between Don Quijote's desire for Dulcinea, the ideal chivalric love object attached to a feudal past, and his desire for "Princess Micomicona," who promises to bring the knight she marries wealth and power and who therefore draws him into the reality of a modern world of money. This reversal is diagramed in Table 4.1.

Here it is the lady Belerma who stands in for a feudal, chivalric past that lives on only as a stagnant, mummified version of itself; she is, as Don Quijote implies, a has-been. Dulcinea, meanwhile, has moved through "enchantment" into the modern world ruled by great capitalists like the Fuggers. She takes the place of "Princess Micomicona" as the love object tied to material reality and monetary considerations. But instead of promising wealth to her knight as "Princess Micomicona" did, this Dulcinea is herself in need of cash. She suggests the ugly side of modernity from which Don Quijote has tried to escape into his chivalric dreams: both literal poverty and the impoverishment of the imagination and of human values when all thoughts turn to money.

But if Don Quijote's vision is gloomy and speaks to the general disenchantment of his world in Part Two, it nonetheless suggests that there is something to be gained by moving from the aristocratic past and its literary representations in Don Quijote's romances of chivalry to the money-ridden present and the new form of the novel that Cervantes is creating. Belerma, Durandarte, and Montesinos keep repeating, four days a week, the same procession of ritual mourning, and Durandarte, lying on his own tomb, can console himself only by saying "Patience and shuffle the cards" ["paciencia y barajar" (690; 707)], suggesting an endless replaying of their story as it becomes more and more out of date. But Dulcinea and her companions are alive. They leap and frisk, and cut capers like goats, and they thus anticipate the little kids—"cabrillas" (820; 836)—with whom Sancho will claim that he played among the Pleiades when he rode on the enchanted horse Clavileño in Chapter 41, a heavenly journey that parallels this descent into the earth in the Cave of Montesinos. To be sure, the goatish comparison may demean Dulcinea-as-peasant still further, and introduce a sexual innuendo as well.[3] But whether Don Quijote realizes it or not, the debased realm into which Dulcinea and he have entered is animated and alive with new possibilities both for him and for his novelistic creator—as opposed to the outmoded and worn-out feudal world of chivalry.[4] This vitality even at what may be the bleakest moment for its hero is symptomatic of Part Two of *Don Quijote*. In its second installment Cervantes repeatedly acknowledges the reduced nature of the everyday world that his novel inherits: its face of ugliness and material need, its narrower scope for the heroic and for the literary imagination. Yet he nonetheless begins to make a case, both ethical and literary, in favor of modern times.

Structure

Cervantes published Part Two of *Don Quijote* in 1615, ten years after the appearance of Part One. In it he revisits and rewrites episodes and the larger structure of the earlier installment of his novel (see Table 4.2 below). Don Quijote's account of his sojourn in the Cave of Montesinos (Chapters 22–23) itself provides an ironic revision of the fantasy of the knight in the underwater world of enchantment he detailed to the Canon of Toledo. The story of Camacho and Basilio's rivalry for Quiteria (Chapters 19–22), as we shall see, recasts on a peasant level elements from the love stories of Part One—Grisóstomo, Cardenio and Luscinda, the "Curioso impertinente." The episode of the water mills (29) offers another, different version of the famous episode of the windmills. The story of Ana Felix and Don Gregorio (54, 63–65) rewrites the Captive's Tale in deliberately abbreviated form: a second attempt to rescue a captive Spaniard by a beautiful Christian Moorish woman devoted to the Virgin Mary and aided by her father's money. It also comments topically on the expul-

TABLE 4.2
Correspondences between Part Two and Part One

Part Two Chapters	Part One Chapters
10 "Enchanted" packsaddle	45 Disputed packsaddle
11 Actor steals Sancho's ass	23 Ginés steals Sancho's ass
17 Transported lions in cage	49 Don Quijote in cage like transported lion
19–21 Basilio at Camacho's wedding	12–14 Grisóstomo; 23–24, 27 Cardenio; 34 Camila
21 Camacho at his wedding to Quiteria	28 Don Fernando at his wedding to Luscinda
21 Quiteria says yes at wedding	27 Luscinda says yes
22–24 Cave of Montesinos	50 Don Quijote's story of enchanted underwater realm
25–27 Braying ass and Ginés (see also Chapters 3–4)	23 Ginés steals Sancho ass
29 Water Mills	8 Windmills
30–57, 68–70 Two stays at the Castle of Duke and Duchess	16–17, 32–47 Two stays at the Inn
31 Welcome of Don Quijote	21, 50 Welcome of knights in Don Quijote's fantasies
38–39, 48 Stories of two sorrowing duennas	28 Dorotea's story
46 Altisidora's practical joke	43 Practical joke of Maritornes and Innkeeper's daughter; 16 Maritornes and her lover
58, 69 Bulls, pigs	18 Sheep
60 Roque Guinart	44–47 Don Quijote as highwayman; 1 Rinaldo
63–65 Ana Félix and Don Gregorio	39–41 Captive's Tale, Zoraida
69 Inquisition of Don Quijote and Sancho Panza; torment of Sancho	6 Inquisition of Don Quijote's library; 17 blanketing of Sancho at the inn
71–72 Sancho flogs himself	52 Disciplinants; 4 flogging of Andrés

sion of the Moriscos between 1609 and 1613 that had intervened between the two parts of Cervantes's novel. In the case of Ana Felix, we are left to wonder whether Zoraida, whose rescue from Islam constituted the high point of modern chivalry in Part One, would not now herself be expelled from Spain.[5]

The stay of Don Quijote and Sancho at the castle or country palace of the Duke and Duchess (30–57, 68–71) is the most transparent case of this rewriting of Part One, for the aristocratic couple have in fact read the published first part of the novel. They shape their reception of Don Quijote on his own fantasies of chivalric hospitality outlined in the earlier book, and their extended practical joke on the knight and his squire makes them authorial rivals to Cervantes who try to write his novel according to their own peculiar taste. When they retain Don Quijote at their castle and send Sancho off to govern his "island," the novel provides a new version of the opposition of arms versus letters explored in Part One.[6] Their burdening of Sancho with the task of disenchanting Dulcinea by flogging himself transfers to him the "penance" done by Don Quijote and Cardenio for their ladies in the Sierra Morena in Part One, and Sancho's final, if fraudulent, accomplishment of this task (72) parallels the last episode of Part One before Don Quijote returns to his village, his meeting with the self-flagellating disciplinants.

Don Quijote's visit with the Duke and Duchess divides the structure of Part Two much as his stay at the inn divides Part One: in both parts of the novel, the knight's picaresque wanderings give way to an extended period of hospitality in one place. The castle or country palace of the Duke and the Duchess quite explicitly recalls and takes the place of the inn of Part One.[7] (The parallel extends to the fact that Don Quijote and Sancho make *two stays* at both the inn and at the Duke's castle, separated in each case by a block of chapters and episodes.) In Part One, Don Quijote mistakes the inn for a castle and its serving wench Maritornes for the castellan's daughter or princess who has fallen in love with him. In Part Two, the far less delusional Don Quijote sees inns as inns, not as castles—so we are told no less than three times in Chapters 24, 59, and 71 (702; 719, 948; 965, 1032; 1050). But, in return, Don Quijote is housed in a real castle, which features a maid-in-waiting, Altisidora, who pretends to be in love with him and who, like Maritornes, plays a nasty prank on the hapless hidalgo. The inn of Part One was for Don Quijote a place of imprisonment, comparable, by the interlaced juxtaposition of stories, to the Algerian captivity of Captain Viedma. The castle of the Duke and Duchess is similarly a kind of prison for the knight, as his remarks on "libertad" and "cautiverio" suggest when he leaves it behind in Chapter 58 (935; 952).[8]

Reading the episodes of Part Two thus requires one to consider their relationship to the fiction of Part One as well as to the ways in which the episodes are linked to one another. Cervantes does not give up the practice of interlace and of the interpolated tale he developed in Part One, but he does claim to modify it. His narrator, Cide Hamete, comments self-consciously on the narrative strategies of Part Two when he complains at the opening of Chapter 44 of "always having to speak of the knight and Sancho, without ever daring to indulge in digressions and episodes of a more serious and entertaining character" ["que siempre había de hablar dél y de Sancho, sin osar estenderse a otras digresiones y episodios más graves y más entretenidos" (833; 848)]. To afford variety to his history, Cide Hamete tells us that he had inserted into Part One the "Curioso impertinente" and the Captive's Tale, which were separate ("separadas") from the incidents that befell Don Quijote. Earlier in Chapter 3 Sansón Carrasco had recorded the complaints of readers of the novel's first installment that the "Curioso impertinente" had nothing to do with Don Quijote's deeds (549; 562); Don Quijote is himself indignant to hear that his history is a hodgepodge. Cervantes now answers these critics through Cide Hamete:

He also felt, as he says that many readers, carried away by their interest in the knight's exploits, would be inclined to neglect these tales, passing over them either hastily or with boredom, thereby failing to notice their elegance and fine craftsmanship, which would have been clearly manifest if they had been published by themselves and not joined to Don Quixote's lunacy and Sancho's fooleries. And therefore, in this second part he resolved not to insert any tales, either detached or patched onto the narrative, *but only some episodes like them*, arising naturally out of the actual course of the events, and even these should be used sparingly and with no more words than necessary to explain them. (833–34, my emphasis)

También pensó, como él dice, que muchos, llevados de la atención que piden las hazañas de don Quijote, no la darían a las novelas y pasarían por ellas, o con priesa, o con enfado, sin advertir la gala y artificio que en sí contienen, el cual se mostrara bien al descubierto cuando por sí solas, sin arrimarse a las locuras de don Quijote ni a las sandeces de Sancho, salieran a luz. Y así, en esta segunda parte no quiso ingerir novelas sueltas ni pegadizas, *sino algunos episodios que lo pareciesen*, nacidos de los mesmos sucesos que la verdad ofrece, y aun éstos, limitadamente y con solas las palabras que bastan a declararlos. (848–49, my emphasis)

With a smile, Cervantes seems to agree with the readers who found the interpolated tales out of place in Part One and therefore failed to appreciate their art; no small part of that art, of course, consisted in the tales' mirroring relationship to the fiction that enclosed them.

In Part Two, Cervantes makes things easier for his reader. He spells out this specular relationship when he has Sansón Carrasco dress himself up as the Knight of Mirrors—"Caballero de los Espejos"—in Chapters 12–15: he is only one of many characters who mirror Don Quijote.[9] But Cide Hamete and Cervantes now claim to introduce these characters and their stories more organically out of the narrative of Don Quijote's adventures. What the readers of Part One wanted, Cervantes appears to have realized, was more of Don Quijote and Sancho Panza, and his two heroes acquire a new prominence: their growing interdependence and affection for one another becomes a central story of Part Two. But the stories of other characters surround them nonetheless, and continue to bear much of the book's burden of meaning. The comments in Chapter 44 precede, pointedly enough, the clearest instance of interlace and juxtaposed narratives in the novel, as the next ten chapters and the novel's perspective switch scenes among Don Quijote at the castle of the Duke and Duchess, Sancho at his governorship, and Teresa Panza back in Don Quijote's village.[10] One model for this section is the interlace of the *Orlando furioso*: Cide Hamete "hears" Sancho calling him away from the castle—"nos está llamando el gran Sancho Panza" (842; 857)—at the end of the chapter, imitating Ariosto's narrator, who responds to the cry of his character Astolfo and drops one strand of the *Furioso* to pick up another (15.9–10). Here Don Quijote's and Sancho's stories are interlaced with each other.

Interlace holds together the groups of episodes and stories of Part Two that precede and follow the meeting of Don Quijote and Sancho with the Duke and the Duchess. Although the novel's second part appears to be more loosely organized than the first, its division into two halves—on the road, at the castle—produces two main thematic clusters. In the first, which is the focus of this chapter, Cervantes radically changes the character of Don Quijote by associating him with the ethos and behavior of a middling social class that is moneyed and peace loving: he comes, in fact, to resemble the members of that class, the hidalgo Don Diego de Miranda and the rich farmer Camacho, to whom he seems initially opposed. In the second, the subject of the next chapter, he appears to be accepted into the knightly world and aristocratic class of his fantasies, as the Duke and the Duchess make him their honored guest.

The historical trajectory we have seen traced by Part One of the novel now seems to be reversed in Part Two. There the path to a modern from a feudal mentality was suggested by the alternative of "Princess Micomicona" substituting for "Dulcinea," of the worldly careers of the soldier and judge for the vocations of knight and monk, of inns for castles. In Part Two, Don Quijote seems, in fact, to have forgotten his fantasy of marrying a princess, as is suggested in his Cave of Montesinos vision by his situating of the needy Dulcinea in what had been the structural place of the rich "Princess Micomicona." The theme of social climbing is transferred to the would-be governor Sancho, who argues with his wife, Teresa, in Chapter 5 about marrying their daughter, Marisancha, up into the nobility.[11] But Don Quijote nonetheless begins to accept and adapt to a modern world around him—only to be virtually kidnapped back into the feudal, aristocratic past, or at least into the fantasy form of that past incarnated in the chivalric romances, at the castle of the Duke and Duchess. These latter are the novel's representatives of the present-day nobility in Spain, and much of the satirical thrust of Part Two, already announced in its first chapter, concerns the gap between their behavior and the knightly ideals that Don Quijote expects of them: they are more sham knights than he is. Stagnant, diseased, and cruel, these aristocrats might be aligned with Durandarte and the lady Belerma, reliving their outmoded past in the Cave of Montesinos. Nevertheless, the Duke and the Duchess control a long stretch of the novel and, by implication, their noble class still maintains an oppressive power over Spanish society.

The two narrative halves of Part Two thus restate the conflict of historical mentalities embodied in Don Quijote's two objects of desire in Part One—the rich princess Micomicona and the ideal lady Dulcinea—and relocate it in his larger society. Don Quijote and Sancho meet on their travels first the representative figures of an emerging moneyed class and its modern values, then the adherents of a still dominant, if atavistic and ethically hollow, feudal nobility. It is a central irony of the novel that Don Quijote's chivalric aspirations now seem more assimilable to the former rather than the latter: he has become a modern knight. Cervantes pointedly opposes the two halves to one another at the opening of Chapter 31, when the sojourn of Don Quijote and Sancho at the castle of the Duke and the Duchess begins. Sancho expects to find there the same hospitality he had been offered first by Don Diego de Miranda and by Basilio in the episode of Camacho's wedding feast—"se le figuraba que había de hallar en su castillo lo que en la casa de don Diego y en la de Basilio" (744; 761). But he and Don Quijote will find quite a different reception from their noble hosts.

The Two Quijotes

The Don Quijote of Part Two is a changed man. In Chapter 72, Cervantes takes a dig at the pseudonymous Alonso de Avellaneda, who had authored a second part of *Don Quijote* and published it in 1614, a year before Cervantes's own, "authentic" sequel was to appear. As a last-minute addition, Cervantes brings into his novel a character from Avellaneda's book, one Don Álvaro Tarfe, who admits and signs an affidavit to the effect that the Don Quijote and Sancho he met there were different and distinct characters from the Don Quijote and Sancho he presently encounters. Earlier in Chapter 59, characters had noted and complained that Avellaneda had changed the name of Sancho Panza's wife to Mari (951; 969); her name in Part One was Juana. To complicate the issue and make a joke out of it, Cervantes appears to have gone back and changed the name himself: she is Teresa Panza in Part Two. But he had already changed the character of Don Quijote more dramatically than by a mere change of name. Avellaneda's Don Quijote may be different from the Don Quijote of Part Two, but that Don Quijote, in turn, is a very different character from the Don Quijote of Part One.[12]

In Part One Don Quijote was a sociopath. His last action there, as we have seen, was to attack the Virgin Mary, or more precisely the penitents who were carrying her image (63). This is the Don Quijote whose highest pleasure is to win battles and to triumph over enemies, and his relationship to others expresses itself in violence. He mostly does harm to himself, but he also inflicts real injuries, and if comic decorum precludes his killing any people in Part One, it is not for his want of trying. He knocks a muleteer unconscious (3); he forces a Benedictine monk to fall from his mule; he overthrows the Biscayan (9); he wounds one of the Yanguesans in the shoulder (15); he kills seven sheep (Chapter 18); he badly wounds the bachelor-priest in the procession of mourners (19); he whacks Sancho when his squire mocks him at the fulling mills (20); he attacks the barber who wears the "helmet of Mambrino" (21). Don Quijote attacks the law itself, wounding the king's commissary and freeing the galley slaves (22).[13] This culminating act of lawlessness is linked in Don Quijote's words to the final one of attacking the disciplinants carrying the image of the Virgin. Of the galley slaves he says that "these men are being taken to their destination by force and not by their own free will" ["esta gente, aunque los llevan, van de por fuerza, y no de su voluntad" (209; 203)], while he takes the Virgin to be "some noble lady who they were carrying away by force. . . . you are bearing her away against her will" ["alguna principal señora que llevaban por fuerza . . . la lleváis contra su voluntad" (509–10; 513–14)]. In the name of the individual will, the anarchic Don Quijote is equally a menace to the state and to the Catholic Faith.[14]

The Don Quijote of Part One quite explicitly identifies himself with such lawlessness. We are told in Chapter 1 that among the knights he encountered in his intense reading of chivalric romances he admired above all others—not, as we might think, Amadis, Palmerin, or Orlando, but—"Rinaldo of Montalban, especially when he saw him sallying out of his castle to plunder everyone who came his way" ["Pero, sobre todos, estaba bien con Reinaldos de Montalbán, y más cuando le veía salir de su castillo y robar cuantos topaba" (59; 38)].[15] It is "Rinaldo of Montalban" that Don Quijote calls himself when he wakes up in Chapter 7, ready to pursue his second sally (94; 77). Rinaldo, as the capsule description suggests, is in the chivalric cycles of the Four Sons of Aymon a kind of outlaw and highwayman—he and his companions are "thieves" ["ladrones" (87; 70)], says the Curate in the review of Don Quijote's library in Chapter 6; in Chapter 1 of Part Two, Don Quijote describes him as "friendly to robbers and to vagabonds" ["amigo de ladrones y de gente perdida" (537; 550)]. This Rinaldo is less an altruistic Robin Hood than a figure of feudal independence and anarchy, a noble clansman who as often rebels against the crown of Charlemagne as he comes to his king's aid and rescue. He is a law to himself in his own domain. Cervantes is suggesting a quite specific historical correlative for Don Quijote's nostalgic taking up of knight-errantry and for the violence that he goes on to inflict on society. Don Quijote wants to go back to the social arrangements of feudalism that preceded the emergence of the modern state and its project of pacifying the nobility, to an earlier time in which riches were to be acquired by force of arms, whether it was called conquest or theft.

Don Quijote's initial identification with the outlaw Rinaldo of Montalban might not merit critical emphasis did Cervantes not continue to develop it through allusion across the course of Part One. In Chapter 10, shortly after Don Quijote has declared to Sancho that no one has ever read of a knight-errant being put to justice, no matter how many homicides he may have committed (112; 98), he makes a vow to lead a life of abstinence until he wins from another knight a helmet as good as the one he has lost in his fight with the Biscayan; he cites as a precedent the helmet of Mambrino, fought over in the *Orlando furioso* (114; 100). Don Quijote famously fulfills his vow in Chapter 21 when he encounters the helmet of Mambrino itself in the form of the basin that its barber owner is wearing on his head and that he quickly relinquishes when he runs away in terror from Don Quijote's lance. Now, the helmet of Mambrino belonged in the romances of chivalry to no one else but Rinaldo of Montalban, whose head was made invulnerable by its enchantment. (Cervantes may be making a silent joke, since it is now too late to protect the head, at least what is going on inside it, of his madman-hero.) The identification of Don Quijote as an outlaw continues throughout Part One. The Curate invents a story in Chapter 29 of how he was set upon by four highwaymen—"nos salieron al encuentro cuatro salteadores" (299; 300)—who were among the galley slaves set free by Don Quijote. When the dispossessed barber shows up at the inn in Chapter 44, demanding his basin, packsaddle ["albarda"], and ass, he accuses Sancho Panza of being a "thief and highwayman" ["ladrón, salteador de caminos" (454; 457)].

The troopers of the state police, the Holy Brotherhood, show up in the following chapter and identify Don Quijote, the liberator of the galley slaves, as a robber and highwayman himself—"robador y salteador de sendas y de carreras" (462; 465)—and in Chapter 47 the Canon of Toledo will take Don Quijote for "some criminal highwayman" ["algún facineroso salteador" (474; 478)] when he sees him imprisoned in his cage. Society indeed needs protection from Don Quijote in Part One, and he needs to be protected from himself.

This aggressive and antisocial behavior largely disappears from the Don Quijote of Part Two, and when near its end in Chapter 60, he meets the Barcelonan bandit Roque Guinart, the leader of a band of "ladrones" (962; 981) and "salteadores" (964; 983), he seems to be meeting a version of a former possible self. Aside from his unhorsing of Sansón Carrasco, when the latter, disguised as the Knight of the Mirrors, lures him into battle, Don Quijote does violence in Part Two only to the pasteboard puppets—"figurillas de pasta" (716; 734)—of Maese Pedro in Chapter 26; Maese Pedro is lucky not to have had his own head inadvertently cut off by Don Quijote "as if it had been made of almond paste" ["que si fuera hecha de masa de mazapán" (716; 734)]. The mutilation of the puppets—the beheaded King Marsilio, the cleft Charlemagne, the noseless Melisendra—is described in some detail, and we should note that Don Quijote indiscriminately harms both Moorish foe and Christian friend; but it stands in for the actual injuries Don Quijote does to others in Part One. The wounds Don Quijote inflicts in the second part of the novel are pointedly unreal, as make-believe as those delivered by the knights-errant he has read about in his chivalric romances and that Don Quijote describes in Chapter 1, a passage that is being recalled and cleverly literalized here: knights, he says, who can slice apart a pagan army of two thousand men as if they were "made of almond paste" ["fueran hechos de alfenique" (531; 544)].

Don Quijote has not only become less violent in Part Two; he has become innocent in the etymological and most literal sense of the word. In his conversation in Chapter 13 with the squire of the Knight of the Mirrors, a squire who is in reality his own neighbor Tomé Cecial in disguise, Sancho Panza describes his master:

> he has a soul as simple as a pitcher; he could do no harm to anyone, but good to all, nor has he any malice in him; why a child would convince him it is night at noonday, and it is on account of this simplicity that I love him as I love the cockles of my heart. (613)

> tiene una alma como un cántaro: no sabe hacer mal a nadie, sino bien a todos, ni tiene malicia alguna: un niño le hará entender que es de noche en la mitad del día, y por esta sencillez le quiero como a las telas de mi corazón. (627)

Sancho's words will be echoed by Don Quijote himself when he offers his own self-assessments in Chapter 25 and again in Chapter 32:

> But whatever I may be, I give thanks to Heaven, which has endowed me with a soft and compassionate heart, always inclined to do good to all and harm to no one. (709)

> My intentions are always directed toward virtuous ends, to do good to all and harm to none. (754)

> pero como quiera que yo me sea, doy gracias al cielo, que me dotó de un ánimo blando y compasivo, inclinado siempre a hacer bien a todos, y mal a ninguno. (725)

> Mis intenciones siempre las enderezo a buenos fines, que son de hacer bien a todos y mal a ninguno. (770)

The Cervantine narrator himself confirms his characters' appraisals when he offers this summation of Don Quijote as the knight lies on his deathbed in the final Chapter 74:

> this gentleman, whether as Alonso Quixano the Good or as Don Quixote of La Mancha, had always been so good-natured and so accommodating that he was beloved not only by his family, but by all who knew him. (1046–47)

> en tanto que don Quijote fue Alonso Quijano el Bueno, a secas, y en tanto que fue don Quijote de la Mancha, fue siempre de apacible condición y de agradable trato, y por esto no sólo era bien querido de los de su casa, sino de todos cuanto le conocían. (1065)

Good to all? Beloved by all? These testimonials would have astounded the various victims Don Quijote left in his wake in Part One. They crucially redefine his character in Part Two. His harmlessness and child-like simplicity sentimentalize the hero, and they would feed the romantic interpretation of Don Quijote that culminated in Miguel de Unamuno's feverish, if influential, musings on the mad hidalgo as a kind of saint and Christ figure.[16]

Good and lovable, the Don Quijote of Part Two is also wise. In Part One characters comment on the good sense—"buen entendimiento"—he speaks when he is not on the subject of his chivalric romances (392; 394, 490; 493), and Part Two opens with Don Quijote, apparently recovered from his adventures of Part One, demonstrating a similar "buen entendimiento" (530; 542) until the Curate steers the conversation back to Don Quijote's obsession with chivalry. But in Part Two, this good sense will become something more, a form of wisdom—"discreción"—evidenced in the conversation that Don Quijote has with Don Diego de Miranda's poet son (18), in his counsels to Basilio (22) and to the page (24), and in his advice to Sancho about Sancho's governorship (42). After the last of these the narrator breaks in at the beginning of Chapter 43 to remark on Don Quijote's mixture of wisdom and madness—"su discreción y su locura" (827; 843); the terms are coupled together throughout the second installment of the novel (649; 663, 767; 783, 943; 961, 965; 984). In effect, the gentler, wiser Don Quijote of Part Two is already evolving into the Alonso Quijano the Good ("el Bueno") that he will become in its last chapter.

The newly wise Don Quijote is, in fact, noticeably less given to his former madness. At least he no longer appears to hallucinate as he did in Part One, where windmills were giants and herds of sheep armies. Even at what may be his most delusional moment, he sees the water mills for what they are in Chapter 29, although he still insists to Sancho that they are really a fortress or prison disguised beneath their mundane appearance (736; 753). He recognizes the herd of bulls in Chapter 58 as bulls, and the herd of pigs in Chapter 68 as pigs, not as enemy squadrons; symptomatic, too, of the change in his character, he does not attack the bulls and pigs as he did the sheep, but he is himself assaulted and bowled over by the stampeding animals. He sees inns as inns instead of castles. As a result, he experiences a general disenchantment of the world.[17]

The key episode in the depiction of the hero's reduced ability to project his fantasies on the world around him comes, of course, at the very beginning of his adventures in Chapter 10, when the tricky Sancho Panza presents him with the vision of the "enchanted" Dulcinea. "I do not see, Sancho," said Don Quijote, "anything except three peasant girls on three asses" ("—Yo no veo, Sancho—dijo don Quijote—, sino a tres labradoras sobre tres borricos" [592; 606]). Cervantes's masterful division of Don Quijote's words in this sentence, so that the first section can stand as an independent clause, indicates that Don Quijote does not see at all, or rather that he sees only what is really before him: he is no longer the visionary—and delusional—seer of Part One. The particular emphasis that Don Quijote lays at the end of the chapter on what appeared to him to be an ass's packsaddle—"albarda" (596; 609)—but which Sancho assures him was Dulcinea's jennet-saddle, returns us to the ass's packsaddle that Don Quijote had won in Chapter 21 of Part One from the same barber from whom he took the "helmet of Mambrino." Don Quijote subsequently attempted to maintain that the packsaddle was a horse's trappings by force of arms, triggering a near riot at the inn in Chapter 45: "the packsaddle remained a horse trapping until the day of judgment, the basin a helmet, and the inn a castle in the imagination of Don Quixote" ["la albarda se quedó por jaez hasta el día del juicio, y la bacía por yelmo y la venta por castillo en la imaginación de don Quijote" (460; 463)]. Now, however, the "albarda" remains an "albarda."

The reversal of the situation in the earlier installment establishes the terms of Part Two. Don Quijote must accept the impostures that others, in this case Sancho, devise to prop up his fantasies of knighthood even as Don Quijote's own powers of fantasy fail him. Cervantes indicates the theatrical nature of the various tricks and practical jokes that these other characters play on Don Quijote by following the episode of the "enchantment" of Dulcinea with the encounter of Don Quijote and Sancho with a troop of costumed actors in Chapter 11, after which knight and squire meet Sansón Carrasco, dressed up as the Knight of the Woods in Chapter 12. The stay at the castle of the Duke and Duchess produces one elaborately staged skit after another, ending in the mock auto-da-fé in Chapter 69, and Don Antonio Moreno also produces a hoax marvel for his guest in the talking head at his house in Barcelona in Chapter 62. The puppet show of Maese Pedro—whose prophetic ape appears to anticipate the talking head—fits into the pattern, too, even if, in this instance, the drawing of Don Quijote into the playlet is not part of its design. Much of what Don Quijote encounters in Part Two is unreal stage show, and he himself becomes a kind of puppet manipulated by others who exploit his chivalric mania. The hero's new passivity partially accounts for his diminished aggression and number of victims. In place of his attempts in Part One to impose his fantasies of knighthood upon the world, which, as in the cases of the "albarda" and the slaughtered sheep, lead to violence, in Part Two these fantasies are fed back upon Don Quijote: he becomes the victim and butt of the jokes, sometimes violent and painful, played upon him.[18]

One cannot insist too much upon the difference between the Don Quijotes of the two parts of the novel. The romantic interpretation and popular reception of *Don Quijote* have tended to read the gentler and wiser Don Quijote of Part Two back into Part One. This reading not only distorts the nature of Don Quijote's character in Part One, suggesting that a good-hearted humanity already coexists there with the antagonism to social constraints that the romantics valued in the hero; that antagonism, in fact, falls away from the nice-guy Don Quijote of Part Two. It also fails to recognize that the transformation of his character is central to the meaning of Part Two and to the novel's larger narrative about modernity.

For Cervantes connects this change in his hero—his becoming good and lovable—specifically to Don Quijote's adaptation to a society whose values and behavior are monitored by the flow of money. If the anarchic outlaw Don Quijote of Part One sought to relive a feudal world that existed before the modern world of the nation-state and of a moneyed economy, the goodness and wisdom of the Don Quijote of Part Two emerge as he is reintegrated into modern society and as he takes on traits that the novel associates with that society's new product: a fluid middling class created by wealth. Part One did not have much good to say for the nascent world of capitalism displacing an older feudal order; despite reservations, Part Two is more sanguine. The chivalric strivings of Don Quijote are first contrasted to the material contentedness and limited imagination of the wealthy Don Diego de Miranda and Camacho, but we also see him adopt their values and behavior: liberality, peaceablity, Christianity. Cervantes's identification with his reformed hero suggests his own rapprochement with his society as the newly successful, if not rich, author of the first part of *Don Quijote*. Both Don Quijote and his creator were joining the middle class.

Don Diego de Miranda and Don Quijote

What happens if we imagine Don Quijote and Sancho Panza with money, a well-off hidalgo and an affluent peasant? The novel answers with Don Diego de Miranda, the "wise gentleman" ["discreto caballero" (629; 642)] of La Mancha whom Don Quijote meets in Chapter 16–18, and "Camacho the Rich" ["Camacho el rico" (658; 671)], the wealthy farmer ["labrador"] whose interrupted wedding feast fills up the succeeding Chapters 19–22. The two episodes are carefully interlaced and connected with each other, and between the two figures—literally between and including their respective social positions—Cervantes depicts and defines a new middling class.

The episode of Don Diego de Miranda depends on a complicated play on the word "caballero," which means "knight" when used by and about Don Quijote and, when initially applied to Don Diego, "gentleman," as a term comprising the aristocracy, high and low. But "caballero" also distinguishes the high nobleman from the "hidalgo," the member of the mere gentry; it is as an "hidalgo" that Don Diego introduces himself (633; 647), and it is the same class to which Don Quijote himself belongs when he is at home.[19] Don Quijote's aspirations to be a knightly "caballero," we have learned earlier, are, in fact, misunderstood as social climbing, and the joke seems to be that nobody understands the word any longer in its older, chivalric meaning. In Chapter 2, Sancho tells Don Quijote that people are talking about him, and complaining that he is pretending to a higher social status than the one to which he is entitled: "The knights ['los caballeros'] say that they don't relish seeing the petty gentry ['los hidalgos'] set themselves up against them" (542; 55); and Don Quijote's niece in Chapter 6 further criticizes him for calling himself a "caballero" in the broader sense of the word: "for though the gentry may be so, the poor cannot!" ["aunque lo pueden ser los hidalgos, no lo son los pobres!" (567; 580)]. Despite his being an hidalgo, she implies, Don Quijote has in his poverty fallen out of the ranks of the nobility altogether.

Don Diego de Miranda is an hidalgo who has no such problem. The narrator describes his house in Chapter 18 as the dwelling of a "caballero labrador y rico" (649; 662); he is a rich gentleman-farmer, even if he is not a "caballero" in the highest ranks of society. But this description suggests the similarity of this gentleman to Camacho, the rich "labrador," in the ensuing episode. We may be reminded of Dorotea, the rich farmer's daughter and social climber in Part One who protests that her family is gradually acquiring "the name of hidalgos, and even of caballeros." Camacho displays no such social ambitions, and perhaps he does not need to do so: his wealth, and the ethical behavior that accompanies it, are enough to liken him to Don Diego. Cervantes does not depict the urban merchants and tradesmen who would create a new moneyed social class—we remember the third brother of the Captive, the merchant conspicuous by his absence in Part One. His landed version of this new class, somewhere in the middle between the high nobleman and the peasant, reflects the conservative limits of his novel's social vision. Nonetheless, these chapters open *Don Quijote* to the existence of a middling social group—already a recognizable forerunner of a future middle class—and to its values.

The life that Don Diego de Miranda professes to lead has been seen by critics alternately as Cervantes's ideal and as the object of his irony. His specular relationship to Don Quijote is suggested by his otherwise common enough Spanish name: the two men stare at one another ["si mucho *miraba* el de lo verde a don Quijote, mucho más *miraba* don Quijote al de lo verde" (631; 645)] in a moment that recalls the mutual staring, as if of recognition, of Don Quijote and Cardenio in Part One—"le estuvo *mirando*, como que quería ver si le conocía" (229; 225).[20] The same age as Don Quijote, a fellow native of La Mancha, and a member of the same hidalgo class, the pious, charitable Don Diego is a possible alter ego of the knight. One critical opinion argues that he shows us how a sane Don Quijote ought to have behaved.[21] As Timothy Hampton sums up this view, "Don Diego is the role-model, the ideal, for members of the group that Don Quixote belonged to before his wits turned. . . . Had Don Quixote been married and perhaps a bit wealthier, he might have become a Don Diego."[22] Yet Hampton's own interpretation of the episode belongs to the opposing critical camp, and he makes perhaps its strongest case for an ironic reading of this role model, called as he is first by Don Quijote and subsequently by the narrator's chapter title, the "Knight of the Green Cloak" ["el Caballero del Verde Gabán" (647; 661)]: a gentleman perhaps, even a wise one, but no knight in armor.[23] The domestic tranquility of Don Diego is made to seem tame compared to the valiant adventures of Don Quijote. It is, moreover, a life hostile to poetry, although Don Diego's son seems ready to supply the lack. These objections, as we shall see, also pertain to Camacho in the ensuing episode, where, according to the masque performed at the wedding feast, Camacho's Wealth stands in opposition to Valor and Poetry.

Don Diego de Miranda nonetheless makes a powerful, ethical case for his existence. He casts irony on Don Quijote's chivalric pretensions just as much as Don Quijote calls his domesticity into question. Furthermore—and this is the point I wish to emphasize—if Cervantes builds the episode through the mirroring opposition of the two figures, the subsequent fiction of Part Two will show Don Quijote becoming more and more *like* Don Diego, as if he or the novel itself had absorbed the latter's moral example.

Don Quijote introduces himself to Don Diego in Chapter 16 as the reviver of chivalry. He is compelled, he says, to sing his own praises when no one else is around to do so, and he boasts of his "valiant and Christian deeds" ["mis valerosas, muchas y cristianas hazañas" (632; 646)], *none* of which we have seen him in fact perform: succoring widows, protecting maidens, relieving orphans, wives, and young children. These have made him worthy, he says, of being the subject of a book, now printed and available in most of the nations of the earth.

It is then the turn of his traveling companion to describe himself:

> I am more than moderately rich, and my name is Don Diego de Miranda. I spend my life with my wife, my children, and my friends. My pursuits are hunting and fishing, but I keep neither hawk nor hounds, but only a tame partridge and a saucy ferret or two. I have about six dozen books, some in Spanish and some in Latin, some historical and some devotional, but books of chivalry have never even crossed my threshold. I read profane books more than devotional, provided they give me honest entertainment, delight me with their language, and startle and keep me in suspense by their plots, though there are very few of this kind in Spain. Sometimes I dine with my neighbors and friends, and very often they are my guests. My table is clean, well appointed, and never stinted. I take no pleasure in murmurs of scandal and allow none in my presence; I do not pry into my neighbors' lives, nor do I spy on other men's actions. I hear Mass every day; I share my goods with the poor, without boasting of my good works, lest hypocrisy and vainglory worm themselves into my heart, for they are foes that subtly waylay even the wariest. I try to make peace between those I know to be at loggerheads. I am devoted to Our Lady and always put my trust in the infinite mercy of Our Lord. (633–34)

> Soy más que medianamente rico y es mi nombre don Diego de Miranda; paso la vida con mi mujer, y con mis hijos, y con mis amigos; mis ejercicios son el de la caza y pesca; pero no mantengo ni halcón ni galgos, sino algún perdigón manso, o algún hurón atrevido. Tengo hasta seis docenas de libros, cuáles de

romance y cuáles de latín, de historia algunos y de devoción otros, los de caballerías aún no han entrado por los umbrales de mis puertas. Hojeo más los que son profanos que los devotos, como sean de honesto entretenimiento, que deleiten con el lenguaje y admiren y suspendan con la invención, puesto que déstos hay muy pocos en España. Alguna vez como con mis vecinos y amigos, y muchas veces los convido; son mis convites limpios y aseados, y no nada escasos; ni gusto de murmurar, ni consiento que delante de mí se murmure; no escudriño las vidas ajenas, ni soy lince de los hechos de los otros; oigo misa cada día; reparto de mis bienes con los pobres, sin hacer alarde de las buenas obras, por no dar entrada en mi corazón a la hipocresía y vanagloria, enemigos que blandamente se apoderan del corazón más recatado; procuro poner en paz los que sé que están desavenidos; soy devoto de nuestra Señora, y confío siempre en la misericordia infinita de Dios, nuestro Señor. (647–48)

When Don Diego finishes, we are immediately provided with one authoritative way to read his declaration. After hearing about such a "good and holy" ["buena y santa"] life, Sancho Panza rushes to kiss his feet and declares him "the first saint I've seen riding in short stirrups" ["el primer santo a la jineta que he visto" (634; 648)]. Sancho's unintended joke only partly dilutes the seriousness of his testimonial. The squire is the novel's usual spokesman for Christian values and, eight chapters earlier, as he and Don Quijote were setting out on their quest in Part Two, Sancho had suggested that they might do better if they were to "set about becoming saints" ["nos demos a ser santos" (582; 595)]. Don Quijote had responded that chivalry is itself a religion—"religión es la caballería" (583; 596). Unamuno's vision of a saintly hero seems to be the result of taking Don Quijote at his word; one upshot, however, of the meeting with Don Diego is to suggest the extent to which Don Quijote's chivalry is opposed to Christian behavior.[24]

Sancho is not wrong to admire the holy precepts that Don Diego professes; the hidalgo's words contain New Testament recollections: "Cum ergo facis elemosynam, noli tuba canere ante te, sicut hypocritae" (Matt. 6:2); "Beati pacifici" (Matt. 5:9). Marcel Bataillon argues that Don Diego embodies the Erasmian ideal of the devout layperson—an ideal, we may add, much associated with a new middle class.[25] Don Diego's insistence on not speaking ill of others and minding his own business does smack of the Erasmus of the *Adagia*, who reminds readers of Christ's injunction in the same Evangelical Discourse of Matthew, "Nolite iudicare" (Matt. 7:1), not to judge lest they be judged. "Begin at home" (1.6.83) is a proverb, Erasmus says, addressed to "critics of the lives of other people whose first duty is to correct the faults of their own dependents and the way they live," while "Spit in your own bosom" (1.6.94) teaches a man "to remember his own private errors and desist from arrogant attacks on the way other men live."[26] This pietistic injunction to turn inward seems to be accompanied in Don Diego's case by a new idea of respecting the privacy of others. In the context of an early seventeenth-century Spain intent on rooting out religious heterodoxy, it may even suggest a liberal tolerance, like that which the Morisco Ricote in Chapter 54 claims to find in Germany, where the inhabitants do not look too curiously—"no miran en muchas delicadezas" (915; 933)—and there is liberty of conscience.

As devoted as Don Diego is to his own household and affairs, he is not, as his critics charge, entirely confined to them. His house invites the outside community, neighbors and friends, into it, and Don Quijote and Sancho are themselves the beneficiaries of his hospitality. And, however modestly, he does good in the world, which is more than can be said thus far for Don Quijote. After listening to Don Quijote, Don Diego replies that he cannot be persuaded "that there is anyone on earth today who favors widows, protects maidens, honors wives, and succors ophans" ["que haya hoy en la tierra quien favorezca viudas, ampare doncellas, ni honre casadas, ni socorra huérfanos" (633; 646)]. The irony is characteristically double-edged: there *should* be someone to aid the weak, but Don Quijote is not that someone, however much he may vaunt his "Christian" deeds. Don Diego does what he can for the poor with his wealth, without boasting of his charity, and he thereby avoids the vainglory that describes Don Quijote, victorious over the Knight of the Mirrors, at the beginning of the preceding chapter: "ufano y vanaglorioso iba don Quijote" (629; 640), the Don Quijote who admits to singing his own praises. Don Diego also, and perhaps more significantly, is a peacemaker who seeks to reconcile enemies, though his attempt to dissuade Don Quijote from fighting the king's lion in the next chapter falls on deaf ears. Finally, Don Diego professes his devotion to Our Lady, the Virgin Mary, and, as in Part One, the contrast is suggested once again with Don Quijote's personal lady; before facing the lion, Don Quijote will recommend himself to God "and then to his lady, Dulcinea" ["y luego a su señora Dulcinea" (642; 656)]. Don Diego's Christianity is contrasted with Don Quijote's chivalry, which may well be a religion, but a religion of the individual ego: boasting, violent, idolatrous—and, at least so far, without good works.

This is only one side of the story, however, as Hampton and others point out. The ensuing episode of the lions in Chapter 17 suggests that the peaceful homebody Don Diego has become as domesticated as the decoy partridge and ferret ["perdigón manso, o algún hurón atrevido" (633; 647)] that he uses in his hunting after small game, and that he lacks physical courage—Don Quijote tells him to return to partridge and ferret as he, Don Quijote, prepares to face the biggest game of all, the king's lion, the king of beasts. Don Diego can be excused for fleeing when the lion's cage is opened and urging on others to flee with him—this is what any sane person would do. Less clear-cut is his decision not to stop Don Quijote from forcing the release of the lions: "not being so well armed, he thought it would be imprudent to fight with a madman" ["viose desigual en las armas, y no le pareció cordura tomarse con un loco" (642; 656)]. Don Diego's reluctance to risk his body is, of course, contrasted to Don Quijote's "valentía" in the face of the noble—"generoso" (643; 657)—lion, who comically turns his shoulders and moons him. It earns Don Quijote a special apostrophe from Cide Hamete: words fail him ["faltarme palabras"] sufficiently to praise this mirror of all valiant men in the world—"espejo donde se pueden mirar todos los valientes del mundo" (643; 657); the chapter title, too, proclaims that the mad hidalgo's unheard-of courage reached its highest point and extreme here in the adventure of the lions—"último punto y estremo adonde llegó y pudo llegar el inaudito ánimo de don Quijote" (638; 652). The apostrophe is tongue-in-cheek and the chapter then goes on to identify this high point of unheard-of courage *also* as the extreme of never-before-seen madness—"Hasta aquí llegó el estremo de su jamás vista locura" (643; 657). The cage and cart bearing the lions may remind us of the similar "jaula" and "carro" in which Don Quijote is imprisoned and brought home at the end of Part One: there the Canon of Toledo, in fact, tells Don Quijote in Chapter 49 that his chivalric mania has reduced him to being carried about "as they transport a lion or tiger from town to town" ["como quien trae o lleva algún león o algún tigre de lugar en lugar" (491; 494)]. The lion, too, is a kind of double of Don Quijote: we may wonder who really belongs in the cage here.[27]

Nevertheless, Don Quijote's mad recklessness may score a point or two off of Don Diego de Miranda's wise discretion. Don Diego tries to dissuade Don Quijote from confronting the lion by noting that "valor that verges on temerity has more of madness about it than bravery" ["la valentía que se entra en la juridición de la temeridad, más tiene de locura que de fortaleza" (641; 654–55)]. When the adventure of the lions is concluded and the two hidalgos join up again, Don Quijote reminds Don Diego that one can err in the other direction. Like all virtues defined in Aristotelian terms, valor, he says, is situated between the vicious extremes of cowardice and temerity; so Sancho Panza had already quoted his master as saying back in Chapter 4: "en los estremos de cobarde y de temerario está el medio de la valentía" (555; 568). Don Quijote continues:

> But it is less harmful for the valiant man to mount to the height of rashness than to sink into the depths of cowardice, for just as it easier for the prodigal man than for the miser to come to be liberal, so it is easier for the daring than for the cowardly to become truly valiant. (646–47)

Pero menos mal será que el que es valiente toque y suba al punto de temerario que no que baje y toque en el punto de cobarde; que así como es más fácil venir el pródigo a ser liberal que el avaro, así es más fácil dar el temerario en verdadero valiente que no el cobarde subir a la verdadera valentía; (661)

With his analogy of valor and liberality, Don Quijote spells out his argument in terms that the wealthy, liberal Don Diego should understand. But these terms are doubly loaded to Don Diego's disadvantage. First, they hint that Don Diego, by failing to rise to temerity, has fallen into cowardice: he did not stop Don Quijote and he ran away. Second, they suggest that if Don Diego acts through liberality while Don Quijote acts through physical valor—however mad and fruitless that valor may be—liberality may be in some way *opposed* to valor: that Don Diego's Christian, moneyed existence is opposed to Don Quijote's military vocation and does not breed valiant men.[28]

To Don Diego's consternation, he *has* bred a poet. The literary vocation of Don Diego's son, Don Lorenzo, seems, however, to be a reaction or filial revolt against, rather than an outgrowth of, his upbringing in his father's house. Don Diego ruefully confesses that he had rather not have a son than see him devoted to poetry instead of to the study of law and theology that would lead to a career in the magistracy or church, shed luster on the family, and bring princely reward (634–35; 548). As a guest in Don Diego's dwelling in Chapter 18, Don Quijote asks Don Lorenzo to recite one of his poems just after the text observes how contented Don Quijote was by the "marvelous silence that reigned through the whole house, which seemed like a Carthusian monastery" ["maravilloso silencio que en toda la casa había, que semejaba un monasterio de cartujos" (652; 666)]. This compliment to the housekeeping of Don Diego's good wife, the symbolically named Doña Cristina, suggests at the same time that the poetry of Don Lorenzo fills a void in this exemplary domestic world. Don Quijote meanwhile proves himself a conoisseur of poetry in his discussions with father and son in Chapters 16 and 18.

Don Diego would rather live a life without poetry, and his imaginative limits make him a limited subject, in turn, for poetry. Unlike Don Quijote, he cannot boast of having had an international best-seller written about his deeds. As critics have pointed out, Cervantes's narrator ostentatiously declines to describe the house of Don Diego, a typical rich farmer's house, for to do so would be to indulge in "dull digressions" ["frías digresiones" (649; 662)]. He then turns around and gives a full description of Don Quijote's clothing: no detail is too small to be insignificant when it comes to the book's hero.[29] All happy families are alike, Tolstoy would later observe, and therefore there is nothing to write about them. Had Don Quijote, like Don Diego, married and devoted himself to family and household, he might have found a fulfillment that would not have left him seeking something more in his chivalric reading and his own knightly quests that lead him away from home. "Get a life, Alonso Quijano, and you will not need to be Don Quijote": this message is twice conveyed to Don Quijote later in Part Two by characters who tell him to go home and look after his estates, wife, and children—"volveos a vuestra casa, y criad vuestros hijos, si los tenéis, y curad de vuestra hacienda" (752; 769); "Vuélvete, mentecato, a tu casa, y mira por tu hacienda, por tu mujer y tus hijos" (973; 991). But in both cases the speakers represent dissenting voices, the ecclesiastic in the household of the Duke and Duchess and the Castilian in Barcelona, who are dismissed by others, those who have already read Part One of *Don Quijote*, who prefer Don Quijote just as he is and derive enjoyment from him. Don Diego, on the other hand, does not appear so much to be amused by Don Quijote as concerned with determining, along with his son, the wisdom or foolishness of his guest— "su discreción o tontería" (649; 663): he is an unimaginative reader of the novel's hero. As for the "discreto" Don Diego himself: he may lead a good, contented life, but not one about which anybody wants to read.

The measurement of Don Diego and Don Quijote against one another suggests the historical divide that Cervantes's novel keeps reexamining in different forms. Don Diego's homely, devout existence conforms to reason and to the Aristotelian mean, a moral terrain that, Cervantes's fiction suggests, corresponds to his position in a new middling class. This is the life of modern virtue, but it appears duller and more restricted than the older aristocratic culture that it is coming to rival and displace. The reader may be encouraged to share something of Don Quijote's own nostalgia for the military tradition of the aristocracy, for its extreme forms of behavior, and for its glamorous individuality—the stuff of poetry. Yet when Don Quijote seeks to revive the aristocratic past in its fantasy version of chivalry, he discloses the madness that lies at its heart: violence disguised as valor, pride masked as individuality—both contrary to Christian ideals of peace and selflessness. Don Diego himself protests to Sancho that he is no saint, but a great sinner (634; 648), an answer that might confirm Sancho's opinion of him or that we can read as mere conventional politeness. But the episode suggests that the culture of Don Diego's middling, moneyed class contests the feudal ethos that preceded it precisely by its modern piety, by the new possibilities it presents for living out Christian values as a layperson. In the contest for our approval that the novel stages between the two hidalgos, the Christianity of Don Diego is the ethical counterweight that may inevitably tip the balance in his favor over the aesthetic interest of Don Quijote.

Camacho and Basilio

The balance, however, appears to shift in the other direction in the ensuing episode of Camacho's wedding, the wedding that does not take place because of the ruse of Camacho's rival Basilio, who instead marries Quiteria, the intended bride. In this episode, which is as elaborately constructed as any in the novel, the rich Camacho and the poor but gallant Basilio repeat the opposition between Don Diego and Don Quijote. As outside observers of the wedding, Don Quijote and Sancho themselves shift positions on the merits of the claims of Camacho and Basilio, but in the end Basilio receives the prize. Furthermore, by casting the rivalry between the two men as a question of Quiteria's marrying for money or for love, the episode looks back and comments on the split in Don Quijote's fantasies that structured Part One: on the one hand his ambition to marry a princess like "Micomicona" that suggests his unacknowledged adherence to the modern world of social mobility, on the other his materially disinterested, if egotistical love for Dulcinea that resists modernity. Quiteria, whose name initially resembles that of the hero, faces a similar alternative, and the victory of Basilio seems not only one of true love, but of more traditional values.[30] Basilio's trick that interrupts the wedding demonstrates that it *is* true love at stake in this case and not the egotism of Don Quijote and of the other lovers—Grisóstomo, Cardenio, the Anselmo of the "Curioso impertinente" who, as we have seen, mirror Don Quijote's desire for Dulcinea in Part One and who victimize the women they claim to love. Cervantes makes Basilio's actions variously recall and roll the stories of those self-centered lovers into one so that Basilio can "correct" them and prove himself worthy of Quiteria.

Camacho, Basilio, and Quiteria are peasants, and the lower-class setting affords a distanced and somewhat unreal literary space in which the novel can explore its social themes. Basilio "wields a sword like the best of them" ["juega una espada con el más pintado" (659; 672)], and therefore wins the initial approval of Don Quijote, who declares him worthy not only of Quiteria, but of Queen Guinivere. But this skill, which, like Basilio's success in peasant games such as wrestling and throwing the bar, hints at his sexual prowess and attractiveness, does not make Basilio a warrior, and certainly not a nobleman, entitled to carry a sword at his side: it only makes him look a bit like one. Similarly, we are told that those who remember everybody's lineage—"que tienen de memoria los linajes de todo el mundo" (658; 671)—declare Quiteria to be higher born than Camacho. What such a distinction can mean in this rural village context is highly doubtful; Sancho Panza's repeated assertions in the novel

TABLE 4.3
The Masque at Comacho's Wedding

Interés	Amor
Liberality/Liberalidad	Poetry/Poesía
Gifts/Dádiva	Wisdom/Discreción
Treasure/Tesoro	Good lineage/Buen linaje
Peaceful possession/Posesión pacífica	Valor/Valentía

that he is an Old Christian—that is, that he has no Jewish or Moorish ancestors—only remind us that he is a peasant nobody. But it nonetheless allows the suggestion that Camacho is a kind of New Man, whose liberal use of his wealth has allowed him to overcome his low birth, just as Sancho has told Teresa Panza in their argument about social climbing in Chapter 5: "So if a person whom Fortune has raised from his lowly state to the height of his present prosperity—these were the words of the preacher—be well bred, liberal, and courteous to all, and if he does not try to vie with those who were noble from ancient times, rest assured, Teresa, that no one will remember what he was, and all will respect him for what he is" ["Y si este a quien la fortuna sacó del borrador de su bajeza (que por estas mesmas razones lo dijo el padre) a la alteza de su prosperidad, fuere bien criado, liberal y cortés con todos, y no se pusiere en cuentos con aquellos que por antigüedad son nobles, ten por cierto, Teresa, que no habrá quien se acuerde de lo que fue, sino que reverencien lo que es" (562; 575–76)]. Through a bit of literary sleight of hand, then, the peasants Camacho and Basilio are made to stand in respectively for the moneyed parvenu and the old-style noble of the sword.

The masque performed at Camacho's wedding, a competition between "Interés" and "Amor," further aligns the two suitors of Quiteria with new and old social groupings. Written by a curate of the village, the masque represents, according to its interpreter Don Quijote, the riches of Camacho versus the talents—"habilidades" (670; 685)—of Basilio as they vie for Quiteria, personified by a damsel in a traditional Castle of Modesty.[31] Thus the nymphs who follow Interés embody, according to the parchment labels they carry on their backs, those qualities of Camacho that attract the material self-interest of Quiteria; those who follow Amor, the attributes of Basilio that awaken her love. Each of the followers of Interés seems to have its opposing counterpart among the followers of Amor (table 4.3).

Don Quijote comments that the curate-author must be a better friend of Camacho than of Basilio (670; 685), perhaps because at one point the purse of Interés succeeds in knocking down the castle of the damsel, although by the end of the masque she is immured in it again while a tie prevails between her two besieging suitors. But the author Cervantes seems to have stacked the deck very much in Basilio's favor, and not only because Basilio will gain Quiteria by the conclusion of the episode. He has made Basilio lovable.

The interlacing with the preceding episode of Don Diego de Miranda redistributes the traits that contrasted Don Diego and Don Quijote. Basilio inherits the poetry and valor of Don Quijote, the qualities in which Don Diego was found wanting. Camacho, on the other hand, inherits the liberality and peaceabilty of Don Diego. The connection between the episodes is reinforced when the nymph personifying Liberality announces that although liberality is the mean that avoids the extreme of prodigality and of its opposite—"Llaman Liberalidad / al dar que el estremo huye / de la prodigalidad / y del contrario" (669; 684)—she will nonetheless be prodigal to show her love for Quiteria. We can hear the echoes of Don Quijote's earlier conversation with Don Diego about extremes and means, and here, too, liberality and valor are placed on opposite sides, corresponding to two distinct cultures. The placing of high birth—"Buen linaje"—on Basilio's side makes it clear that his virtues are associated with the traditional social order; this in spite of the fact that it is Quiteria, not Basilio, who is said to have the advantage of birth over Camacho. Camacho can counter such advantages only with Treasure, his new money. But the surprising feature of the masque is its attribution to Basilio, and not to Camacho, of "Discreción," the wisdom and prudence that had defined the "discreto caballero," Don Diego. At the end of the episode, when Basilio and Quiteria depart together in Chapter 21, they are described as virtuous and wise, if poor ["los pobres virtuosos y discretos"] while Camacho is simply one of the rich ["ricos" (677; 693)].

Basilio, then, inherits not just the features that separate Don Quijote from Don Diego—liberality and poetry—but also those that may separate the hidalgo Don Diego from the peasant Camacho—good lineage and wise discretion. We can map the social coding of the two episodes (table 4.4).

If the two episodes work, as I have argued, to delineate a new middling social group and a common culture shared by the rich farmers Don Diego and Camacho, there is still a distinction to be drawn between the noble and the wealthy peasant: the two may share a roughly equivalent economic position, but not the same social status nor all of the same traits. Wealth and its uses are all that Camacho appears to have in common with Don Diego, and all that he and the new moneyed class have to offer: the liberality manifest in their hospitality and the "peaceful possession" and enjoyment of property that may suggest something of the dull quiet of Don Diego's household. The attributes that make Basilio inspire love, on the other hand, are those money cannot buy—the wisdom of the modern

TABLE 4.4
A Middle Class between Hidalgo and Peasant

Moneyed Peasant Camacho	Moneyed Hidalgo Don Diego	Old Nobility "Caballero" Don Quijote	Basilio
Liberality	Liberality	Valor/Violence	Valor
Peaceability	Peaceability	Poetry/Fantasy	Poetry
	Good Lineage		Good Lineage
	"Discreción"		"Discreción"

gentleman as well as the gallantry of the old-fashioned soldier-noble, both allied to the good lineage that is the basis of a traditional caste society. Quiteria's eventual wedding for Love instead of for Interest, a banal enough literary plot, is less significant in itself than in its culturally conservative coding. If *Don Quijote* depicts in the figure of Camacho the emergence in Spain of a socially fluid class created by wealth, in Basilio it suggests the persistent prestige of an older, feudal aristocratic culture that the new class cannot enjoy. As a corollary to the novel's preference of Don Quijote as its hero over Don Diego, here Basilio is allowed to play the hero at Camacho's own wedding.

If Camacho tries to buy Quiteria, Basilio earns her precisely by playing the heroic role of a literary lover, ready, it seems, to kill himself for her sake. More precisely, the literary lovers on whom his behavior is modeled come from no place else but Part One of *Don Quijote*.[32] He is first introduced to the reader in the title of Chapter 19 as an "enamored shepherd" ["pastor enamorado" (657; 670)], a phrase that recalls Grisóstomo, the make-believe shepherd who commits suicide for the sake of Marcela. The structure of the episode, where Don Quijote and Sancho Panza join some travelers headed for the wedding of Camacho, resembles the earlier episode where knight and squire travel to attend Grisóstomo's funeral. The wedding seems indeed to be turning into the funeral of Basilio, who turns up dressed in black and with a garland of black cypress (673; 688–89), like the mourners at the burial of Grisóstomo (135; 122). After apparently running himself through on a blade hidden in his shepherd's staff, Basilio refuses to take confession unless Quiteria will marry him at the hour of his death. Calling on Quiteria rather than God in his last moments, he is "about to die like a heathen rather than a Christian" ["dando muestras de morir como gentil y no como cristiano" (675; 691)], just as the funeral rites of the suicide Grisóstomo seem heathenish—"parecen de gentiles" (123; 110).

Basilio and his story recall still more closely the lovelorn Cardenio of Part One. We are told in Chapter 19 that Basilio and Quiteria grew up as neighbors like Pyramus and Thisbe (658; 672). The motif contributes to the interlacing of the episodes of Don Diego de Miranda and of Camacho's wedding, for Don Lorenzo, the poet son of Don Diego, has in the previous chapter recited a sonnet he has composed about Pyramus and Thisbe (654–55; 668–69).[33] But it also reminds us of the childhood lovers Cardenio and Luscinda, whom Cardenio similarly described in Chapter 24 of Part One as reliving the story of Pyramus and Thisbe: the father of Quiteria stops Basilio from his ordinary comings and goings into her house ["acordó el padre de Quiteria de estorbar a Basilio la ordinaria entrada que en su casa tenía" (658; 672)] just as Luscinda's father, like the mythical Thisbe's father, felt obligated to stop Cardenio—"obligado a negarme la entrada de su casa" (232; 227). In both cases, material considerations persuade the fathers to marry Quiteria and Luscinda to the richer suitor rather than to the childhood sweetheart. When he learns that Quiteria has been betrothed to Camacho, Basilio heads into the countryside and descends into madness: "at other times he fixes his eyes on the ground in such a distracted way that he resembles a clothed statue . . . we who know him are convinced that when tomorrow the fair Quiteria says *yes* will be his death sentence" ["otras veces clava los ojos en la tierra, con tal embelasamiento, que no parece sino estatua vestida . . . tememos todos los que le conocemos que el dar el sí mañana la hermosa Quiteria ha de ser la sentencia de su muerte" (660; 673–74). The description echoes that which the shepherds of the Sierra Morena give of the intermittently mad Cardenio, who has headed for the mountains after witnessing the wedding of Luscinda and Don Fernando: "he fixed his eyes to the ground, while we held our breath, wondering where the poor lad's distraction would end" ["clavó los ojos en el suelo por un buen espacio, en el cual todos estuvimos quedos y suspensos, esperando en qué había de parar aquel embelesamiento" (228; 223)].

Basilio's intervention at the wedding of Quiteria and Camacho further rewrites the story of Cardenio, who, we remember, failed to come out of his concealment and intervene at the marriage of Luscinda and Don Fernando. Cardenio recalls that he should have come out from behind the tapestry where he was hidden in Luscinda's house and have said, "Take warning that this *yes* means instant death for me" ["Advierte que el decir tú *sí* y el acabárseme la vida ha da ser todo a un punto" (272; 270)]; nonetheless, he hears Luscinda say "Sí quiero," and appear to consent to her marriage with Fernando before she faints away. Cardenio also says that he should have protested that he and Luscinda were already sworn man and wife—"Considera que no puedes cristianamente llegar al fin de tus deseos, porque Luscinda es mi esposa, y yo soy su marido" (272; 270).

Basilio does step forward to proclaim that he and Quiteria are married in the eyes of God and that she cannot wed while he is still alive—"conforme a la santa ley que profesamos, que viviendo yo, tú no puedes tomar esposo" (673; 689); he then stabs himself, as if to clear the way for his rival, Camacho. Now nothing more is required, Don Quijote breaks in to say, than a "sí" from Quiteria, not to the bridegroom Camacho, but to Basilio's request that she marry him as he lies in extremis. Quiteria takes her time to study the situation and decide, but she agrees to wed Basilio of her own free will; when it all turns out to have been a trick, Camacho and his followers "realized that they had been fooled and mocked" ["se tuvieron por burlados y escarnidos" (676; 692)]. When Don Fernando read the letter that Luscinda had written, declaring that despite her apparent consent at the ceremony, she nonetheless remained the wife of Cardenio, the jilted groom felt that Luscinda had similarly fooled and mocked him—"pareciéndole que Luscinda le había burlado y escarnecido y tenido en poco" (286; 286).

Basilio's wounding of himself is a trick, not a miracle, as he himself says after he has sprung to his feet and taken the blade out of the carefully prepared tube he had concealed on his body: "¡No 'milagro, milagro', sino industria, industria!" (676; 692).[34] It is an actor's ploy, and we are reminded of the trick that the adulterous Camila plays on her husband, Anselmo, in the tale of the "Curioso impertinente" in Chapter 34 of Part One: she does indeed stab herself, but not fatally, in the little scene she and his rival Lotario act out for Anselmo's audience of one. The textual echoes are once again evident: Camila is seen "lying on the ground bathed in her own blood" ["tendida en tierra y bañada en su sangre" (360; 360)]; so Basilio lies "bathed in his own blood and stretched on the ground" ["bañado en su sangre y tendido en el suelo" (674; 689)]. When Lotario leaves the playlet in Anselmo's house, he crosses himself in amazement at the "industria" (360; 361) of its author and principal actress, Camila.

What are we to make of these highly self-conscious revisions of the episodes of Part One? If any further proof were needed, Basilio's repetition of the motifs of the stories of Grisóstomo, Cardenio, and Camila indicates how these stories are themselves interrelated in Part One as part of what I have called the "Dulcinea" narrative cluster, stories that reflect on Don Quijote's love for his ideal lady. Basilio's story is also a corrective of those stories, particularly of the egotism of the male lovers in them and of their victimization of women. Unlike Grisóstomo, he does not actually kill himself for love, the ultimate act of egotism and idolatry, and place his soul in jeopardy. Unlike Cardenio, he does not stand back and watch, but instead comes forward at the wedding to claim his beloved and rescue her from a loveless marriage. Unlike Anselmo and Lotario, he does not force the woman he loves to put on a duplicitous charade of sacrifice, but stages that sacrifice himself. What is missing here, above all, is the sense in those earlier stories of Part One that the loved woman herself counts for less than triumph over one's male rival—whether the purely imaginary rival for Marcela whom Grisóstomo conjures up in his jealousy, the Don Fernando over whom Cardenio wants to be chosen by Luscinda, the Lotario whom Anselmo deliberately makes into a rival for his wife Camila's affections. Basilio's performance is directed to persuading and winning Quiteria, and its claim that he wishes to be wedded to her even when there can be no question of the marriage's consummation is a profession of the selflessness of his love. The meaningful words with which she exchanges vows and her new confirmation of the validity of the marriage after Basilio's trick is revealed lead the bystanders to think that Quiteria was in on the plot (676; 692). We are informed in the following Chapter 22 that Basilio had not, in fact, prearranged his fake suicide with her (678; 694), but it is left open whether she may have seen through the trick. The scene does at the least portray a meeting of minds, and it justifies Camacho's conclusion that Quiteria had loved and was still in love with Basilio (677; 693).

With its false container of blood, Basilio's trick comes right out of the theater in which Cervantes tried to make a career as a professional playwright, and the romantic melodrama that he puts on is itself a rival to the ceremonial wedding masque that Camacho has previously staged between Interés and Amor. Once again, Basilio wins on aesthetic points: he is an altogether more exciting performer than the rather pallid Camacho. Yet, upstaged as Camacho is, and even with so much stacked against him, he does not fare so badly in the fiction and gains a measure of the reader's sympathy. As Kathleen Bulgin has argued, the episode still makes a case for Camacho and for the Interés he represents.[35]

For one thing, the sympathies of Don Quijote and Sancho Panza themselves switch back and forth between the two rivals. In Chapter 19, both take the side of Basilio, but Don Quijote immediately qualifies his support by defending the rights of parents to choose marriage partners for their children; otherwise, he says, daughters might throw themselves after some "good-for nothing swashbuckler" ["desbaratado espadachín" (659; 673)], potentially turning Basilio, just praised for his swordsmanship, into a version of the Vicente de la Rosa who ran off with Leandra in Part One. At the smell of the cooking for Camacho's wedding feast in Chapter 20, Sancho changes allegiance, and claims that the best foundation in the world is money—"el mejor cimiento y zanja del mundo es el dinero" (665; 679); dazzled by the largesse of the banquet, Sancho later comments that "what you have is what you are worth" ["tanto vales cuanto tienes, y tanto tienes cuanto vales" (670; 685)]. The squire's materialism may be crass, but in Chapter 22, after the success of Basilio's "industria" and his marriage to Quiteria, Don Quijote himself advises Basilio to give up his athletic and poetic talents—precisely the talents that helped him win Quiteria's love—because they do not make money ["no le daban dineros" (678; 694)]. It is now time, Don Quijote continues, for Basilio to build his fortune by lawful and *industrious* means—"por medios lícitos e industriosos" (679; 694); he is to transform the nature of his "industria" into work and worldly success—that is, to become more like Camacho.

Camacho plays a small enough role at his own wedding, but his behavior nonetheless counts in his favor. In Part One, when Don Fernando found himself "burlado y escarnecido" at his marriage to Luscinda, he had reached for his sword to kill her rather than let her wed another. Camacho and his followers, too, draw swords, but he soon desists from violence, persuaded by Don Quijote's intervention, but even more by his own reasoning and that of the attending priest:

> So deep an impression did Quiteria's disdain produce upon Camacho that it caused him to banish her from his thoughts in an instant. The persuasive words of the priest, who was a man of wisdom and good sense, prevailed upon him, and in this way he and his followers were pacified. They put away their swords and blamed Quiteria's inconstancy more than Basilio's ingenuity. Camacho reflected that if Quiteria as a maiden loved Basilio, she would still love him after marriage, and so he should rather give thanks to Heaven for having taken her away from him than for having given her to him.
>
> As Camacho and his group were consoled and pacified, all those in Basilio's calmed down, and the rich Camacho, to show that he felt no resentment at the trick that had been played upon him, insisted that the festivities should continue as if he were really getting married. (677)

> y tan intensamente se fijó en la imaginación de Camacho el desdén de Quiteria, que se la borró de la memoria en un instante; y así, tuvieron lugar con él las persuasiones del cura, que era varón prudente y bien intencionado, con las cuales quedó Camacho y los de su parcialidad pacíficos y sosegados; en señal de lo cual volvieron las espadas a sus lugares, culpando más a la facilidad de Quiteria que a la industria de Basilio; haciendo discurso Camacho que si Quiteria quería bien a Basilio doncella, también le quisiera casada, y que debía de dar gracias al cielo más por habérsela quitado que por habérsela dado.

> Consolado, pues, y pacífico Camacho y los de su mesnada, todos los de la de Basilio se sosegaron, y el rico Camacho, por mostrar que no sentía la burla, ni la estimaba en nada, quiso que las fiestas pasasen adelante como si realmente se desposara. (693)

We must remember that both Camacho and Basilio are peasants and cannot be expected to share the murderous sense of emulative honor of their aristocratic betters; perhaps that is why their story of rivalry for the same woman can reach a happy ending. But Camacho's case is more socially particular: the relative ease with which he is rendered "pacífico"—the adjective is insisted upon by its repetition—seems to be an outgrowth of his culture of Interés. The "Posesión pacífica" that was described as one of its attributes in the wedding masque now reads less like a description of quiet domestic life than of an ethical disposition.

In the opposition of Amor and Interés, Cervantes appears to have anticipated by over a century the apologies for a middle-class ethos fostered by early capitalism that Albert Hirschman described in his classic study, *The Passions and the Interests*:

> One set of passions, hitherto known variously as greed, avarice, or love of lucre, could be usefully employed to oppose and bridle such other passions as ambition, lust for power, or sexual lust. . . . [O]nce money-making wore the label of "interests" and reentered in this disguise the competition with the other passions, it was suddenly acclaimed and even given the task of holding back those passions that had long been thought to be much less reprehensible.[36]

According to this line of thinking, the rational pursuit of economic advantage could soften and tame the violent passions of aristocratic culture; at least it might offer an alternative to that culture. In Cervantes's fiction, where Interest is already the name that redescribes this alternative ethos, Camacho the Rich quickly takes stock of his situation and makes his peace with it. This calculation readily lends itself to the prudent counsels of the priest; in his forebearance not only from vengeance but even from resentment, in his thanking Heaven, Camacho appears to share the Christianity of that other representative of moneyed, middling values, the pious and peacemaking Don Diego de Miranda. However unheroic he may be, Camacho's victory over himself is nonetheless impressive in its own way.

A New Don Quijote

In both of these interlaced episodes Cervantes places members of a new social group—a middle class in the making—against bearers of heroic attributes associated with a traditional aristocratic society: Don Diego de Miranda versus Don Quijote, Camacho versus Basilio. From the hindsight of literary history, we can detect a time lag in *Don Quijote*. Cervantes intuits that the novel form he is inventing is conditioned by a moneyed economy that is displacing aristocratic culture and offering up new cultural models and values—for which, only now in Part Two, does he find positive things to say. The members of the new class are allowed to make powerful moral claims for their peaceful and humane, if unexciting, lives. And, if Don Diego de Miranda, who does not read chivalric romances, but nonetheless prefers secular, entertaining books to devotional ones, is representative, they also constitute an emerging audience for the new genre of the novel.[37] *Don Quijote* is not ready, however, for a middle-class hero: *that* lies in the novel's future.[38] Neither does Cervantes return to the aristocratic heroes of epic and chivalric romance. Instead, he presents heroes who repeat the gestures of aristocratic heroism, but who are not real aristocrats. Don Quijote is a poor hidalgo and a madman dressed up in antiquated chivalric armor; Basilio is a peasant in need of a job and he, too, puts on a charade to win his love.

The Don Quijote of Part Two is nonetheless more of a middle-class hero than he might initially appear from these two episodes. In ensuing chapters he begins to exhibit traits the novel has just associated with Don Diego de Miranda and Camacho. By the end of the block of episodes that precede Don Quijote's meeting with the Duke and the Duchess and that constitute the first half of Part Two, Don Quijote becomes liberal, pacific, prudent, Christian.

First of all, the impoverished Don Quijote carries cash on hand. I earlier asked us to imagine Don Quijote and Sancho Panza with money, and proposed that they would look like Don Diego de Miranda and Camacho. But, in fact, Cervantes already has his heroes take money along with them on their quest in Part Two. This is the final detail that we learn at the end of Chapter 7, before Don Quijote and Sancho set off on their adventures (576; 589). Now we see the money put to use. It is true that in his vision of the Cave of Montesinos in Chapter 23 Don Quijote is unable to come up with more than four reals for the enchanted Dulcinea (694; 711), and the running of his stocking in Chapter 44 occasions Cide Benengeli's execration upon poverty (837; 852). But after he has destroyed the puppet show of Maese Pedro in Chapter 26, Don Quijote remunerates both the puppeteer and the innkeeper. His recognizing inns as inns is accompanied by his even more important readiness to pay for the hospitality he receives in them, and marks his entrance into and acceptance of the world of money: at the end of Chapter 29, just before Don Quijote and Sancho meet the Duke and Duchess, Don Quijote similarly pays the fishermen for the "enchanted boat" he has wrecked in the Ebro (738; 755); and one chapter earlier Don Quijote has finally agreed to pay the wages to Sancho (730; 747) that he had ruled out of the question in Chapter 7 (573; 585–86).

This Don Quijote who pays as he goes is praised by Maese Pedro in Chapter 26 for his "unheard of Christian spirit" ["inaudita cristiandad" (718; 736)] when he offers to compensate for the damaged puppets. We may hear an echo and a revision of the "inaudito ánimo" that describes Don Quijote in the heading of Chapter 17 where Don Quijote faced the king's lions. Don Quijote is similarly admired by the innkeeper of Chapter 26 for his "liberalidad" as well as for his madness, and the narrator also comments:

> And so the puppet-show squall passed and all took supper in peace and good companionsip at Don Quijote's expense, for he was liberal in the extreme. (720)

> En resolución, la borrasca del retablo se acabó y todos cenaron en paz y en buena compañía, a costa de don Quijote, que era liberal en todo estremo. (737)

It is now Don Quijote who assumes the role of host earlier taken by Don Diego de Miranda and Camacho and whose Christian bounty provides the peaceful meal and communion at the inn: a companionship that is literally the eating of bread together.[39] His extreme liberality, the defining virtue of Camacho, also reminds us of his speech to Don Diego on the means and extremes of virtue, and of the desirability of leaning toward prodigality. It is confirmed a few sentences later when Don Quijote gives twelve reals to the page who is going off to become a soldier, a pointed contrast to the "espilorchería," the stinginess, of the page's previous employers at Court (701; 718).

The peace achieved by the meal accords with another new role for Don Quijote. He intervenes between the followers of Basilio and those of Camacho to urge that the latter "have no right to exact vengeance" ["no es razón toméis venganza" (676–77; 692)] for the wrongs wrought by love. In Chapter 27, he again preaches against vengeance when he confronts the villagers whose braying aldermen have been mocked by their neighbors; the entire village is now up in arms and and spoiling for a fight. Don Quijote's precepts turn evangelical:[40]

> Besides, to take unjust vengeance—and no vengeance can be just—goes directly against the sacred law we profess—which commands us to do good to our enemies and to love those who hate us, a commandment that, though it may seem rather difficult to obey, is only so for those who have less of God than of the world and more of the flesh than of the spirit. For Jesus Christ, God and true man, who never lied, nor could, nor can lie, for He is our lawgiver, said that His yoke was easy and His burden light. He would not then have commanded us to do anything that was impossible to perform. So, my dear sirs, you are bound by laws both divine and human to keep the peace. (725)

> cuanto más que el tomar venganza injusta, que justa no puede haber alguna que lo sea, va derechamente contra la santa ley que profesamos, en la cual se nos manda que hagamos bien a nuestros enemigos y que amemos a los que nos aborrecen; mandamiento que, aunque parece algo dificultoso de cumplir,

no lo es sino para aquellos que tienen menos de Dios que del mundo, y más de carne que de espíritu; porque Jesucristo, Dios y hombre verdadero, que nunca mintió, ni pudo ni puede mentir, siendo legislador nuestro dijo que su yugo era suave y su carga liviana; y así, no nos había de mandar cosa que fuese imposible el cumplirla. Así que, mis señores, vuesas mercedes están obligados por leyes divinas y humanas a sosegarse. (742–43)

This most explicitly Christian moment of the entire novel is characteristically anticipated much earlier by Sancho Panza, who refuses to take vengeance for wrongs done to his ass by the actors in Chapter 11: "a good Christian never takes it for wrongs," Sancho concludes, and declares his aim "to live in peace as long as Heaven grants me life" ["no es de buenos cristianos tomarla de los agravios . . . vivir pacíficamente los días que los cielos me dieren de vida (602; 616)]. In this subsequent episode, where an ass or asininity are again at stake, Don Quijote becomes a Christian peacemaker; he recalls the pious Don Diego de Miranda, who seeks to make peace between those in discord: "procuro poner en paz los que sé que están desavenidos" (634; 648).

This effort at Christian mediation seems about to succeed when Sancho insists on adding his two cents; he recalls how much he enjoyed braying himself and gives an example on the spot. Thinking themselves mocked once again, one of the villagers strikes Sancho down with a pole. Don Quijote finds it impossible to avenge his squire—"no fue posible vengarle" (726; 744)—in the face of a shower of stones and the crossbows and muskets aimed toward him:

> he turned Rozinante's reins and departed from them as fast as he could gallop, beseeching God with all his heart to be delivered from that peril and fearing at every step that a bullet would enter his back and come out through his chest. (726)

> volvió las riendas a Rocinante, y a todo lo que su galope pudo, se salió de entre ellos, encomendándose de todo corazón a Dios, que de aquel peligro le librase, temiendo a cada paso no le entrase alguna bala por las espaldas y le saliese al pecho. (744)

The irony that the Don Quijote who has just preached against vengeance now seeks to find it is quickly succeeded by the comic ignominy of his turning his back in headlong flight and leaving Sancho in his peril. The scene reminds us that the gunpowder revolution has put an end to the chivalric heroism Don Quijote attempts to revive: point a gun at him and the knight is helpless.[41] But his running away also repeats the flight of Don Diego de Miranda, Sancho, and the muleteer at the moment when Don Quijote insisted on facing the lions: they "did not stop fleeing and looking behind them at every step, urged on by the gentleman in green" ["no dejaban de huir ni de volver la cabeza a cada paso, todos en tropa y antecogidos del hidalgo" (644; 658)]. And, in the following Chapter 28, Don Quijote justifies his "retreat" with the very argument of Don Diego that he had earlier contested: "you must know, Sancho, that valor that is not based upon prudence is called rashness, and the achievements of the rash are rather to be ascribed to good luck than courage" ["has de saber, Sancho, que la valentía que no se funda sobre la basa de la pruden- cia se llama temeridad, y las hazañas del temerario más se atribuyen a la buena fortuna que a su ánimo" (728; 745)]. The Don Quijote who earlier had asserted that it is better to err on the side of rashness than of coward- ice now finds that a prudent mean between the two is the best policy for the man of valor. This reversal, which the tongue-in-cheek narrator echoes at the opening of the chapter when he observes that prudent men save themselves for better occasions—"es de varones prudentes guardarse para mejor ocasión" (727; 744)—comes at Don Quijote's expense and defini- tively bursts the bubble of pride that surrounded him after his victories over Sansón Carrasco and the lion.

The scene completes a much larger reversal that Don Quijote's charac- ter has undergone in these episodes. The dialectical structure of Cervan- tes's fiction first places Don Quijote's chivalry in opposition to an emer- gent middle-class culture and then finds in its hero a synthesis of the two: with whatever degree of consciousness, the hero now assumes the values and imitates the behavior of Don Diego de Miranda and Camacho. He shares their humane Christianity, their peaceability and generosity, even their prudence that smacks of a want of valor and heroism. And this likeness makes him more likable.

Don Quijote's absorption of the ethos of the new moneyed class paral- lels and, now we can see, contributes in no small part to the change in character that has made a new man of him in Part Two: less violent, more good-hearted, innocent—"un ánimo blando y compasivo, inclinado siem- pre a hacer bien a todos, y mal a ninguno" (709; 725). This gentler Don Quijote, the spokesman against the code of vengeance and honor that lies at the basis of an older feudal culture, now apppears to be a product of a new social group, whose influence may create a gentler, more Christian way of life: he is an honorary member of the modern middle class. His partnership with Sancho Panza that makes him a kind of composite hero only confirms his placement in the same middling group, comprising and also somewhere between hidalgo and rich peasant, that Don Diego de Miranda and Camacho occupy. To this extent Don Quijote appears to have adapted to a new world of money and of compromised, more medio- cre heroism that will be the future domain of the novel.[42] Don Quijote is now a peacemaker, and we may assume from Part Two that his creator, Cervantes, has also made his peace with modernity.

Preaching to the Bandits

Just how far this Don Quijote has come from Part One, where he identi-
fied with the bandit Rinaldo of Montalban and was himself taken for a
highwayman, is measured late in Part Two when he meets the bandit
Roque Guinart.[43] A real-life bandit who operated outside of a feud-ridden
Barcelona in the first decade of the sixteenth century, Roque's existence
presents a modern version of the chivalric career that Don Quijote professes; its "constant sequence of adventures and accidents, all of them
perilous" ["nuevas aventuras, nuevos sucesos, y todos peligrosos" (962;
981)] are just the sort of perilous adventures—"peligrosas aventuras"
(646; 660)—that Don Quijote much earlier claimed to be seeking. Cervantes's Roque is romanticized and indeed highly chivalrous: he displays
rough justice to his fellow bandits, liberality and magnanimity to those
he robs, gallantry to Claudia Jerónima, a damsel-in-distress. The opposition of Don Quijote and Roque suggests that the old feudal world that
Don Quijote hopes to relive in his chivalry still lives on in modern times—
atavistically and vestigially—in the form of banditry and vendetta; it also
hints that such chivalry may all along have been little more than feudal
anarchy and lawlessness.

Timothy Hampton has noted that Don Diego de Miranda and Roque
Guinart are symmetrical figures placed toward the beginning and ending
of Part Two; their models, passive and active, demonstrate the limited
and marginalized possibilities for heroism open to Don Quijote in his
modern times. Don Diego's unheroic virtue is confined to his domestic
sphere, whereas the example of Roque suggests that were Don Quijote
indeed capable of acting out his chivalric ideals, he could only do so outside the law at the edge of society—as indeed Don Quijote is treated as
an outlaw by the forces of the state in Part One.[44] This is a valuable observation, but I would argue that by the point his narrative reaches Roque
both Don Quijote and the larger novel have preferred and assimilated the
model of the Christian homebody over that of the chivalrous bandit. For
while Don Diego may be contented to the point of complacency, the fiction insists on the misery of Roque's life, from the macabre opening of
the episode in Chapter 60, where Don Quijote and Sancho encounter
thirty-odd bandits dangling from the trees, on which they have been
hanged by the king's justice (956; 974), to the narrator's final verdict on
Roque in Chapter 61: "His was indeed a nerve-wracking and unhappy
life" ["vida, por cierto, miserable y enfadosa" (966; 985)].

Roque claims to be good at heart—"soy compasivo y bien intencio-
nado" (962; 981)—that is, he is as potentially good-natured as the "compasivo" Don Quijote himself. But he has been led into his life of outlawry,

he tells us in the same passage, by uncontrollable desires for vengeance—
"deseos de venganza." How disordered such desires may be has just been
demonstrated by the episode-within-the-episode of Claudia Jerónima,
who, disguised as a man, has ridden up to Roque's camp, and implored
his protection. In a kind of Romeo and Juliet story, Claudia has loved and
received a pledge of marriage from Don Vicente Torrellas, a member of
the enemy faction with which her family is feuding. On learning that Don
Vicente is about to wed another woman, one Leonora, the daughter of
the rich Balvastro, she intercepts him on his way to the ceremony and
puts two bullets into him, washing her honor clean in his blood. The only
problem with this satisfactory scenario of revenge is that when Claudia
Jerónimo and Roque reach the dying Don Vicente, they learn that the
news of the impending marriage was greatly exaggerated: he had not betrayed her at all. Claudia Jerónimo has been misled into killing her intended husband; with his last breath, Don Vicente asks Claudia Jerónima
to give him her hand and marry him—"aprieta la mano y recíbeme por
esposo" (960; 979)—as he expires.

"Roque was confused and did not know what to do" ["Confuso estaba
Roque y no sabía qué hacerse" (960; 979)]. Everything in this brief vignette is confused: the lovers who come from enemy families to begin
with, the faithful bridegroom who is mistakenly thought to be untrue, the
combination of murder and marriage, even the woman Claudia Jerónima
dressed as a man. The tragic story of jealousy aroused by the prospect of
the intended about to marry a rich rival, the daughter of "el rico Balvastro" rewrites the comedy of Camacho's wedding ["Camacho el rico"].[45]
Its climax, where Don Vicente asks for Claudia Jerónima's hand in marriage, echoes the trick of Basilio, who, only pretending to be dying of his
self-inflicted wound, calls on Quiteria to take his hand and be his wife—
"darme en este último y forzoso trance la mano de esposa" (674; 690).
This contrast is pointed and reinforces the symmetry that Hampton finds
between Don Diego de Miranda and Roque Guinart—the mock violence
and peaceful conclusion of Camacho's wedding are part of Don Diego's
middle-class sphere while the real violence and mad passions of Claudia
Jerónima belong to Roque's dark world of noble vendetta and banditry.
Roque can do nothing about them.

When Roque returns to his bandit followers, he finds "Don Quijote
among them, mounted on Rozinante and making them a speech in which
he urged them to give up their way of life, as perilous for the soul as well
as the body" ["don Quijote entre ellos, sobre Rocinante, haciéndoles una
plática en que los persuadía dejasen aquel modo de vivir tan peligroso así
para el alma como para el cuerpo" (963; 980)]. For all that it falls upon
deaf ears, this speech—or sermon—is a remarkable moment, and shortly
thereafter Don Quijote plays spiritual doctor to the more receptive Roque

himself. Roque makes a kind of confession—"le confieso"—to Don Quijote about his existence as a bandit: there is no life more unquiet, he says—"no hay modo de vivir más inquieto." And he explains that the wish to avenge an insult overcomes all his good inclinations—"el querer vengarme de un agravio que se me hizo, así da con todas mis buenas inclinaciones en tierra, que persevero en este estado" (962; 981). Don Quijote, like a good father confessor, responds that the important thing is to acknowledge one's sins, and to trust in God, the superior physician of the soul—"nuestro médico" (963; 982); he then suggests as penance—"penitencia"—the life of a knight-errant. This last advice causes Roque to smile and brings a jokey conclusion to this scene of contrition. Nonetheless, it has shown Don Quijote as a kind of priestly figure—a "thologian" ["tólogo"(726; 743)], as Sancho earlier dubs him when the peacemaking Don Quijote sermonized against vengeance to the villagers of the braying aldermen. He preaches Christianity to the bandits and tries to convert them and Roque from their life of crime and from the dark passions, revenge above all, that dominate it.

This preaching seems equally directed to a former self of Don Quijote and indicates a conversion already effected: his turning his back upon the outlaw like career to which he had aspired in Part One. Much closer now in spirit to Don Diego de Miranda than to Roque Guinart, this change in the character of Don Quijote between the two installments of the novel speaks to the larger historical change that it charts: the supersession of a feudal-aristocratic order by a modern society and the gentler values of its moneyed, middling class. We are nearing the end of the novel and the final conversion of Don Quijote away from his dreams of chivalry: his return to his mediocre existence as petty-noble hidalgo, and his death, both as man and as hero.

FIVE

ARISTOCRATS

D ON QUIJOTE MEETS Roque Guinart in Chapter 60 between his two stays at the castle of the Duke and the Duchess (Chapters 30–57, 68–70), and the bandit comments as much on that noble couple as he does on the mad hidalgo. Roque and the Duke and the Duchess represent two fates of an older aristocratic world in modern society. In Roque the violent and independent way of life of aristocratic feudalism persists at this society's margins in the atavistic vendettas of feuding clans and banditry. The Duke and the Duchess remain at the center of the society's power, and the courtly palace life of these grandees represents a far more successful adaptation of the aristocracy to modern times. Roque is marginal to Cervantes's novel itself, occupying only one and a half of its chapters, while the Duke and the Duchess control most of the action of the second half of Part Two.

The noble couple re-create the romance world of Don Quijote's fantasies. In doing so, they lay claim themselves to be the modern heirs of chivalry. When the Duchess first appears, hawk in hand and mounted on a "very white palfrey or hackney" ["un palafrén o hacanea blanquísima" (739; 756)], she seems to have stepped out of a Burgundian tapestry—or out of one of Don Quijote's romances, where, as Cervantes's contemporary, the lexicographer Covarrubias, tells us, palfreys are the chosen steeds of damsels.[1] The Duchess reminds Sancho that the Duke is a knight in Chapter 33 (769; 785), and in Chapter 36, the Duke himself professes his knighthood (793; 808). The chivalry that is apparently absurd when practiced by the mad hidalgo is still part of noble identity, something the Duke and the Duchess like to half-believe in, even if they do not believe in its literal truth, as does Don Quijote.[2] It is part, we might say, of the class *ideology* of the Spanish aristocracy.[3]

As a consequence, the demystification of chivalry in *Don Quijote* turns into social satire in the extended episode of the Duke and the Duchess. Cervantes may not envision, nor desire, the end of a dominant aristocratic class (though the Duke and the Duchess appear to be childless.) But he does sharply criticize its culture. He exposes the cruelty, idleness, and injustice of a present-day high nobility that appears to have given up its martial and chivalric past and become an indolent courtier class. Ironically, it is the bandit Roque Guinart in whom the novel finds an *ethical* survival of aristocratic chivalry: he is the modern equivalent of the knight Don Quijote dreams to be, the defender of distressed damsels like Claudia Jerónima and the dispenser of justice to his men. But a similar mirroring relationship between Don Quijote and the self-professed modern knight, the Duke, and his lady, the Duchess, reveals these nobles to be neither chivalrous nor just: distressed damsels need not apply to *them*, as the daughter of the duenna Doña Rodríguez can attest. The Duke and the Duchess allow Don Quijote to live out his chivalrous ideals and raise Sancho to be governor and judge of his "island," only to thwart them both when they succeed against expectations. Don Quijote and Sancho turn out to be better representatives of knighthood and justice than their noble patrons—and so does the noble bandit Roque. Moreover, if Roque directs the traditional violence of his aristocratic class against rival clans and against the forces of the state, the Duke and the Duchess train this violence upon those who cannot strike back, exhibiting cruelty to animals and to their own servants and dependents. It is into the ungentle hands of this noble couple that Cervantes delivers Don Quijote and Sancho Panza for much of the remainder of Part Two.

The Duke and the Duchess know from their reading of Part One just what Don Quijote expects in the way of hospitality from the two miniature chivalric romances he tells to Sancho in Chapter 21 (the knight and the beautiful daughter of the king) and to the Canon of Toledo in Chapter 50 (the knight in the enchanted underwater garden); both are fantasies of lavish aristocratic entertainment. In Don Quijote's scenarios, the king had given the knight a rich scarlet mantle ["un rico manto de escarlata" (204; 197)] and in the enchanted garden a damsel throws over the shoulders of the knight a priceless mantle ["echarle un mantón sobre los hombros" (497; 501)]. When Don Quijote arrives at the country palace of the Duke and the Duchess in Chapter 31, he is met by two beautiful maidens ["hermosas doncellas"] who throw a large mantle of the very finest scarlet cloth over his shoulders ["echaron sobre los hombros a Don Quijote un gran manto de finísima escarlata" (744; 761)]. Don Quijote had told Sancho that the king would order his knights to ride out and welcome the flower of chivalry—"a recibir a la flor de la caballería" (204; 197). A chorus of the servants of the Duke and the Duchess welcome Don Quijote as the flower and cream of knights-errant—"¡Bien sea venido la flor y la nata de los caballeros andantes!" (745; 762) The damsels of the enchanted garden bathed the visiting knight and gave him a new shirt (497; 501). Six "doncellas" are assigned by the Duke and the Duchess to strip Don Quijote and clothe him with a new shirt, but he refuses their help out of modesty (746–47; 764). The bathing is subsequently burlesqued, without the knowledge of the Duke and the Duchess, when four "doncellas" wash

Don Quijote's beard in Chapter 32 (757; 773). The king's daughter, the princess, falls in love with the visiting knight and they meet by the railings—"rejas" (205; 198)—of a garden adjoining her sleeping chamber. The scene is reenacted in Chapters 44 and 46 when Altisidora, the servant of the Duchess, pretends to be in love with Don Quijote outside *his* bedroom window with its "reja" (838; 853) overlooking a lovely garden. In Chapter 31, we are told of Don Quijote that "for the first time he felt himself to be thoroughly convinced that he was a real knight-errant in fact and not in imagination" ["y aquél fue el primer día que de todo en todo conoció y creyó ser caballero andante verdadero, y no fantástico" (744; 762)]. The Duke and the Duchess have brought his fantasies to life.

There is something regressive and infantilizing in this bathing and dressing of Don Quijote. The Duke and the Duchess seek to arrest the development of both hero and novel. As readers who enjoyed Part One, they now attempt to carry the new Don Quijote of Part Two back to the first installment of the novel, fostering his illusion that he is a knight at their "castle" even as he no longer mistakes inns for castles. Their intervention into the fiction of *Don Quijote* creates a reverse mirroring relationship between its two parts. In Part One a Don Quijote who sets out to revive chivalry finds himself imprisoned by a modern world of money and law; he eventually winds up in a cage. In Part Two, a Don Quijote who seems to have adapted some of the more peaceable and moderate traits of that world's emerging middle class finds himself imprisoned by his old chivalric delusions, fed back to him by the Duke and the Duchess; he and Sancho are literally kidnapped and made prisoners—"presos" (1013; 1033)—in Chapter 68 when they are brought back to the ducal palace. This regressive movement of Part Two thus has a historical correlative. Cervantes's novel discovers a new social formation whose values compete with those of an older feudal-aristocratic order. The Duke and the Duchess, representatives of an aristocracy whose power is still entrenched and socially dominant, drag *Don Quijote* back toward the past. Their class may exert a similar drag on Spanish society and culture as a whole.

Cruel Readers

Vladimir Nabokov professed to be appalled by the cruelty that solicits laughter in *Don Quijote*. What could be funnier, he asked in his lectures at Harvard in 1951–52, published posthumously in 1983, than Don Quijote's losing half an ear in Part One "except of course losing three quarters of an ear"?[4] He listed the beatings that Don Quijote and Sancho Panza undergo as well as the injuries that Don Quijote himself inflicts, and kept a kind of running scorecard. In his reading, the Duke and the Duchess are the chief promoters of the novel's cruelty in Part Two. Their castle is a "torture house," and they take over the role of the persecuting enchanters whom Don Quijote uses to explain his setbacks. In fact, the Duchess manages to persuade Sancho that Dulcinea really *is* enchanted in Chapter 33.

A second line of criticism of *Don Quijote*, reacting no less than Nabokov to a romantic, sentimental reading of the novel, insists upon its comedic nature. Don Quijote's sufferings are the result of the *burlas*, practical jokes or plain mishaps that, as Anthony Close maintains, "form the backbone of incident in the age's comic literature."[5] There is little acknowledgment of the cruelty or painfulness of these slapstick *burlas*: to complain about them, instead of just laughing along, would be to commit an act of critical anachronism. By this logic, too, the relatively benign Duke and the Duchess are merely continuing what Cervantes started in Part One. They keep the jokes coming.[6]

These diametrically opposed readings nonetheless agree that the Duke and the Duchess are the agents of Cervantes.[7] But the novel in fact opens up a distance between these noble readers of Part One and the author, a distance finally spelled out in Chapter 70 when the narrator Cide Hamete declares that these jokers are no less mad than their victims—"tiene para sí ser tan locos los burladores como los burlados" (1023; 1041). At issue are the *burlas* themselves. It is not a romantic or modern-day anachronism to call into question the nature of one's laughter at watching the antics of slapstick. Cervantes sardonically comments at the end of Chapter 56 on the reactions of the spectators to one of the jokes orchestrated by the Duke and the Duchess that fails to come off, the duel that never takes place between Don Quijote and the lackey Tosilos:

> most of the spectators were disappointed and depressed because the eagerly awaited combatants had not hacked one another to pieces, just as boys are sorry when the man they are expecting is not brought out to be hanged because he is pardoned either by the injured party or by the judge. (930)

> y los más quedaron tristes y melancólicos, de ver que no se habían hechos pedazos los tan esperados combatientes, bien así como los mochachos quedan tristes cuando no sale el ahorcado que esperan, porque le ha perdonado, o la parte, o la justicia. (947)

The author asks his readers what *they* were hoping to see happen to Don Quijote: did they want to see a kind of public execution, and were they disappointed to see the hero mercifully spared? In this light, it is no coincidence that the final torment inflicted by the Duke and the Duchess on Don Quijote and Sancho comes in the form of a mock auto-da-fé with Sancho dressed up for the flames of the stake. Cervantes appears to build the Duke and the Duchess into the fiction of *Don Quijote* to raise just

such questions about reader response: as we watch and criticize their enjoyment at the infliction of pain on others, we have to confront our own
laughter. Nabokov, that is, responded to something real enough in the
novel, but he failed to give credit to Cervantes, who had anticipated him
in reflecting upon the cruelty that lies at the basis of its physical comedy.

The Duke and Duchess are the first readers of Part One of *Don Quijote*,
apart from Sansón Carrasco in Chapters 12–14, whom Don Quijote and
Sancho encounter after they leave their village. While Sansón's project is
to bring Don Quijote's wandering and the novel to an end, a project in
which he finally succeeds in Chapter 64, the Duke and the Duchess want
to extend the novel on their own terms, and even continue it after Sansón
has defeated Don Quijote and sent him home: they seize Don Quijote
and Sancho by force in Chapter 68 to carry the pair back for a second
visit to their palace. Cervantes suggests that these noble readers have tried
to abduct and take over his novel itself. As rivals, rather than simple
agents, of the author Cervantes, the Duke and the Duchess already anticipate the real-life pseudonymous Alonso de Avellaneda and his second part
to *Don Quijote*. This "spurious" continuation of their story comes to
the attention of Don Quijote and Sancho in Chapter 59 when they are
dining at an inn that promises much in the way of fare, but only delivers
cow's heels for consumption: an emblem itself of the emptiness of Avellaneda's book.[8]

The Duke and the Duchess, too, construct a sequel to Part One of *Don
Quijote*. The reception they give to Don Quijote appears to answer Don
Quijote's craving for recognition as a knight and, simultaneously, Cervantes's own desire for recognition as Don Quijote's creator. They are generous aristocratic patrons of the kind Cervantes needed and only rarely
found: their steward bestows two hundred crowns on Sancho when they
first take their leave of the castle in Chapter 57 (932; 949), doubling the
take of one hundred crowns that Sancho lifted from Cardenio's saddle-
bags and brought home with him in Part One. But their further treatment
of Don Quijote and Sancho suggests that the Duke and the Duchess responded to Cervantes's novel in their own particular way. They seem to
have enjoyed above all the beatings and violence suffered by the knight
and his squire in Part One—as if this violence were a comic end in itself.
Like all readers of sequels, the Duke and the Duchess want more of what
they found to their taste in the original, and they construct their new
version of Part One as a series of pratfalls.[9]

The gentler Don Quijote of Part Two is much less the instigator of
violence than he was in Part One, and the Duke and the Duchess have to
devise their own schemes to visit pain on his body and on the body of
Sancho Panza. The struggles that Don Quijote and Sancho undergo to
realize themselves as characters and to escape from the confining plots

handed to them by the Duke and the Duchess correspond to Cervantes's attempt to make his novel, particularly its second part, something more and different than a mere slapstick comedy that some readers of the first installment took it to be.[10] The reductive readers in this case are aristocrats, and Cervantes's critique of his bad readers joins here with his satire on noble culture. The enjoyment that the Duke and the Duchess derive from physical cruelty—whether they read about it or whether they have it carried out themselves—makes them apt representatives of a class habituated to exercising its power on the bodies of others.

Don Quijote and Sancho first encounter the Duke and the Duchess in Chapter 30 when she is out hawking—it is not clear whether the Duke, who later joins her, is also participating in this noble pastime. Indeed, while both of this noble couple are avid hunters, the Duchess seems more avid. When they go out hunting again in Chapter 34, this time for big game, and take Don Quijote and Sancho Panza with them, only the Duke can prevent the Duchess from stepping in front of all the rest of the party to cast her spear at the oncoming boar (775; 790). The Duke explains to the unconvinced Sancho that such woodland hunting is the particular reserve of the elite:

> hunting is the most suitable and necessary exercise of all for kings and princes. The chase is the image of war; it has its stratagems, wiles, ambushes, by which one can overcome the enemy in safety; in it we have to bear extreme cold and intolerable heat; indolence and sleep are scorned; bodily strength is invigorated; the limbs of one who takes part in it are made supple; indeed, it is an exercise that can be taken without harm to anyone and with pleasure to many. And the best point about it is that it is not for everybody, as other kinds of sports are, excepting hawking, which is also reserved for kings and great lords. Therefore, O Sancho, change your opinion, and when you are governor, follow the chase and you will soon find that one loaf will do you as much good as a hundred. (776–77)

> el ejercicio de la caza de monte es el más conveniente y necesario para los reyes y príncipes que otro alguno. La caza es una imagen de la guerra: hay en ella estratagemas, astucias, insidias para vencer a su salvo al enemigo; padécense en ella fríos grandísimos y calores intolerables; menoscábase el ocio y el sueño, corrobóranse las fuerzas, agilítanse los miembros del que la usa, y, en resolución, es ejercicio que se puede hacer sin perjuicio de nadie y con gusto de muchos; y lo mejor que él tiene es que no es para todos, como lo es el de los otros géneros de caza, excepto el de la volatería, que también es sólo para reyes y grandes señores. Así que ¡oh Sancho!, mudad de opinión, y cuando seáis gobernador, ocupaos en la caza y veréis como os vale un pan por ciento. (791–92)

The Duke cites the two-thousand-year-old justifications for hunting as a defining aristocratic activity that derive from Xenophon's *Cynegeticus*. The hunt is a kind of basic training that prepares the nobleman for war, toughening up his body and teaching him tactics and strategy.[11]

Renaissance moralists, however, attacked the aristocratic hunt precisely because of this link to war. In his commentary on the adage "dulce bellum inexpertis" (war is sweet to those who have not experienced it), the pacifist Erasmus depicts hunting as the historical first step in the brutalization of humankind that led to war, and Erasmian literature would repeatedly point to the paradox that princes and noblemen wanted exclusive rights to an activity that was indistinguishable from the trade of the common butcher.[12] Thomas More's antiaristocratic *Utopia*, where butchery itself is consigned to slaves, ascribes the attraction of hunting to the enjoyment of physical cruelty: "the hunter seeks nothing but pleasure from the killing and mangling of a poor animal."[13] Montaigne follows this line in his essay on cruelty, where he registers his distaste for hunting and asserts that he has "not been able without distress to see pursued and killed an innocent beast which is defenseless and which does us no harm."[14]

The peasant Sancho Panza appears to be the heir of this polemic against the hunt and against the violent aristocratic culture that fosters it. When the boar is at bay, Sancho runs away, climbs a tree where his new hunting suit gets caught and ripped on one of its branches, leaving him helplessly suspended above the ground. He subsequently comments:

> If it had only been hunting hares or little birds, my suit wouldn't be in such a pickle; I can't see what pleasure there is in lying in wait for an animal that may murder you with his tusk if he gets a go at you. . . . I'd sooner kings and princes didn't expose themselves to such dangers for the sake of a pleasure that, in my opinion should not be one at all, for it consists in killing an animal that has committed no crime. (776)

> Si esta caza fuera de liebres o de pajarillos, seguro estuviera mi sayo de verse en este estremo. Yo no sé qué gusto se recibe de esperar a un animal que, si os alcanza con un colmillo, os puede quitar la vida. . . . [N]o querría yo que los príncipes y los reyes se pusiesen en semejantes peligros, a trueco de un gusto que parece que no le había de ser, pues consiste en matar a un animal que no ha cometido delito alguno. (791)

Cervantine irony does not allow us to detach this criticism of hunting from Sancho's cowardice: Don Quijote bravely faces the boar, shield and sword in hand, while his squire runs away. Sancho distinguishes between this hunting for big and potentially dangerous game, the sport of princes and high aristocrats, and the more moderate, safer hunting for smaller beasts and birds of the kind that he and his disguised neighbor Tomé

Cecial discussed back in Chapter 13 (611; 625), the pastime of common, rural classes. This is also the pastime, we remember, of the moderately wealthy Don Diego de Miranda, who tells Don Quijote in Chapter 16 that he has neither hawk nor hounds, but keeps only a tame decoy partridge and a saucy ferret (633; 647); Don Quijote mockingly recalls them as he goes to confront a quarry that is worthy of *him*: the king's lions. In that earlier episode Don Diego fled, along with Sancho, as far as possible (642; 656) from the lions, just as Sancho now runs as fast as possible (775; 790) from the boar. These mirroring episodes distinguish two modes of hunting that characterize the social classes who participate in them. The middling sort hidalgo, Don Diego, engages in hunting as a peaceable diversion that does not require physical courage. The high aristocrats, the Duke and Duchess, hunt against beasts which, as potentially dangerous adversaries, turn their pastime into the mirror of warfare. And they, the Duchess in particular, want to be in at the kill.

For all of his cowardice, Sancho's criticism still strikes home: the beast has committed no crime and is therefore unjustly killed by the hunter. It acquires further force when the violence inflicted on the beasts of the hunt is juxtaposed in the same episode with Sancho's own love for animals, especially for his dappled donkey, "el rucio."[15] He holds back from the hunt at first because of his fears for the donkey, "lest some mishap befall him" ["porque no le sucediese algún desmán" (775; 790)]. The donkey does not desert him when Sancho is caught in the tree, and "Cide Hamete says that he rarely saw Sancho without Dapple or Dapple without Sancho, such was the friendship and good faith between them" ["y dice Cide Hamete que pocas veces vio a Sancho Panza sin ver al rucio, ni al rucio sin ver a Sancho: tal era la amistad y buena fe que entre los dos se guardaban" (777; 791)]. Three chapters earlier, Sancho causes a run-in with Doña Rodríguez when he asks the duenna to look after "el rucio," who, he says, is scared of being left alone (745; 762). Later, when he and the donkey fall into some old ruins in Chapter 55, he shares his own bread with the animal (921; 938) and, when he is rescued, refuses to see the Duke until the donkey is stabled (924; 941). Cervantes, of course, gets a lot of comic mileage out of the asininity that links Sancho—and Don Quijote, too—to "el rucio." But when in Chapter 53 Sancho, disillusioned and physically beaten at the end of his governorship, gives his donkey a kiss of peace on the forehead (909; 926), this moment of Christian communion between creatures offers an effective contrast to the cruelty meted out on Sancho by the Duke's human agents. The faithful relationship between master and beast, moreover, parallels Sancho's relationship to his own master, Don Quijote: when the two quarreled over wages in Chapter 28, the repentant Sancho promises to serve his master as a donkey, tail and all—"y le serviré como jumento" (731; 749)—for the rest of his life.

Sancho Panza's tenderness toward animals—one should also note his fantasy of playing with the little kid-goats of the Pleiades that he recounts after his celestial "voyage" on the magic horse Clavileño in Chapter 41 (820; 836)—is linked to his function in the novel as the embodiment of the body itself. His last name, of course, means "stomach," and as two disappointed readers of Avellaneda's sequel suggest in Chapter 59, he can be easily misread reductively as a mere peasant glutton—"comedor" (951; 969). But Sancho, fleshly where Don Quijote is lean, is the spokesman for the animal part of man. This is nowhere clearer than in Chapter 54, in an episode that is calculatedly interlaced between Sancho's bestowing his kiss of peace on his donkey and his later sharing his bread with the beast. After declaring on leaving his government in Chapter 53 that he came naked into the world and finds himself naked (910; 926) at present, Sancho literally strips to nakedness—"en pelota" (913; 930)—with his old Morisco neighbor Ricote and the German "pilgrims" who are with him and look suspiciously like Protestants, but who are, Ricote says, very peaceable—"muy apacible gente" (913; 930)—while they eat bread and drink wine.[16] Religious differences disappear in this irenic communion of men revealed in their common bodily humanity. Sancho reasons that "when in Rome, do as the Romans do" ["cuando a Roma fueres, haz como vieres" (914; 931)]—while the scene intimates a community that is more catholic than institutional Catholicism. In their broken Spanish, the Germans say, "*Español y tudesqui, tuto uno: bon compaño*" and bring home the etymological force of "companion," one with whom we eat bread.[17] The narrator comments that cares have little power over us when we eat and drink—"sobre el rato y tiempo cuando se come y bebe, poca jurisdición suelen tener los cuidados" (914; 931). Sancho echoes the sentiment in one of his characteristic proverbs in the next chapter as he gives his bread to his donkey: "all sorrows with bread are good ones" ["todos los duelos con pan son buenos" (921; 938)]. The companionship that Sancho feels with animals is thus inseparable from a vision of peaceful human fellowship based on a shared animal nature—the fellowship of the common man—and it is set in contrast to the violence of the aristocratic hunt, a violence that the Duke and the Duchess will extend from the beasts they prey on to human beings.

It is, in fact, Sancho Panza's bodily kinship with animals, as well as his subordinate status as peasant and servant, that makes him the primary target of the cruel pranks of the Duke and the Duchess.[18] He has more of a body to abuse than does Don Quijote, and the noble pair act accordingly. The most important and long-lasting of the jokes they play comes at the end of the day of the hunt. A nocturnal pageant appears, bearing the enchanted Dulcinea, and a figure of Merlin proclaims in verse that she will be disenchanted only after Sancho gives himself three thousand, three hundred lashes on his bare buttocks:

> es menester que Sancho, tu escudero,
> se dé tres mil azotes y trecientos
> en ambas sus valientes posaderas
> al aire descubiertas . . .   (784; 798)

When Sancho proves reluctant to carry out the prescribed whipping, the page disguised as Dulcinea addresses him as an "animal" and as a beast intent only on eating and more eating—"bestión . . . que a sólo comer y más comer te inclina" (785; 800). The aristocrats are hardly less crude readers of Sancho than the rival author Avellaneda. He is reduced to a gluttonous peasant body, suitable, like the boar that has just been killed during the hunt, for the suffering of pain.[19]

Fat backsides such as Sancho's are irresistible, conventional targets for slapstick comedy. Cervantes's fiction invites us to laugh, but also to wonder just what we are laughing at. There is no disguising the sexual component in the pleasure that the Duke and the Duchess take in this proposed whipping of Sancho's buttocks. This "penance," which is to make Sancho like one of the self-flagellating disciplinants in the final chapter of Part One, contains a streak of infantile sadism and it is, in fact, likened by "Dulcinea" to a schoolboy's punishment (785; 800). The Duchess insists in Chapter 36 that a mere handslapping will not do, and she appears to be a conoisseur of whips when she teasingly tells Sancho to make himself a scourge of thorns or a cat-of-nine-tails in order to draw blood (790; 804). The same sadism is trained on the unfortunate Doña Rodríguez when she discloses to Don Quijote the secret illness of the Duchess, the dropsy that requires her to have a drain in each leg through which she discharges diseased bodily humors.[20] The duenna's skirts are lifted and she receives a slippering on her bottom, while Don Quijote is himself pinched by mysterious tormentors in the darkness (871; 886). The Duke will complete this motif of flagellation by ordering one hundred lashes to be given to his lackey, Tosilos, who has disobeyed him by not putting up any resistance in the judicial combat he was supposed to fight with Don Quijote (1003; 1022).

The Duke and the Duchess freely inflict pain on the bodies of their servants, and they seek to make Sancho Panza another of their dependents. The Duke makes clear (787; 902), although the Duchess will mendaciously deny it one chapter later (792; 806), that such mortification is the price Sancho has to pay for the governorship that has been promised him. Still, one may take the command that Sancho inflict three thousand, three hundred blood-raising lashes upon himself as a joke that no one really expects to be carried out. Perhaps, as some critics suggest, there is more play than harm in these aristocrats.

The story of how Doña Rodríguez's husband suffered at the hands of her duchess-mistress suggests otherwise, whether or not this "Doña Casilda" is the same Duchess as the one whom Don Quijote and Sancho meet in the novel. The text is notoriously unclear on this point, but from its satirical perspective, one duchess is much like another. According to the story the doleful duenna tells in Chapter 48, her husband, who was a "squire," like Sancho, in the household of the Duchess in Madrid, was riding a mule through the city one day, carrying his mistress behind him on the animal's crupper. At the entrance to a narrow street, he meets an "alcalde," a city justice of the peace, mounted on horseback, accompanied by two constables. He gives way, despite both the indignation of the lady and the judge's own yielding of precedence to them:

> However, my husband, cap in hand, insisted on waiting upon the judge. Seeing this, my lady, full of rage and spite, drew out a large pin—or, I believe, a bodkin—out of its sheath and ran it into his loin, whereupon my husband gave a loud cry and his body writhed so violently that he tumbled to the ground with his lady. . . . My mistress went away on foot and my husband ran into a barber's shop, crying that his bowels had been pierced through and through. My husband's courteousness became so proverbial in the city that boys would run after him in the streets, and because of this and because he was somewhat shortsighted, my lady dismissed him. The sorrow this caused him, without any doubt, hastened the calamity of his death. I was left a widow. (869)

> Todavía porfiaba mi marido, con la gorra en la mano, a querer ir acompañando al alcalde; viendo lo cual mi señora, llena de cólera y enojo, sacó un alfiler gordo, o creo que un punzón, del estuche, y clavósele por los lomos, de manera que mi marido dio una gran voz y torció el cuerpo, de suerte que dio con su señora en el suelo. . . . vínose a pie mi ama, y mi marido acudió en casa de un barbero diciendo que llevaba pasadas de parte a parte las entrañas. Divulgóse la cortesía de mi esposo, tanto, que los muchachos le corrían por las calles, y por esto y porque él era algún tanto corto de vista, mi señora la duquesa le despidió, de cuyo pesar, sin duda alguna, tengo para mí que se le causó el mal de la muerte. Quedé yo viuda. (883–84)

Aristocratic pride leads to aristocratic violence. Offended at seeing her pride of place yielded to a mere man of law—an upstart from the urban middle class—the Duchess attacks her servant. Only subsequently is it suggested that Doña Rodríguez's husband may, in his shortsightedness, have mistaken the judge, escorted by his attendants, for another nobleman of the lady's own rank. Here, too, the violence is directed to the lower anatomy and is even more sexually charged. With her daggerlike pin ["alfiler"], the Duchess strikes her man seated in front of her in the loins ["lomos"], and he complains that she has pierced his bowels ["entrañas"]: the scene suggests a sadistic anal penetration with a reversal of gender roles. We may think back, too, on the hunting scene and the Duchess with her spear ready to be the first to stab the boar. The result here is similarly fatal, whether the duenna's husband dies of his wound or from the even crueler blow of his dismissal from Doña Casilda's service.

Such scenes of cruelty, by which the novel's aristocrats physically exercise on social inferiors the power vested in their rank, and which further intimate the sadistic enjoyment they find in doing so, cast a disturbing light on the practical jokes that the Duke and the Duchess play on their guests, Don Quijote and Sancho Panza. Cervantes's readers are asked to what extent their own laughter at the characters' pratfalls and beatings makes them complicit with tyrannical power and cruelty, to what extent, too, this laughter derives from unacknowledged sado-sexual impulses. The question is recursive: did they, too, read Part One of *Don Quijote* predominantly as slapstick comedy, the slapstick that the noble couple now impose on Part Two?

After the relatively benign soaping of the beards of Don Quijote and Sancho in Chapter 32—the latter's beard is soaped with dirty dishwater—the *burlas* at the palace of the Duke and the Duchess become more violent and even get out of hand. The wooden horse Clavileño blows up, casting Don Quijote and Sancho on the ground, and scorching them in Chapter 41. Don Quijote is mauled and scratched by cats in Chapter 46 and is laid up in bed for five days. Sancho is so badly beaten and bruised in the fake battle that ends his government that he faints away in Chapter 53. In these latter two cases, the perpetrators indeed feel that their jokes have gone too far—"tan pesada" (854; 869, 909; 925). When knight and squire are kidnapped and brought back to the country house of the Duke and the Duchess, they are subjected to a mock auto-da-fé in Chapter 69, where, in order to resuscitate the "dead" Altisidora, it is ordered (1017; 1036) that Sancho be slapped in his face, pinched, and finally subjected to pinpricks ["alfilerazos"] in his arms and his loins ["lomos"]. *That is, Sancho is to receive the same treatment as Doña Rodríguez's husband,* who was pierced in the loins by the "alfiler" of Doña Casilda and subsequently died. This culminating torture proves too much, however, for Sancho; he refuses to bear it, and thus avoids that other squire's fate. The deliberately interlaced recollection belies, however, any notion that the *burlas* of the Duke and the Duchess are so much harmless fun.

The auto-da-fé setting of this final elaborate joke played by the Duke and the Duchess continues their idea that Sancho should whip himself in the role of a penitent, here one of the "penitenciados" (1016; 1035) of the

Inquisition. But it also brings into the open the role of the Duke and the Duchess as readers who take control over Cervantes's novel. In Part One, the Curate and the Barber, the spiritual and physical doctors of Don Quijote, carry out a kind of inquisition of the chivalric romances in Don Quijote's library, consigning the culprit books to be burnt, as the Curate puts it, by the "secular arm of the housekeeper" ["brazo seglar del ama" (91; 74)]. In Chapter 6 of Part Two, Don Quijote's niece, in an evocation of that episode, wishes that chivalric romances would be wrappped in a sanbenito, the robe in whch the Inquisition dressed penitents, as a warning to potential readers (566; 579). In the auto-da-fé performed for the Duke and the Duchess, where Sancho is made to wear a miter and a sanbenito painted with flames of fire, it is the book *Don Quijote* itself that is in question. Cervantes glances nervously at real state and church censors, readers with the power to determine the contents and the very survival of books. He has already shown the real Inquistion shutting down the talking head of Don Antonio Moreno in Chapter 62. In the Duke and the Duchess, seated next to the kingly figures who preside over the mock auto-da-fé, he places readers with analogous social power inside his novel itself.

Books are in no small part what their readers make and get out of them, and the Duke and the Duchess have sought to impose their reading on *Don Quijote*, reducing it finally to the crude physical comedy of slaps and pinpricks on the fat body of Sancho Panza. This reading, Cervantes satirically intimates, is in keeping with the cruel tastes of their aristocratic class, a class that takes pleasure in the physical violence it has the power to inflict on social subordinates. In their own particular way, the Duke and the Duchess have taken the place here in Part Two of the Canon of Toledo in Part One, who tried to lay down rules for literature to the caged Don Quijote and who also expressed the normative social views of an aristocratic, hierarchical society. Both the hero and the novel *Don Quijote* have to escape the clutches and narrow tastes of a noble audience. Cervantes dismisses the Duke and the Duchess as no less mad than Don Quijote himself. His final dismissal of inquisitorial impositions on the novel comes in Chapter 73, when Sancho uses the sanbenito and miter to dress up his dappled ass.

Courtiers versus Knights

The satire on the high aristocracy in Part Two is already set in place in its first seven chapters set in Don Quijote's village. These chapters are a kind of prologue that announce thematic clusters that run through the novel's second part: the question of the social mobility of both Don Quijote and Sancho (2, 5, 6), the existence of Part One and its readers in the world

(3), the relationship of valor to discretion (3, 4), Sancho's desire for wages (7).[21] In Chapter 1, Don Quijote additionally introduces the issue of what has become of Spain's nobility:

> Most of our knights nowadays prefer to rustle in the damasks, brocades, and other rich silks they wear than in armored coats of mail. . . . Today sloth triumphs over industry, idleness over labor, vice over virtue, arrogance over bravery, and theory over the practice of arms, which only lived and flourished in the Golden Age and among knights-errant. (535)

> Los más de los caballeros que agora se usan, antes les crujen los damascos, los brocados, y otras ricas telas de que se visten, que la malla con que se arman. . . . Mas agora ya triunfa la pereza de la diligencia, la ociosidad del trabajo, el vicio de la virtud, la arrogancia de la valentía, y la teórica de la práctica de las armas, que sólo vivieron y resplandecieron en la edades del oro y en los andantes caballeros. (547–48)

The passage speaks to the general transformation of the European aristocracy in the early-modern period from an independent, warrior nobility to a courtier class attendant on centralizing monarchs, a phenomenon described alternately by Lawrence Stone as a "crisis of the aristocracy," and by Norbert Elias as a "civilizing process."[22] Contemporaries were quick to criticize the new court formation and the elaborate codes of comportment it imposed on the nobleman; Don Quijote parrots the literature of dispraise of courtly life that goes back in the Spanish Renaissance to the *Menosprecio de Corte y Alabanza de Aldea* (1539) of Antonio de Guevara.[23] Castiglione's vastly influential *Book of the Courtier* (1528), translated into Spanish by Juan Boscán in 1534, already sounded the warning note that courtiership, devoted to "elegance of dress . . . and other such things as pertain to women and love," can effeminize the nobleman to the point that in Italy "there are but few who can be found who dare, I will not say to die, but even to place themselves in danger."[24]

Don Quijote suggests that the Spanish nobility has similarly traded in its armor for fancy clothes. Cervantes plays again on the multiple meanings of "caballero": the nobleman (of the high nobility rather than the hidalgo class) is no longer a knight, committed to the old martial tradition of the aristocracy, but has taken up the indolent and women-pleasing, hence effeminizing, life of the courtier. The theme returns in Chapter 6, when his housekeeper asks Don Quijote why he does not go to serve his king, like other "caballeros" at court, and he expounds the difference between "cortesanos," who expend neither their fortunes nor their bodies, and *true* knights-errant—"caballeros andantes verdaderos" (565; 578)—who expose themselves to the elements and to the enemy. The implication is that only the knight-errant is a true and proper knight/"caballero."

The polemic against the courtier in Part Two revises and adds a third term to the opposition of arms versus letters in Part One. There Cervantes's novel principally opposed the knight-errant to the monk and then found their modern versions in the professional soldier and the judge, incarnated in the two Viedma brothers, the man of arms versus the man of letters.[25] The dichotomy of arms and letters is played out again in Part Two when Sancho Panza leaves Don Quijote to become governor and judge of his "island." Sancho's plans to marry his daughter Sanchica up into elite society remind us of Clara, the daughter of the rich Judge Viedma, who is promised to Don Luis, the duke's son, in Part One. But in the meantime, Part Two tells a different story of what has happened to the knight in modern times: a whole aristocratic class appears to have settled into a courtly life of ease. (Professional soldiers reappear only briefly and very late in the second part of the novel in the galley scene and sea battle in Chapter 63.) In the hands of this courtier nobility, letters no longer have a practical function, preparing one for a career in the law courts or the church, but have become an object of consumption and a cultural ornament marking elite status. Cervantes may already hint at this development in Don Lorenzo, the son of the hidalgo Don Diego de Miranda: Don Diego wished him to study law or theology (635; 648), but Don Lorenzo has become an *aficionado* of poetry (650; 663).

In Part One, the modern knight to whom Don Quijote had been juxtaposed was the soldier Captain Viedma; the fiction of Part Two juxtaposes him to the "caballero" of the present, the Duke, who is a carpet-knight. If the comparison to Captain Viedma in Part One was greatly to Don Quijote's disadvantage, his mad heroics contrasted to the captain's true military career, his opposition to the Duke in Part Two will reflect badly, by contrast, on the idle aristocrat—and on his consort as well. The pairing of the Duke with his Duchess is, in fact, indispensable to the satire: it suggests that the way of life of the contemporary nobleman has been reduced from the battlefield to courtly amusements entertaining to women.[26]

Don Quijote's conversation with his housekeeper and niece in Chapter 6 develops into his disquisition on the nature of nobility. In this context, "caballero" now takes on its amplest meaning and designates "nobleman" or "gentleman," the aristocracy high and low. Not all noblemen are truly noble, Don Quijote maintains:

> Nor are all who call themselves gentlemen [*caballeros*] to be taken at their own valuation, for some are of gold, others are of base alloy, and all look like gentlemen, but not all are able to stand the touchstone of truth. There are low men who blow themselves up to bursting point to appear gentlemen, and others of exalted rank who seem to be dying to pass for men of the vulgar

herd. The former rise through ambition or virtue; the latter sink through indolence or vice. And it is necessary to have knowledge and discernment in order to distinguish between these two kinds of gentlemen, so alike in name and so different in actions. (566)

Ni todos los que se llaman caballeros lo son de todo en todo; que unos son de oro, otros de alquimia, y todos parecen caballeros; pero no todos pueden estar al toque de la piedra de la verdad. Hombres bajos hay que revientan por parecer caballeros, y caballeros altos hay que parece que aposta mueren por parecer hombres bajos; aquéllos se levantan o con la ambición o con la virtud, éstos se abajan o con la flojedad o con el vicio; y es menester aprovecharnos del conocimiento discreto para distinguir estas dos maneras de caballeros, tan parecidos en los nombres y tan distantes en las acciones. (579)

This subtly constructed passage begins by suggesting that all that glitters is not gold, and that the world is filled with false noblemen. A natural first reading would suppose that Don Quijote is complaining of baseborn impostors who pretend to noble birth, common characters in Spanish fiction of the period.[27] The figure of gold versus baser metals that distinguishes high from low birth goes back as far as Plato's *Republic*. This reading seems indeed confirmed in the first clause of the next sentence, where lowborn men puff themselves up in order to pass themselves off as noble.

But the second clause suddenly changes perspective: there are high aristocrats who are just dying to appear baseborn, and they, it seems, are the real false nobles in question. For while lowborn men may rise through "ambition or virtue," those of high birth can lower themselves by "sloth or vice," and, as the last sentence concludes, one judges both by their actions. The use of "parecer" five times in the passage, in fact, changes the nature of nobility from something innate to a matter of appearances and, more importantly, of outward behavior: noble is as noble does. By the end of his speech, Don Quijote has shifted the basis of nobility from birth to virtue and virtuous deeds: this, too, is a venerable commonplace, and it contains an implicit attack on aristocratic privilege and a defense of social mobility.[28] Thus Don Quijote repeats it when he advises Sancho on the eve of the latter's assuming his governorship in Chapter 42: "virtue in itself is worth more than noble birth" ["la virtud vale por sí sola lo que la sangre no vale" (825; 841)]. Don Quijote goes on to assert in Chapter 6 that there is great confusion in the lineages of the world—that is, all men are of mixed, "alchemical" birth. Those families that *appear* great and illustrious are those that *show* the virtue, wealth, and liberality of their members—"solos aquéllos parecen grandes y ilustres que lo muestran en la virtud, y en la riqueza y liberalidad de sus dueños" (568; 581).

The "or"s should be understood as "and"s in the couplings of ambition/virtue and sloth/vice, for this discussion of nobility repeats the contrast between active, errant knights versus idle, sedentary courtiers that begins Chapter 6. Antonio de Guevara, in his *Menosprecio de Corte*, similarly links sloth and vice together:

> There is nothing in this life so inimical to virtue as is idleness, for the beginning of dissolute men is found in idle moments and superfluous thoughts. We should have great compassion on the courtier who occupies himself in his house only with eating, drinking, gambling, and loafing, because if in the court he went about surrounded by enemies, he will be crowded by vices in the country.

> No hay en esta vida cosa que sea tan enemigo de la virtud, como es la ociosidad, porque de los ociososos momentos y superfluos pensamientos tienen principio los hombres perdidos. Al cortesano que no se ocupa en su casa sino en comer, beber, jugar, y holgar muy gran compasión le hemos de tener, porque si en la corte andaba rodeado de enemigos andarse ha en aldea cargado de vicios.[29]

Guevara discusses the nobleman who retires from court to the countryside but does not engage in the work of supervising and laboring on his property—a figure who bears some resemblance to Cervantes's Duke in his country palace. Cervantes makes an equation or syllogism. Idleness—whether the novel calls it "ociosidad," "reposo," "pereza," "flojedad," "holgazanería"—is the principal satirical charge against court life. Idleness causes the decadence of noble families because it opposes the virtue that is the basis of true nobility. The transformation of the Spanish aristocracy into an idle courtier class thus imperils its very nobility, which has now become a name without substance. This early chapter of Part Two asks the reader already to be suspicious of all those who call themselves "caballeros" and to employ a "conocimiento discreto" as a touchstone to judge who is really noble. Twenty-five chapters later, the test applies to the idle Duke and his Duchess.

Cervantes keeps the issue alive in the intervening chapters. In Chapter 17, Don Quijote returns to the contrast between courtier-knight and knight-errant as he explains his chivalric calling to Don Diego de Miranda. The courtier, it is emphasized three times in the passage, devotes himself to the service of women:

> it is a fine sight to see a knight, all armed in burnished armor, pace the lists in merry jousts before the ladies, and it is a fine sight to see all those knights who in military exercises or the like, entertain, cheer, and if one may say so, honor the courts of their princes. . . . [I]t is a finer sight, I say, to see a knight-

errant succoring a widow in some lonely waste than a courtier knight dallying with a maiden in the cities. . . . [L]et the courtier serve the ladies, lend pomp and circumstance by his gay liveries, support poor knights at his beautiful table, arrange jousts, maintain tourneys, and show himself, generous, liberal and lavish, and a good Christian above everything, for in this way he will fulfill his precise obligations. (646)

bien parece un caballero, armado de resplandecientes armas, pasar la tela en alegres justas delante de las damas, y bien parecen todos aquellos caballeros que en ejercicios militares, o que lo parezcan, entretienen y alegran, y, si se puede decir, honran las cortes de sus príncipes. . . . Mejor parece, digo, un caballero andante socorriendo a una viuda en algún despoblado que un cortesano caballero requebrando a una doncella en las ciudades. . . . [S]irva a las damas el cortesano; autorice la corte de su rey con libreas; sustente los caballeros pobres con el espléndido plato de su mesa; concierte justas, mantenga torneos, y muéstrese grande, liberal y magnífico, y buen cristiano, sobre todo, y desta manera cumplirá con sus precisas obligaciones. (660)

The last injunctions about liberality and the fulfilling of Christian duties appear to link the pious hidalgo Don Diego to this model courtier. It is another example of the multiple ironies and interlaced unity of Cervantes's text. Don Quijote inappropriately lumps Don Diego's liberality and Christianity—qualities, that, as we have seen, Don Quijote will himself take up—to the idle and effeminate frivolousness of the courtier.[30] But the passage does point forward nonetheless to the courtly Duke and Duchess. At their palace Don Quijote will attempt to succor a widow— Doña Rodríguez—while he resists the erotic entanglements of the supposedly lovestricken maiden Altisidora. He will, indeed, be made there an object of court entertainment, to amuse the Duchess as well as her husband.

Don Quijote's anticourtier polemic is also endorsed and actualized in the brief vignette of the page whom Don Quijote and Sancho meet in Chapter 24. The page, in whom Cervantes glances back at his younger self, has rejected the court service he recently pursued. He reveals the emptiness of court splendor, the "libreas" that Don Quijote praised earlier to Don Diego, when he tells how his masters, once their business was done, took back from him the livery that they only dressed him in for show—"las libreas que por sola ostentación habían dado" (701; 717). (Don Quijote takes up the issue of liveries yet again and finds a middle ground in the advice that he offers to the governor-designate Sancho in Chapter 43 to spend an equal amount on the poor as he spends on decking out his servants in plain rather than fancy suits of clothing [828; 843]).

Now the page is going off to become a soldier, thus making a real-life career choice that conforms to Don Quijote's own pursuit of knight-errantry instead of courtiership, to his opposition of genuine military valor to the mere appearances of military exercise—"ejercicios militares, o que lo parezcan"—in the jousts and diversions carried out at court.

The hunting of the Duke and Duchess, an "ejercicio" that the Duke praises as the image of war ["una imagen de la guerra"] is involved in this same polemic. When the Duke urges Sancho to pursue the chase when he becomes governor, Sancho responds that a governor should stick to his business and that hunting and pastimes are more fitting for idlers—"Mía fe, señor, la caza y los pastatiempos más han de ser para los holgazanes que para los gobernadores" (777; 792). The exchange neatly distinguishes the attitudes of a leisure-class nobility from those not so much of the peasant who Sancho is as from the *letrado* class of judges and administrators to which he aspires to belong. The latter do the work of government while the old aristocracy stagnates on its estates. While the Duke maintains that hunting lessens idleness and sleep ("menoscábase el ocio y el sueño"), Sancho suggests that, to the contrary, it is idleness itself, the diversion of "holgazanes."

These are the same idlers whom Sancho is determined to remove from his island-state when he pursues his rounds as governor in Chapter 49:

> for I'm dead set on clearing this island of all kinds of rubbishy tramps, idlers, and sharpers, for I want you to know, friends, that lazy loungers in a state are like drones in a hive of bees; they eat up the honey the worker bees gather. (874)

> que es mi intención limpiar esta ínsula de todo género de inmundicia y de gente vagamunda, holgazanes y mal entretenida; porque quiero que sepáis, amigos, que la gente baldía y perezosa es en la república lo mesmo que los zánganos en las colmenas, que se comen la miel que las trabajadoras abejas hacen. (888)

The rounds, unlike Sancho's other judgments as governor, are unscripted by the agents of the Duke and the Duchess: he is facing the real world of his "island." Nonetheless, he finds his quarry soon enough in two squabbling gamesters, one of whom claims to belong to the nobility ("hombres principales") and who is accustomed to live by the tips he receives for standing by and regulating the gambling, since he was brought up by his parents as a man of honor to hold neither occupation nor benefice—"pues sabe que yo soy hombre honrado y que no tengo oficio ni beneficio, porque mis padres no me le enseñaron ni me le dejaron" (875; 889). Sancho banishes this parasite on his state and is determined to close the gambling house itself. But Sancho's notary informs him that the house in question cannot be touched because it belongs to a "gran personaje," one of the realm's "caballeros principales" (876; 890–91), who maintains it even though he continues to lose his money at cards. Thus it is not merely self-proclaimed gentlemen like the kibitzing bystander demanding his tip but the real nobility who consume their patrimony and live without occupation and function. Corruption and idleness begin at the top, and this "caballero" ruining himself in gaming reflects on the Duke himself, who, we have learned through Doña Rodríguez one chapter earlier, is in debt (870; 884).[31] Drones on the state come in various forms, but they all call themselves noblemen.

The novel stops just short, as Sancho does in his exchange on hunting, of accusing the Duke and the Duchess of being such "holgazanes," but the inference is nonetheless clear. The supposedly lovelorn Altisidora also indirectly implicates her noble masters when Don Quijote attributes her crush on him to idleness—"la ociosidad descuidada" (851; 867)—in the song that he sings in Chapter 46 in response to Altisidora's own earlier serenade. As he and Sancho prepare to leave the Duke and the Duchess for the second and final time in Chapter 70, Don Quijote returns to his advice: "this damsel's malady proceeds from idleness. The remedy for that is honest and continuous occupation" ["todo el mal desta doncella nace de ociosidad, cuyo remedio es la ocupación honesta y continua" (1026; 1045)]. The Duchess promises to keep Altisidora busy at needlework ["labor blanca"]; there may be an ironic reminder that the Duchess has by now sent away one of the few productive workers at her castle, the duenna Doña Rodríguez, whom she employed precisely for her skill as a worker in "labor blanca" (868; 882, 869; 884). Don Quijote's counsel is, of course, thoroughly conventional—idle hands make the devil's work—but its application extends farther than Don Quijote understands. Altisidora's "love," like all of the pranks that the Duke and the Duchess play on Cervantes's heroes, springs from the general idleness at their country palace. Cervantes addresses *Don Quijote* in Part One to the "Desocupado lector," something for the reader's spare time (41; 19); now two readers with seemingly no occupation at all take over his novel and threaten to turn it into a reflection of their empty courtly existence.

So Don Quijote himself understands his experience at the castle of the Duke and the Duchess. When he is designated to take up the quest presented to him by the doleful duenna Countess Trifaldi in Chapter 36, Don Quijote swells with pride and contrasts himself as a vitally needed knight-errant to the lazy courtier—"perezoso cortesano" (795; 809). But by the time he prepares to leave their castle at the beginning of Chapter 57, he realizes that the Duke and the Duchess have made him into just such an idle appendage of their household:

Don Quijote thought it high time to leave the idle life he led in the castle, for he felt that he was much to blame for allowing himself thus to be shut up and for living indolently amid the tempting dainties and delights provided for him, a knight-errant, by the duke and duchess. (931)

Ya le pareció a don Quijote que era bien salir de tanta ociosidad como la que en aquel castillo tenía; que se imaginaba ser grande la falta que su persona hacía en dejarse estar encerrado y perezoso entre los infinitos regalos y deleites que como a caballero andante aquellos señores le hacían. (948)

Now Don Quijote is leading the lazy—"perezoso"—life that he had earlier condemned. We catch a brief glimpse of Don Quijote as courtier in Chapter 46 when he bedecks himself with his new finery—scarlet mantle, green cap, silver lace—and strides affectedly ["con gran prosopopeya y contoneo" (850; 866)] to meet his noble patrons. His growing unease appears in his letter to Sancho in Chapter 51 where he announces that he intends to leave the idle existence he is leading, for he was not born for it—"yo pienso dejar esta vida ociosa en que estoy, pues no nací para ella (895; 912)—a life that he has decided at the beginning of Chapter 52 is directly contrary to the order of chivalry he professes (899; 915). Don Quijote thus lives out the contrast between courtier and knight-errant that he has spent so much time expounding earlier in the novel. The court-castle of the Duke and the Duchess becomes a place of confinement—Don Quijote feels "encerrado"—and at the opening of Chapter 58 he sings the praises of liberty after he and Sancho have left the "captivity" ["cautiverio" (935; 952)]—of their hospitality. Don Quijote has been caged again, as he was in Part One, however golden the cage of Part Two may appear to be.

The immobility of Don Quijote contrasts in these chapters with the dramatic social mobility of Sancho Panza, his sudden rise and equally sudden fall as governor. But the indictment of the aristocrats who supervise both narratives is much the same. This Spanish nobility will not continue the heroic, knightly traditions of its past now that it has become a courtier class, enjoying a life of indolent luxury and ease. Thus, if the hospitality of the Duke and the Duchess initially promises to realize Don Quijote's fantasies of being a knight-errant and to carry him back into that heroic past, it soon turns out to transform him into the knight-errant's opposite, the modern courtier. Nor will the nobility allow the emergence of new men, like the unexpectedly wise judge, Sancho; so the rage of Doña Casilda already attested when her squire yielded precedence to the lowborn judge in Madrid. The agents of the Duke bring Sancho's brief governorship down. Its aristocracy condemns Spanish society to a stagnation that mirrors its own—just as the Duke and the Duchess stymie both Cervantine heroes, knight and squire.

Justice

Cervantes's technique of interlace is nowhere more obvious and didactic than in the stories of the first and second "dueña Dolorida," whose relationship to one another is announced in the titles of Chapters 36, 37, 38 and Chapter 52. Cervantes spells out, so that his reader cannot miss them, the parallels between the story that the first doleful duenna, the Duke's bearded steward disguised as "Countess Trifaldi," tells in the skit that the Duke and the Duchess have arranged in Chapters 38 and 39 and the story of the second, real-life duenna, Doña Rodríguez, who recounts her woes in the darkness of Don Quijote's bedchamber in Chapter 48. "Countess Trifaldi" describes how the jokily named Princess Antonomasia, daughter of Queen Maguncia in far-off Candaya, was seduced into secret marriage by the courtly skills and poetry of a private gentleman, Don Clavijo, and became pregnant by him, and how the wedded couple have been enchanted and turned into metal statues of beasts by the disdainful giant Malambruno, Maguncia's cousin. Don Quijote and Sancho take a ride, blindfolded, toward Candaya on the enchanted hobby-horse Clavileño in Chapter 41. The ride itself has been enough, they are told, to appease the giant and restore Antonomasia and Don Clavijo to their human form and regal state.

Doña Rodríguez, heretofore merely a figure of ridicule, acquires a new pathos in Chapter 48. She narrates how her daughter has been seduced, under promise of marriage, then jilted by the son of a rich farmer who lives nearby in one of the Duke's villages. Doña Rodríguez's attempts to persuade the Duke to order the young man to marry her daughter have fallen on deaf ears because the Duke is in debt to the farmer. In Chapter 51 Doña Rodríguez appeals to Don Quijote to be her champion—just as "Countess Trifaldi" had done for Antonomasia. The parallel suggests that any daughter appears to be a princess in the eyes of her doting mother. It is not clear whether Doña Rodríguez is too dim-witted to be in on the shared practical joke on Don Quijote and actually believes that he is a knight, or whether, in her desperation, she is willing to grasp at any straw to obtain justice. Don Quijote seems to win a husband for the duenna's daughter in Chapter 56 at the mock judicial combat that the Duke arranges to settle the dispute. The Duke has substituted his lackey Tosilos for the farmer's son, who has fled to Flanders to avoid becoming the son-in-law of Doña Rodríguez. Tosilos falls in love with her daughter and refuses to fight; he offers instead to marry her. The girl, who, if the parallel to Princess Antonomasia holds, is in a family way and desperate to wed, is prepared to accept him. Both stories end without Don Quijote needing to complete the trials he has undertaken. Two apparent successes, nonetheless, for the valor of Don Quijote, the defender of widows and damsels in distress.

The matched stories also take us back to Part One, where Dorotea's story of her seduction and abandonment by Don Fernando was paired with the story, which she herself made up and playacted, of Princess Micomicona threatened by another giant, Pandafilando. The elements of Dorotea's own story are variously redistributed: she was a rich farmer's daughter, while it is a rich farmer's son who seduces the daughter of Doña Rodríguez; Don Fernando bribes the servants of Dorotea as Don Clavijo corrupts Countess Trifaldi herself; Dorotea kept the accounts—"tenía yo la cuenta" (280; 279)—of her father's estates, while Doña Rodríguez sings the praise of her daughter who keeps accounts like a miser—"cuenta como un avariento" (869; 884).

Dorotea's story was also a tale of social climbing, and as Princess Micomicona, she appeared to offer to Don Quijote the occasion to realize his own fantasy of chivalry as a career and of rising through marriage from private knight to emperor. Sancho evokes that fantasy again in Chapter 39 to comment on the story that "Countess Trifaldi" tells about Don Clavijo and Antonomasia. "Just as they make bishops of lettered men," he says, "they can make kings and emperors of knights, especially knights-errant" ["así como se hacen de los hombres letrados los obispos, se pueden hacer de los caballeros, y más si son andantes, los reyes y los emperadores" (805; 819)]. This pairing of letters and arms reminds us of Sancho's worries in Part One that Don Quijote might choose to be archbishop rather than emperor. But the first doleful duenna's story, in keeping with the polemic against modern courtiers and courtliness in Part Two, suggests that nowadays it is neither the knight-errant nor the learned man of letters who has the best chance of raising his social status. Don Clavijo is an Italianate courtier—"un caballero particular que en la corte estaba"—who is equipped with the lady-pleasing graces ["gracias" (802; 816)] of music and poetry outlined in Castiglione's *Book of the Courtier* and who cites the love poetry of Serafino d'Aquila, the fifteenth-century court poet recalled in Castiglione's pages.[32] This lovemaking idler—"vagamundo" (802; 816)—wins the princess, as Cervantes's fiction again wryly acknowledges that the present-day "caballero" has turned courtier, and that the best career path may now be found not on the battlefield, nor in the church or law courts, but among the crowd of prince- and lady-pleasers at court.

As Joaquín Casalduero noted long ago, art imitated life in Part One as Dorotea invented the menacing giant Pandafilando as a thinly disguised version of her false lover Don Fernando; in Part Two, real life imitates art as Doña Rodríguez seeks redress as "Countess Trifaldi" sought relief from the giant Malambruno.[33] The figure who corresponds to this second giant who blocks the marrriage of Don Clavijo and Antonomasia is none other than the Duke, who refuses to compel his vassal's son to carry out his promise to marry the duenna's daughter. In both parts of the novel, the villain of the piece is the highest-ranking social member; Don Fernando is the second son of a duke, in Part Two we meet a full-fledged Duke and Duchess.

Cervantes's antiaristocratic bias cannot be clearer, and despite its comedy *Don Quijote* in this section becomes an angry book.[34] In both parts of the novel, a nobleman partakes in the emblematic act of aristocratic tyranny, the seduction of a woman of a lower class who should be under his protection, as well as in the cardinal crime against comedy, the obstruction of marriage. Don Fernando plays the role of aristocratic seducer himself, while the Duke countenances the seduction carried out by another. Dorotea made clear what was at stake when, like a heroine in a Golden Age *comedia* defending the democracy of honor, she proclaimed to Don Fernando: "I am your vassal, not your slave, and your noble blood has not, nor ought to have the right to dishonor and insult my humility, and I consider myself, a country girl and a farmer's daughter, as good as you, a gentleman and lord" ["Tu vasalla soy, pero no tu esclava; ni tiene ni debe tener imperio la nobleza de tu sangre para deshonrar y tener en poco la humildad de la mía; y en tanto me estimo yo, villana y labradora, como tú, señor y caballero" (282; 282)].[35] The duenna's daughter invokes a similar scenario when she proclaims her preference to be the legitimate spouse of the lackey Tosilos rather than the seduced mistress of a "caballero," even though, she adds, the rich farmer's son is not a nobleman— "más quiero ser mujer legítima de un lacayo que no amiga y burlada de un caballero, puesto que el que a mí me burló no lo es" (930; 947): a secondary implication is that no such seducer can be noble, whether nobly born or not. Dorotea finally converted Don Fernando and persuaded him to acknowledge his marriage to her by an appeal precisely to his nobility, for true nobility, she reminded him, consists in virtue—"la verdadera nobleza consiste en la virtud" (375; 376); if he were to deny what he justly owed her, she argued, she would be nobler than he. In the comic resolution of her story, Don Fernando lived up to his noble rank, went from being very bad to very good, and assumed for the rest of Part One the benevolent leadership of the little community at the inn.

If Don Fernando was capable of reform, the same cannot be said for the Duke and his Duchess. The interlacing of the stories of the two duennas produces a remarkable moment in Chapter 36 when the Duke pledges his own assistance to the make-believe "Countess Trifaldi":

> And likewise you may say to her on my behalf that if my help is necessary, it shall not be lacking, for I am bound by my knighthood to help her. By it I am compelled to favor every sort of women, in particular widowed duennas in sorrow and distress, such as her ladyship must be. (794)

y asimismo le podréis decir de mi parte que si mi favor le fuere necesario, no le ha de faltar, pues ya me tiene obligado a dársele el ser caballero, a quien es anejo y concerniente favorecer a toda suerte de mujeres, en especial a la dueñas viudas, menoscabadas y doloridas, cual lo debe estar su señoría. (808)

The Duke claims to be a knight like Don Quijote, and echoes the latter's earlier boast to Don Diego de Miranda that he has succored widows and protected damsels—"socorriendo viudas, amparando doncellas" (632; 646). The passage plays once again on the ambiguity of "caballero," knight and/or nobleman. The Duke may be simply declaring himself to be a nobleman. He may additionally be a member of one of the now largely honorific knightly Orders of Santiago or Calatrava.

The irony of the Duke's pledge to defend women and widows is not readily apparent. It only sinks in twelve chapters later when the second, real widowed duenna Doña Rodríguez (possibly widowed, we remember, by the Duke's own Duchess, or by a duchess like her!) reveals to Don Quijote in Chapter 48 that the Duke refuses to come to *her* aid. In Chapter 52, she repeats that it is useless to expect the Duke, her lord, to do her justice—"porque pensar que el duque mi señor me ha de hacer justicia es pedir peras al olmo" (900; 916)—and the Duke and Duchess, in fact, treat her and her daughter as strangers ["forasteras" (901; 918)] while they await the judicial combat that will decide their cause. The Duke, in fact, doubly acts against them. He both substitutes Tosilos for the real culprit, his wealthy vassal's son, and fixes the duel so that Don Quijote will lose.

But the full extent of the Duke's injustice and tyranny only emerges still later in the novel, another ten chapters after the appointed duel itself fails to take place and the duenna's daughter seems to have found an alternative husband in Tosilos, a result that leaves the Duke extremely angry—"colérico en estremo" (928; 946). Don Quijote and Sancho meet the lackey in Chapter 66, and Tosilos recounts how once Don Quijote and Sancho had left the ducal castle, the Duke ordered that he be given one hundred lashes for disobeying his order to fight; the daughter of Doña Rodríguez has ended up in a convent, and the duenna herself has returned to Castile. In their pique at having their will opposed, the Duke has blocked the marriage of the daughter and the Duchess has discharged her widowed duenna.[36] The apparent comic resolution of the story is destroyed, and the doleful duenna's daughter has been exiled from life like the tragic heroine Claudia Jerónima, who retires to a convent in the episode of Roque Guinart.[37] The delays in the narrative are part of the strategy of indirection by which Cervantes satirizes the aristocracy in the persons of the Duke and the Duchess. The noble couple progressively emerge in their true colors. Cruel, idle, and now unjust, they may finally not be "noble" at all. They lack the chivalry they profess, and we may feel that it is they and their class, rather than the novel's hero, who are the real impostor knights of its story.

In pointed contrast, Don Quijote finally emerges as a genuine knightly champion of justice for widows and damsels when he takes up the cause of Doña Rodríguez and her daughter and succeeds against the expectations and plans of the Duke and the Duchess. The interlaced parallel, of course, is the success of Sancho Panza in his insular government, where, partly as a result of Don Quijote's tutelage in Chapters 42 and 43, partly through his own wits and good nature, Sancho proves to be a wise and merciful judge. Both knight and squire stand for justice—against their noble patrons who overturn the verdict of the judicial combat just as their agents violently overturn Sancho's good government.

In fact, Don Quijote's greatest moment of moral courage emerges in the letter he writes to Sancho in Chapter 51, placed in the narrative *before* he agrees to be the champion of the doleful duenna:

> A certain matter has arisen that I believe will involve me in disgrace with the duke and the duchess. But though it concerns me, it does not affect my decision at all, for after all, when it comes to the point, I must comply with my profession rather than with their pleasure, for as the saying goes, *Amicus Plato, sed magis amica veritas*. I say it in Latin, for I suppose that since you have become a governor you have learned it. (896)

> Un negocio se ma ha ofrecido, que creo que me ha de poner en desgracia destos señores; pero aunque se me da mucho, no se me da nada, pues, en fin en fin, tengo de cumplir antes con mi profesión que con su gusto, conforme a lo que suele decirse: *amicus Plato, sed magis amica veritas*. Dígote este latín porque me doy a entender que después que eres gobernador lo habrás aprendido. (912)

The final Cervantine joke about Latin aside, Don Quijote shows that he fully understands the seriousness of what he is about to do in going against the will of his noble hosts. Sancho understands it too, and tries to dissuade his master in his return letter, fearing that it will redound negatively upon him—"redundar en mi daño" (897; 914). In the Renaissance, and the situation has not much changed since, it required real bravery to oppose one's social superiors, the powerful and the rich. Don Quijote actually does nothing, except to show up, at the actual judicial combat: the lovestruck Tosilos does the rest. But this clearheaded decision to stand up for justice is the ethical high point of Don Quijote's career. At this moment, he becomes a true hero.

In the end, however, Don Quijote cannot make justice prevail. As soon as Don Quijote leaves the castle—"así como vuestra merced se partió de nuestro castillo" (1003; 1022)—the Duke orders Tosilos to be flogged.

The action, the wording, and the technique of narrative delay recall the very first adventure of Don Quijote, his meeting with the peasant boy Andrés, whom he finds tied to a tree and being flogged by his rich farmer master, Juan Haldudo, in Chapter 4 of Part One.[38] Andrés had asked for his back wages and instead been whipped for losing sheep—we may assume that the shepherd has not simply lost, but stolen the missing sheep to get back at his master and to compensate for his unpaid salary. What Don Quijote meets in his first knightly encounter with the world is the social order of class oppression and warfare. With the point of his lance he forces Juan Haldudo to agree to pay back wages to his servant and rides off. Much later in Chapter 31, however, Andrés tells how as soon as Don Quijote left the wood—"así como vuestra merced traspuso del bosque" (317; 318)—Juan Haldudo tied him back to the tree and whipped him worse than before, denying him the wages Andrés says he might have finally obtained had Don Quijote not intervened. Andrés, like Doña Rodríguez and her daughter, has lost his position, and now sets out to find his fortune in Seville. At opposite ends of the novel, Don Quijote attempts to bring about justice for the weak and the oppressed. For a moment he appears to triumph, only subsequently to learn that he has not succeeded at all.

We might want to read in both of these stories Cervantes's understanding of the powerlessness of his fiction, the novel *Don Quijote* as well as the character, to change an unjust society. Once Don Quijote leaves the scene—that is, once we step outside his book—masters return to whipping their servants.

Much of Don Quijote's pretensions to bring about justice, especially in Part One, are bound up with his crazy egotism. His claim in Chapter 20 of Part One to revive the Age of Gold in an Age of Iron—"nací, por querer del cielo, en esta nuestra edad de hierro, para resucitar en ella la de oro, o la dorada" (186; 179)—is so madly grandiose that Sancho can cite it back to his master in mockery (198; 188) when the daunting noise that sounds in the darkness like the rasping of irons and chains—"crujir de hierros y cadenas" (186; 178) turns out to be a fulling mill in the morning light.

Nonetheless, there is an undeniable redemptive element in Don Quijote's mad fantasy of himself as a messianic redeemer, the basis for the romantic interpretation of the novel as the struggle between an idealist and a stubborn reality. At least, the character and the novel can point to society's need for justice.[39] Don Quijote's chivalry causes him to champion the weak, the peasant being beaten instead of being paid, or, much more equivocally, the convicts in Chapter 22 being sent off to the galleys in their real iron chains—"una gran cadena de hierro" (209; 202)—the emblem of a real Iron Age.[40] When Don Quijote is upbraided by the Curate in Chapter 30 for his releasing of the convicts, he tartly replies that it is not the business of a knight-errant to inquire why the afflicted, enchained, and oppressed he meets have come to suffer their condition, only to relieve it: "solo le toca ayudarles como a menesterosos" (300; 301). The brief reappearance of Andrés in the following chapter typically interlaces and juxtaposes the two scenes of rescue and allows us to consider whether the servant boy has not escaped a situation that is tantamount to the convicts' servitude: perhaps exposure to Don Quijote can after all bring about a kind of social liberation, painful as it may be.

The last "rescue" in this series, however, is Don Quijote's attempt to free the image of the Virgin Mary, the true source of redemption, from the penitents at the end of Part One. That final episode reminds us forcefully that Don Quijote's plan to right the wrongs of the world is a mad delusion, and doomed to be frustrated. And yet . . . The irony remains double-edged. There may be no more moving nor pointed moment in the novel than when Don Quijote, imprisoned in his own cage in Chapter 49, half-confused and half-persuaded that he is under the spell of enchantment, declares to the skeptical Sancho:

> I know, and I am convinced that I am enchanted, and that is enough for the peace of my conscience. If I were not enchanted, I would be greatly perturbed to think I had let myself be cooped up in this cage like a lazy coward when there are, at this very moment, so many distressed in the world who are in extreme need of my protection. (488)

> Yo sé y tengo para mí que voy encantado, y esto me basta para la seguridad de mi conciencia; que la formaría muy grande si yo pensase que no estaba encantado y me dejase estar en esta jaula perezoso y cobarde, defraudando el socorro que podría dar a muchos menesterosos y necesitados que de mi ayuda y amparo deben tener a la hora de ahora precisa y estrema necesidad. (492)

Few passages so implicate the reader of Cervantes's fiction. The mad Don Quijote may be imprisoned and enchanted, but what is to stop the sane reader, who is free to do so, from bringing aid to the many who are afflicted and in need? The potential social impact of *Don Quijote*—of literature itself—lies in this question.

Paying Up

The repetition of the story of Andrés in the hundred lashes inflicted on Tosilos suggests that the Duke and the Duchess have institutionalized in their noble household the injustice that Don Quijote encounters in his first adventure. The Duke's aristocratic tyranny over his servants is the more striking for its gratuitousness. The affair of Doña Rodríguez's daughter could have ended with the happy compromise of her marriage to Tosilos, but the Duke will tolerate no affront to his authority and pride. The parallel with Andrés also connects the perversely comical interest of the Duke and the Duchess in flogging Sancho Panza to a larger oppression of the weak by the strong. Their introduction of this method of disenchanting Dulcinea opens a rift in the human relationship that exists between Don Quijote and Sancho, a divide that they physically enact when they send Sancho off to govern his "island" while Don Quijote remains behind at the ducal castle in Chapters 44–54.[41] The Duke and the Duchess design the "resurrection" of Altisidora, who is supposed to have died for love of Don Quijote, to convince Don Quijote further of the magic potential of punishing Sancho's body. By making Don Quijote himself desire the flogging of Sancho, the Duke and the Duchess tempt him to treat his squire as the Duke and the Duchess treat their own servants, Doña Rodríguez and Tosilos, as semifeudal household retainers whom they can beat and whip at will. In Chapter 60, Don Quijote tries, in fact, to remove the sleeping Sancho's trousers in order to inflict the disenchanting lashes, asserting feudal privilege as his squire's "natural lord and master" ["tu amo y señor natural" (956; 973)]. Sancho wakes up, however, and overpowers his master, an episode that immediately precedes the meeting with the bandit Roque Guinart: the juxtaposition suggests an analogy between domestic revolt and Roque's outlaw violence against the forces of the state.

In the ultimate resolution of the issue of Dulcinea's disenchantment, the novel points a way out of the old feudal patterns of violent domination and class conflict. As they leave the castle of the Duke and the Duchess for a second time in Chapter 71, Don Quijote proposes to pay Sancho Panza for each lash he inflicts upon himself and lets Sancho set his price. The transaction smacks of religious parody, of a donor paying monastics for prayers to be said in order to free the dead from purgatorial time—and the version of Dulcinea's "enchantment" that Don Quijote claims to have seen in the cave of Montesinos looks like a kind of Purgatory.[42] In keeping with this idea, Don Quijote plans to count out on his rosary the lashes that Sancho will receive (1030; 1049). Sancho, in fact, tricks his master by flogging the trees of the woods rather than himself. His faked cries of anguish nonetheless cause the compassionate Don Quijote to rush to his squire and take the whip from his hand. He urges Sancho not to kill himself with his exertions, and postpones the completion of the disenchantment so that, Don Quijote says, their "business can be concluded to the satisfaction of all parties" ["para que se concluya este negocio a gusto de todos" (1031; 1050)].

At the beginning of his adventures, Don Quijote sees the master Juan Haldudo giving his servant Andrés a whipping when the latter demands his back wages. At the end of these adventures—Sancho Panza completes his penance in Chapter 72 just before the two reach their village—Don Quijote the master pays money for his servant to whip himself. The opposition suggests that if *Don Quijote* cannot change the social order, the novel nonetheless bears witness to social and historical change—perhaps the larger story it has been repeatedly telling.

At first glance, not much seems to have changed. Money seems to have replaced force, but to effect the same result: the pain felt on the bodies of social underlings. Andrés had testified, too, that, once his master had had the satisfaction of whipping him, he would have paid him his wages: another version of the exchange of money for lashes seen at the novel's end.[43]

Still, the difference is real and ethically charged. Power no longer rests solely with the master. It is now a matter of negotiation between master and servant. As Carroll Johnson has pointed out in a fine analysis of this episode, Don Quijote's payment to Sancho comes at the end of Sancho's drawn-out attempts to gain wages for his squirely service. Johnson further remarks that Don Quijote's recognition of Sancho as an economic agent preserves the human solidarity of the two characters.[44]

This solidarity might have been supposed to inhere in the "natural," paternalistic master-servant relation of feudalism, upon which Marx and Engels would look back with a historical memory brightened by the contrast with the savage greed of capitalism.[45] Don Quijote repeatedly calls Sancho his son, and the loyalty and affection that the two men demonstrate for each other is genuine. But Cervantes's depiction of the household of the Duke and the Duchess shows that he has few illusions on this score. Such an idyllic relation is no longer the norm; probably it never was, and was most likely as much a fantasy as the chivalric romances' idealized depictions of faithful squires and generous knights who reward them with islands. Instead, this final episode suggests that fellowship between master and servant may be fostered by a willingly entered into contractual relationship that ensures "satisfaction" to both parties. As it heals the divide that the Duke and the Duchess have sought to create between Don Quijote and Sancho, this business agreement completes the novel's satire on aristocratic culture and once again announces the new social formation that is coming to rival and supersede it. By such negotiations, men and women can make use of one another and, at the same time, retain and build affective ties. Don Quijote takes the whip from Sancho because he is afraid his squire may kill himself and thus never complete the disenchantment of Dulcinea—and also because he has come to love Sancho.[46]

In the final episode of his chivalric career, Don Quijote acknowledges and enters fully into modern times. He has already paid his way at the inns of Part Two, and now he accomplishes his last mission, the one dearest to his heart, by spending money. The cash that he could not come up with to loan the "enchanted" Dulcinea in his vision in the Cave of Montesinos now buys her disenchantment. The irony and paradox of this payment are clear: Dulcinea is redeemed from a debased world ruled by money, and restored to her idealized chivalric form, precisely by Don Quijote's agreeing to partake in that world's monetary transactions. His very act of paying up seems to put an end to another kind of enchantment: the transforming power of his own fantasy. For Don Quijote now returns to his village, to recover his sanity and to die as Alonso Quijano.

Don Quijote finally catches up with modern times and with the realistic world of the novel that has surrounded him all along. Or do they finally catch up with him and defeat his attempt to escape into a fantastic past of chivalry? The book ends with an experience of gain or loss: how one looks at it is not so much an issue of the hero's sanity or madness as a judgment on history, a judgment on the right and wrong of feudal bonds and on the transition to commercial society. A dominant, if decaying, aristocratic culture, still vested with martial and aesthetic glamour, is yielding ground to a mundane culture in which everything, including human values, is up for sale.[47] Virtually the last thing we learn about the novel's hero is that the grief that Don Quijote's heirs feel at his imminent death is effaced or tempered by the thought of their inheritances; the loyal Sancho Panza actually rejoices—"se regocijaba" (1049; 1066). This is the new way of the world. And in its glare, the death of Don Quijote looks like the demise, in a crazy and vestigial form, of heroism and of the imagination. It raises the question whether heroism and imagination can survive in any form at all in a world regulated by money—or in the genre of the novel that Cervantes is inventing to describe it.

Part Two of Don Quijote has given us reasons for hope. Cervantes continued, as he did in Part One, to satirize without mercy the tales of chivalry the Spanish nobility liked to tell about themselves. He has had no other aim than to demolish them, so he affirms in the last sentence of his book. And they have been replaced, he says, by Don Quijote itself, a new form of literature directed to a different audience. Part One of the novel separated riches from heroism: Don Quijote resisted the fantasy temptation of Princess Micomicona, and the real jewels of Zoraida were thrown overboard in the Captive's Tale. Part Two marks a new acceptance of money, no longer disguised as fabulous wealth beyond the telling. It features a new kind of hero, a much less violent and much kindlier Don Quijote, a cash-carrying hero, too, who mirrors the prosperous Don Diego de Miranda and Camacho the Rich. Cervantes is now sympathetic to the good life—humane, peaceable, and Christian—that moderate wealth can obtain. Money may not free Dulcinea from the ugliness of everyday life, but it can promote the friendship of Don Quijote and Sancho Panza. The future of the novel will chronicle the stories of middling people like Don Diego, like Camacho, and now like Don Quijote himself, and of their quiet, imperfect heroism, rather than tales of great captains and kings. Among such people the novel will find its readers. Cervantes does not unquestioningly embrace the emerging money relations of his time. But he has shown beyond challenge that the attempt to return to the past is madness. The modern world of money is here to stay. It is up to modern men and women, novelists included, to make the best of it.

NOTES

PREFACE

1. Martín de Riquer, *Aproximación al Quijote* (Barcelona: Teide, 1967), p. 124.

2. Vladimir Nabokov, *Lectures on Don Quixote*, ed. Fredson Bowers (San Diego, New York, and London: Harcourt Brace Jovanovich, 1983), pp. 28–29.

3. A developed argument can be found in Carroll B. Johnson's *Cervantes and the Material World* (Urbana and Chicago: University of Illinois Press, 2000), which reached me while I was writing this book. Johnson's conclusions about the transitional historical moment described in Cervantes's works are similar to my own, and he aptly reminds his reader of the "stillborn" nature of capitalism in early-modern Spain. Our critical approaches to *Don Quijote* are very different.

CHAPTER ONE
CERVANTES'S METHOD AND MEANING

1. All citations from *Don Quijote* are taken first from the English translation of Walter Starkie, *Don Quixote of La Mancha* (1957; reprint, New York: New American Library, 1979), then from the Spanish text of Martín de Riquer *Don Quijote de la Mancha*, 2 vols. (Barcelona: Editorial Juventud, 1971). I have occasionally altered Starkie's translation. The citations from the Spanish text appear in brackets. Page numbers in parentheses refer first to the English, then to the Spanish text. All other translations, unless specified, are my own.

2. Edwin Williamson notes some of these parallels in "Romance and Realism in the Interpolated Stories of the *Quixote*," *Cervantes* 2 (1982): 43–67. See also John Weiger, "The Curious Pertinence of Eugenio's Tale in *Don Quijote*," *Modern Language Notes* 96 (1981): 260–85. In a further interlaced parallel, which will be discussed in Chapter Three, Leandra's suitor, Vicente de la Rosa, is aligned with Diego García de Paredes (504; 507), the braggart-soldier whose "modest" account of his own life and superhuman exploits is drawn out of the trunk at the inn in Chapter 32, along with the history of his commander, Gonzalo Hernández de Córdoba, the Great Captain, whose title and true history align *him* with Captain Viedma.

3. The role that the tales have in the architecture of Part One is discussed by Raymond Immerwahr, "Structural Symmetry in the Episodic Narrative of *Don Quijote*," *Comparative Literature* 10 (1958): 121–35.

4. Criticism has often agreed that the interpolated tales must fit into the larger narrative of Part One of the *Quijote*, but most analyses nonetheless treat the tales as self-contained. For a thoughtful discussion, see Williamson, "Romance and Realism." Vicente Gaos usefully questions the sincerity of the apparent "retraction" on the part of the Cervantine narrator in Chapter 44 of Part Two, who seems to regret having included the tales in Part One and who forswears such interpolations in the second installment of the novel; see the chapter "El *Quijote*

y las novelas interpoladas," in Gaos, *Cervantes: Novelista, dramaturgo, poeta* (Barcelona: Planeta, 1979), pp. 47–57. Ana L. Baquero Escudero compares the stories of Marcela, of the Captive and Zoraida, and of Leandra in "Tres historias intercaladas y tres puntos de vista distintos en el primer *Quijote*," *Actas del Segundo Coloquio Internacional de la Asociación de Cervantistas: Alcalá de Henares, del 6 al 9 de noviembre de 1989* (Barcelona: Anthropos, 1991), pp. 417–23.

5. This critical disposition informs the most recent monument of Cervantes scholarship, the now indispensable commentary assembled by Francisco Rico to the edition prepared for the Centro para la Edición de los Clásicos Españoles, *Don Quijote de la Mancha* (Barcelona: Instituto Cervantes, Crítica, 1998). The commentary is organized into separate treatments of individual chapters of *Don Quijote*.

6. For another account of how *Don Quijote* emerges as a different kind of novel from the picaresque novel even as it adapts many features of picaresque fiction, see Walter Reed, *An Exemplary History of the Novel: The Quixotic versus the Picaresque* (Chicago and London: University of Chicago Press, 1981), esp. pp. 71–92; for Reed, it is the revelation of the "insufficiencies of literature" that distinguishes Cervantes's contribution to the novel.

7. Edward C. Riley, "Romance, Picaresque, and *Don Quixote I*," in *Studies in Honor of Bruce W. Wardropper*, ed. Diane Fox, Harry Sieber, and Robert Ter Horst (Newark, Delaware: Juan de la Cuesta, 1989), pp. 237–48.

8. Claudio Guillén, *Literature as System: Essays toward the Theory of Literary History* (Princeton: Princeton University Press, 1971), p. 84.

9. See Edwin Williamson, *The Half-Way House of Fiction* (Oxford: Clarendon Press, 1984), p. 163: "This interweaving of plot and episode suggests that in search of variety Cervantes was experimenting with a species of *entrelacement* so typical of medieval and Renaissance romances." This study will attempt to flesh out Williamson's critical observation.

10. For remarks on the technique of interlace in medieval romance with particular application to the *Amadís de Gaula* and *Don Quijote*, see Williamson, *The Half-Way House of Fiction*, pp. 34–50, 163–65. See also Ferdinand Lot, *Étude sur le "Lancelot en Prose"* (Paris: Champion, 1918); Eugene Vinaver, *The Rise of Romance* (Oxford: Clarendon Press, 1971).

11. See for example the quests of Yvain and Bors in the prose *Lancelot* in *Lancelot-Grail: The Old French Arthurian Vulgate and Post-Vulgate in Translation*, ed. Norris J. Lacey (New York and London: Garland, 1995), 3:171–82; for another, more ironic juxtaposition, compare the quests of Hector, who kills a tyrant who dishonors women, and of Yvain, who kills a knight who has stolen a sparrowhawk from a damsel, at 3:103–8.

12. It is worth pointing out a further interlaced parallel in this episode. Dorotea is supposed to play the damsel-in-distress Princess Micomicona in order to cure Don Quijote, or at least to help the Curate and Barber bring him home (291; 292). The appearance on the scene of the distressed real-life Dorotea *does*, in fact, cure the other madman of the episode, Cardenio, who champions her cause.

13. On Dorotea and her story, see Francisco Márquez Villanueva, *Personajes y temas del "Quijote"* (Madrid: Taurus, 1975); Joaquín Casalduero, *Sentido y forma del "Quijote"* (Madrid: Ediciones Insula, 1949), pp. 142–43; Ruth El Saf-

far, *Distance and Control in "Don Quixote": A Study in Narrative Technique* (Chapel Hill: University of North Carolina Press, 1975), pp. 66–68.

14. For a related discussion of the debt that Cervantes owes to Ariosto's formal techniques, see Thomas Hart, *Cervantes and Ariosto: Renewing Fiction* (Princeton: Princeton University Press, 1989), pp. 16–38. I have published an earlier version of the present argument in "Narrative Interlace and Narrative Genres in *Don Quijote* and the *Orlando Furioso*," *Modern Language Quarterly* 58, no. 3 (1997); 241–68. See also Margot Kruse, "Ariost und Cervantes," *Romanistisches Jahrbuch* 12 (1961): 248–64; Maxime Chevalier, *L'Arioste en Espagne* (Bordeaux: Féret and Fils, 1966), pp. 461–63.

15. Marco Praloran discusses the innovations of this technique, particularly the suspension of the outcomes of individual episodes, in the narrative practice of Ariosto's predecessor, Matteo Maria Boiardo, in "Il modello formale dell'entrelacement nell'*Orlando innamorato*," in *Tipografie e romanzi in Val Padana tra Quattro e Cinquecento*, ed. Riccardo Bruscagli and Amedeo Quondam (Modena: Panini, 1992), pp. 117–27; in his further extension of his narratological analysis to the *Furioso*, Praloran's focus is less on interlace itself than on the temporal loops in the poem: see "Temporalità e tecniche narrative nel *Furioso*," *Studi italiani* 6, no. 1 (1994): 5–54. Valuable analyses of Ariosto's interlace at work are offered by Elissa Weaver, "Lettura dell'intreccio dell'*Orlando furioso*: Il caso delle tre pazzie d'amore," *Strumenti critici* 11 (1977): 384–406; Robert Durling, *The Figure of the Poet in Renaissance Epic* (Cambridge: Harvard University Press, 1965), pp. 140–76; and Albert Russell Ascoli, *Ariosto's Bitter Harmony: Crisis and Evasion in the Italian Renaissance* (Princeton: Princeton University Press, 1987). On the suspensions of the narrative of the *Furioso*, see Daniel Javitch, "*Cantus Interruptus* in the *Orlando Furioso*," *Modern Language Notes* 95 (1980): 66–80.

16. Chevalier, *L'Arioste en Espagne*, p. 463. L. A. Murillo labels these chapters as "interlace" in *A Critical Introduction to "Don Quixote"* (New York: Peter Lang, 1988), pp. 215–20; see Williamson, *The Half-Way House of Fiction*, p. 179.

17. E. C. Riley discusses the issues of variety and unity, episode and whole in Cervantes's own literary culture in *Cervantes's Theory of the Novel* (1962; reprint, Newark, Delaware: Juan de la Cuesta, 1992), pp. 116–31; see also Riley's earlier essay, "Episodio, novela, y aventura en *Don Quijote*," *Anales Cervantinos* 5 (1955–56): 209–30.

18. A critical treatment of this theme is found in Michel Moner, *Cervantès: Deux thèmes majeurs (L'amour. Les Armes et les Lettres)* (Université de Toulouse-Mirail: France-Iberie Recherche, 1986), pp. 71–136; for Part One of *Don Quijote*, pp. 71–85. The social reality is treated in Javier Salazar Rincón, *El mundo social del "Quijote"* (Madrid: Gredos, 1986), pp. 120–37. For a discussion of Don Quijote's discourse on arms and letters in Chapter 38, see Elsa Leonor di Santo, "Análisis de los discursos sobre la edad dorada y las armas y las letras," in *Cervantes: su obra y su mundo: Actas del I Congreso Internacional sobre Cervantes*; ed. M. Criado de Val (Madrid: EDI-6, 1981), pp. 799–808. See also the comments in Américo Castro, *El pensamiento de Cervantes* (1925; reprint, Barcelona: Noguer, 1972), pp. 215–19.

19. See Jean-Marc Pelorson, Les "letrados" juristes castillans sous Phillipe III (Le Puy-en-Velay: Université de Poitiers, "L'Eveil de L'Haute Loire," 1980).

20. On student life in Golden Age Spain, see Richard L. Kagan, Students and Society in Early Modern Spain (Baltimore: Johns Hopkins University Press, 1974).

21. For remarks along the same lines about this third brother, see Caroll B. Johnson, Cervantes and the Material World (Urbana and Chicago: University of Illinois Press, 2000), p. 82; see also Salazar Rincón, El mundo social, pp. 123–24.

22. This point is also noted by Moner, Cervantès: Deux thèmes majeures, p. 80.

23. The episode is analyzed by Jean-Marc Pelorson in "Le discours des armes et lettres et l'épisode de Barataria," Les Langues Néo-Latines 212 (1975): 41–58.

24. Timothy Hampton has emphasized the importance of the nation-state and its institutions in his analysis of Don Quijote in Writing from History (Ithaca and London: Cornell University Press, 1990), pp. 237–96. See also Luis Rosales, Cervantes y la libertad (1960; reprint, Madrid, Cultura Hispánica, 1985).

25. Burckhardt, Jacob, The Civilization of the Renaissance in Italy, trans. S.G.C. Middlemore (1860; English trans. Hammondsworth: Penguin, 1990), p. 104.

26. I am suggesting that Don Quijote already anticipates developments in the novel one century later. The classic account that aligns the growth of the English novel with the emergence of a middle-class and its economic individualism is Ian Watt, The Rise of the Novel (Berkeley and Los Angeles: University of California Press, 1957). On marriage and social mobility in this genre, see pages 138–48, 220–28. See also Michael McKeon, The Origins of the English Novel, 1600–1740 (Baltimore and London: Johns Hopkins University Press, 1987), pp. 286–87.

CHAPTER TWO
"DULCINEA"

1. Among the many studies of Don Quijote's love for Dulcinea see Anthony Close, "Don Quixote's Love for Dulcinea: A Study of Cervantine Irony," Bulletin of Hispanic Studies 50 (1973): 237–55; Luis Rosales, Cervantes y la libertad, vol. 2 of Obras completas (1960; Madrid: Trotta, 1996), 380–463; E. C. Riley, Don Quixote (London: Allen and Unwin, 1986), pp. 135–40; José Angel Ascunce Arrieta, Los Quijotes del "Quijote": Historia de una aventura creativa (Kassel: Reichenberger, 1997): 404–23.

2. For a different critical take on this description of Dulcinea, see Robert Alter, Partial Magic: The Novel as a Self-Conscious Genre (Berkeley, Los Angeles, and London: University of California Press, 1975), pp. 25–27.

3. Augustin Redondo advances a carnivalesque reading of the relationship between Aldonza Lorenzo and Dulcinea in Otra manera de leer "El Quijote": Historia, tradiciones culturales y literatura (Madrid: Castalia, 1997), pp. 231–49.

4. Walter L. Reed discusses some of these parallels in An Exemplary History of the Novel: The Quixotic versus the Picaresque (Chicago: University of Chicago Press, 1981), 79–81; as does Helena Percas de Ponseti, Cervantes y su concepto del arte (Madrid: Gredos, 1975), 1: 214–17. See also Myriam Yvonne Jehenson,

"The Dorotea-Fernando/Luscinda-Cardenio episode in *Don Quijote*: A Postmodernist Play," *Modern Language Notes* 107 (1992): 205–19.

5. René Girard, *Deceit, Desire, and the Novel: Self and Other in Literary Structure*, trans. Yvonne Freccero (1961; English trans., Baltimore and London: Johns Hopkins University Press 1965). Eve Kosofsky Sedgwick has adapted Girard's model in *Between Men: English Literature and Male Homosocial Desire* (New York: Columbia University Press, 1985) to explore the relationship between the two desiring men in the erotic triangle, a relationship that is uncertainly described as a latent or not-so-latent homosexuality. Sedgwick's arguments have some resonance for Cervantes's stories of two sets of friends—especially the two inseparable friends Anselmo and Lotario in the "Curioso impertinente." I am more interested in the ways in which Cervantes dramatizes the consequences of triangular desire for the women who are its ostensible objects.

6. Girard, *Deceit, Desire, and the Novel*, pp. 49–52, applies his model of triangular desire to the "Curioso impertinente" and the characters of Anselmo, Lotario, and Camila. Cesáreo Bandera, in *Mimesis conflictiva: Ficción literaria y violencia en Cervantes y Calderón* (Madrid: Gredos, 1975), pp. 81–111, follows Girard and analyzes the relationship of Cardenio, Don Fernando, and Luscinda in similar terms. He does not, however, compare the two stories or note the parallels between them; Bandera *does* compare the Cardenio-Luscinda story to the earlier story of Marcela and Grisóstomo. Louis Combet is similarly indebted to Girard in *Cervantès ou les incertitudes du désir* (Lyon: Presses Universitaires de Lyon, 1980); his project, announced on page 199, is to fill the gap between Girard's account of the "Curioso impertinente" and the other love intrigues of the novel. It is an approach complementary to my own.

7. Viktor Shklovsky, *Theory of Prose*, trans. Benjamin Sher (Ann Arbor, Michigan: Ardis, 1979).

8. Ruth El Saffar notes the incompleteness of Cardenio's and Dorotea's narratives in *Distance and Control in "Don Quixote": A Study in Narrative Technique* (Chapel Hill: University of North Carolina Press, 1975), pp. 63–65.

9. For a discussion of the critical tradition on the "Curioso impertinente," see Percas de Ponseti, *Cervantes y su concepto del arte*, pp. 182–202. On the relationship of the tale of the "Curioso impertinente" to the larger novel, see Bruce W. Wardropper, "The Pertinence of *El curioso impertinente*," *PMLA* 72 (1957), 587–600; Juan Bautista Avalle-Arce, *Deslindes cervantinos* (Madrid: Edhigar, 1961), pp. 121–61; Juergen Hahn, " 'El curioso impertinente' and Don Quijote's Struggle against 'Curiositas,' " *Bulletin of Hispanic Studies* 49 (1972): 128–40; Hans-Jörg Neuschäfer, "*El curioso impertinente* y el sentido del *Quijote*," *Anthropos* 98–99 (1989): 104–7. There are also comments on the tale in Félix Martínez-Bonati, *"Don Quixote" and the Poetics of the Novel*, trans. Dian Fox (Ithaca and London: Cornell University Press, 1992), pp. 202–14.

10. Bandera, *Mimesis conflictiva*, pp. 101–2, insists on Cardenio's knowing collusion in the creation of Don Fernando as his rival. I do not think that Cardenio's story supports this reading.

11. Don Quijote's imitation of Cardenio is discussed by Carroll B. Johnson, *Madness and Lust: A Psychoanalytical Approach to "Don Quixote"* (Berkeley, Los Angeles, and London: University of California Press, 1983), pp. 112–14; Tim-

othy Hampton, *Writing from History: The Rhetoric of Exemplarity in Renaissance Literature* (Ithaca and London: Cornell University Press, 1990), pp. 261–64; Francisco Márquez Villanueva, *Personajes y temas del "Quijote"* (Madrid: Taurus, 1975), pp. 46–51; John G. Weiger, *The Substance of Cervantes* (Cambridge: Cambridge University Press, 1985), pp. 70–73.

12. Henry Higuera discusses the significance of Amadis's self-abnegation in similar terms in *Eros and Empire: Politics and Christianity in "Don Quixote"* (London: Rowman and Littlefield, 1995), pp. 97–100.

13. Garci Rodríguez de Montalvo, *Amadís de Gaula*, ed. Juan Bautista Avalle-Arce (Madrid: Colleción Austral, 1991), p. 546.

14. Stephen Gilman notes that "imitation of Orlando's fury would therefore be a form of chivalresque slander" in *The Novel According to Cervantes* (Berkeley, Los Angeles, and London: University of California Press, 1989), p. 153; see also Hampton, *Writing from History*, pp. 262–63. Alexander Welsh analyzes Don Quijote's choice between models in a discussion of the problem of the hero's identity in *Reflections on the Hero as Quixote* (Princeton: Princeton University Press, 1981), pp. 171–73.

15. One exception among readers of Cardenio is Arthur Efron in *"Don Quixote" and the Dulcineated World* (Austin and London: University of Texas Press, 1971), pp. 126–27: "Cardenio's is a sought-for sorrow of pure spirit, only incidentally related to a woman named Luscinda." Gilman, *The Novel Accordng to Cervantes*, pp. 151–64, offers a nuanced view of Cardenio; both he and Joaquín Casalduero, *Sentido y forma del "Quijote"* (Madrid: Insula, 1949), pp. 118–19, 128–29, see the character as trapped by his social inferiority to Don Fernando. Salvador de Madariaga reduces Cardenio's character to cowardice in *Don Quixote* (1934; reprint, London: Oxford University Press, 1966), pp. 94–105; Robert L. Hathaway discusses Cardenio's unreliability as a narrator in "Cardenio's Twice-Told Tale," *Cervantes* 19, no. 1 (1999): 4–26.

16. See Michael André Bernstein, *Bitter Carnival: Ressentiment and the Abject Hero* (Princeton: Princeton University Press, 1992).

17. Though we do not go over many of the same details, my readings agree in a general way with the observations of Myriam Yvonne Jehenson in two essays: "*Masochisma versus Machismo*: Camila's Re-writing of Gender Assignations in Cervantes's *Tale of Foolish Curiosity*" *Cervantes* 18, no. 2 (1998): 26–52; and "The Pastoral Episode in Cervantes's *Don Quijote*: Marcela Once Again," *Cervantes* 10, no. 2 (1990): 15–31. Diana de Armas Wilson makes an argument for Cervantes as a protofeminist thinker and author who attacks "the logic of male violence and female complicity," with regard to his novel, the *Trabajos de Persiles y Sigismunda* in "Cervantes's *Labors of Persiles*: Working (in) the In-Between," in *Literary Theory/Renaissance Texts*, ed. Patricia Parker and David Quint (Baltimore and London: Johns Hopkins University Press, 1986), pp. 150–81, and in "Cervantes's Last Romance: Deflating the Myth of Female Sacrifice," *Cervantes* 3 (1983): 103–20; her thesis is expanded in *Allegories of Love: Cervantes's "Persiles and Sigismunda"* (Princeton: Princeton University Press, 1991). A different construction of Cervantes's treatment of women in his fiction is found in Ruth El Saffar, *Beyond Fiction: The Recovery of the Feminine in the Novels of Cervantes* (Berkeley, Los Angeles, and London: University of California Press, 1984).

18. The wound that Camila gives herself and the blood that spurts forth as the sign of her "authenticity" give a final twist to the appearance-and-reality features of the "Curioso impertinente," what I take to be its minor thematic link to the rest of the novel—as opposed to the major link afforded by its erotic psychology. The blood suggests the hymeneal bleeding of the wedding night and makes Camila a pure, virginal bride once more in the eyes of Anselmo. For similar observations and associated Renaissance medical doctrine, see Georgina Dopico Black, "La herida de Camila: La anatomía de la evidencia en *El curioso impertinente*," in *En un lugar de La Mancha: Estudios cervantinos en honor de Manuel Durán*, ed. Georgina Dopico Black and Roberto González Echevarría (Salamanca: Ediciones Almar, 1999), pp. 91–107. Walter Reed, *An Exemplary History of the Novel*, p. 80, notes the similarity to Don Quijote's stabbing the wineskins in the following Chapter 35, and spilling the "blood" of the giants he thinks them to be.

19. Jehenson, "*Masochisma versus Machismo*," p. 43.

20. See the observations of Georges Güntert in "*El curioso Impertinente*, novela clave del *Quijote*," in *Cervantes: Su obra y su mundo*, Actas del I Congreso Internacional sobre Cervantes, ed. Manuel Criado de Val (Madrid: EDI-6, S. A., 1981), pp. 783–88.

21. Critical discussions of the Marcela episode can be found in Hermann Iventosch, "Cervantes and Courtly Love: The Grisóstomo-Marcela Episode of *Don Quixote*," *PMLA* 90 (1975): 64–76; Alban Forcione, "Marcela and Grisóstomo and the Consummation of *La Galatea*," in *On Cervantes: Essays for L. A. Murillo*, ed. James A. Parr (Newark, Delaware: Juan de la Cuesta, 1980); Avalle-Arce, *Deslindes cervantinos*, pp. 97–119; Jehenson, "The Pastoral Episode"; Thomas Hart, *Cervantes and Ariosto* (Princeton: Princeton University Press, 1989), pp. 73–88; Paul Alpers, *What Is Pastoral?* (Chicago and London: University of Chicago Press, 1996), pp. 160–64; Michael D. McGaha, "The Sources and Meaning of the Grisóstomo-Marcela Episode in the 1605 *Quijote*," *Anales Cervantinos* 16 (1977): 33–69; El Saffar, *Beyond Fiction*, pp. 60–63; Harry Sieber, "Society and Pastoral Vision in the Marcela-Grisóstomo Episode of *Don Quixote*," *Estudios literarios de hispanistas norteamericanos dedicados a Helmut Hatzfeld con motivo de su 80 aniversario*, ed. J. M. Solà-Solé, A. Crisafulli, and B. Damiani (Barcelona: Hispam, 1974); Javier Herrero, "Arcadia's Inferno: Cervantes' Attack on Pastoral," *Bulletin of Hispanic Studies* 55 (1978): 289–99.

22. The parallels between Grisóstomo and Don Quijote are noted in El Saffar, *Distance and Control*, pp. 45–46; Efron, *Don Quixote and the Dulcineated World*, 102–3; L. A. Murillo, *A Critical Introduction to "Don Quixote"* (New York: Peter Lang, 1988), pp. 49–50.

23. Américo Castro argued that Grisóstomo is a suicide in "Los prólogos al *Quijote*," *Revista de Filología Hispánica* 3 (1941): 314–38, reprinted in *Hacia Cervantes* (Madrid: Taurus, 1957), pp. 262–301. A counterargument is made by Avalle-Arce, *Deslindes cervantinos*, 104–19, who asserts that Cervantes leaves the nature of the shepherd-poet's death deliberately ambiguous. Herman Iventosch defends Castro and demonstrates the problems with Avalle-Arce's evidence in "Cervantes and Courtly Love." Casalduero, *Sentido y forma*, p. 129, contrasts Cardenio's survival to the suicide of the despairing Grisóstomo.

24. Gordon Braden provides the finest recent account of this tradition in *Petrarchan Love and the Continental Renaissance* (New Haven and London: Yale University Press, 1999). John Freccero describes how Petrarch's erotic desire for Laura becomes assimilated with the quest for poetic fame in "The Fig Tree and the Laurel: Petrarch's Poetics," in *Literary Theory/Renaissance Texts*, ed. Patricia Parker and David Quint (Baltimore and London: Johns Hopkins University Press, 1986), pp. 20–32.

25. See the analysis in Jehenson, "The Pastoral Episode."

26. Renato Poggioli reads Marcela's quest for solitude as the beginning of a new, secular interest in inwardness, a "pastoral of the self." See Poggioli, *The Oaten Flute: Essays on Pastoral Poetry and the Pastoral Ideal* (Cambridge: Harvard University Press, 1975), pp. 166–81 (chap. 8).

27. For anti-Marcela positions, see Hart, *Cervantes and Ariosto: Renewing Fiction*, 79–88; Sieber, "Society and Pastoral Vision"; McGaha, "The Sources and Meaning." Forcione, "Marcela and Grisóstomo," pp. 56–57, is more nuanced, but still hostile to the shepherdess. Even the feminist El Saffar, in *Beyond Fiction*, p. 62, accuses Marcela of lack of self-knowledge.

28. Forcione, "Marcela and Grisóstomo," p. 62; Murillo, *A Critical Introduction*, p. 50.

29. Robert L. Hathaway relates the different attitudes of Eugenio and Anselmo to the question of whether or not Leandra has been robbed of her virginity; see Hathaway, "Leandra and That Nagging Question," *Cervantes* 15 no. 2 (1995): 58–74.

30. Forcione, "Marcela and Grisóstomo," p. 61.

31. The reconciliation of Cardenio, Don Fernando, Luscinda, and Dorotea is a stereotypical comic denouement that owes a large debt to the contemporary stage; it is the nature of such comic dramatic endings to sweep previous problems and conflicts under the rug, even at the price of bad faith. The theatricality of the scene is emphasized by L. A. Murillo in *A Critical Introduction*, pp. 107–11. Murillo reads the episode without irony, however, and his conclusions are very different from my own.

32. Louis Combet, *Cervantès ou les incertitudes du désir*, pp. 201–2, makes the most interesting case for the importance of the difference of rank between Cardenio and Don Fernando. Cardenio does indeed accuse Luscinda, though mistakenly, of preferring Don Fernando over him out of a desire for social advancement. However, *his own* desire for Luscinda is not based on material factors, but rather on being chosen over—and thereby besting—his rival.

33. For an application of René Girard's triangular desire to the whole system of chivalry, see Eugenio Donato, "'Per Selve e Boscherecci Labirinti': Desire and Narrative Structure in Ariosto's *Orlando Furioso*," in *Literary Theory/Renaissance Texts*, ed. Patricia Parker and David Quint (Baltimore and London; Johns Hopkins University Press, 1986); Donato points out that not only women, but horses, swords, and shields become objects over which knights can contend to prove their superiority over one another. The moment that Donato discusses, p. 40, when all of these pretexts for dueling explodes in the *Orlando furioso*, the discord in Agramante camp in Canto 26, is explicitly recalled and reenacted in the fight over the barber's packsaddle in Chapter 45 of Part One of *Don Quijote*.

The model of the most important predecessor text for *Don Quijote* is of further interest here, because the *Orlando furioso*, too, suggests how a new social order is rising to destroy the system of chivalry. The poem's hero and various other knights desire and fight over Angelica, but she surrenders herself to a lower-class foot soldier, Medoro.

34. Johan Huizinga, *The Autumn of the Middle Ages*, trans. Rodney J. Payton and Ulrich Mammitzch (1919; English trans., Chicago: University of Chicago Press, 1996), p. 25.

CHAPTER THREE
"PRINCESS MICOMICONA"

1. For comments on the economic rationality of these episodes in the *Orlando furioso*, see Alberto Casadei, *Il percorso del "Furioso": Ricerche intorno alle redazioni del 1516 e del 1521* (Bologna: il Mulino, 1993), pp. 81–82; Sergio Zatti, *Il "Furioso" fra epos e romanzo* (Lucca: Maria Pacini Fazzi, 1990), pp. 105–6.

2. For the contrary critical view, see Louis Combet, *Cervantès ou les incertitudes du désir* (Lyon: Presses Universitaires de Lyon, 1980), pp. 201–2, and note 32 to Chapter 2 above.

3. Much the best critical discussion of the Captive's Tale remains that of Leo Spitzer in "Linguistic Perspectivism in the *Don Quijote*," in *Linguistics and Literary History: Essays in Stylistics* (Princeton: Princeton University Press, 1967), pp. 41–85. Francisco Márquez-Villanueva provides an important treatment of the tale in relationship to its literary sources in *Personajes y temas del Quijote* (Madrid: Taurus, 1975), 77–146. See also Gustavo Illades, *El discurso crítico de Cervantes en "El cautivo"* (Mexico City: Universidad Nacional Autónoma de Mexico, 1990); Jürgen Hahn, "*El Capitán Cautivo*: The Soldier's Truth and Literary Precept in *Don Quijote*, Part I," *Journal of Hispanic Philology* 3 (1979): 269–303; L. A. Murillo, "Cervantes' *Tale* of the Captive Captain," in *Florilegium Hispanicum: Medieval and Golden Age Studies Presented to Dorothy Clotelle Clark*, ed. John S. Geary (Madison, Wisconsin: Hispanic Seminary of Medieval Studies, 1983), 229–43; and Maxime Chevalier, "*El cautivo* entre cuento y novela," *Nueva revista de filología hispánica* 32 (1983): 403–11.

4. Rober Alter discusses Cervantes's writing himself into his novel, as well as the fairy-tale aspects of the Captive's Tale, in *Partial Magic: The Novel as a Self-Conscious Genre* (Berkeley, Los Angeles, and London: University of California Press, 1975), pp. 15–16.

5. See John J. Allen, "Autobiografía y ficción: El relato del capitán cautivo (*Don Quijote* I, 39–41)," *Anales Cervantinos* 15 (1976): 149–55.

6. For the issue of the decline of Spain and the ways that it was perceived in the seventeenth century, see J. H. Elliott, *Spain and Its World, 1500–1700* (New Haven and London: Yale University Press, 1989), pp. 213–86.

7. For the technical force of Don Fernando's terms, see E. C. Riley, *Cervantes's Theory of the Novel* (1962; reprint, Newark, Delaware: Juan de la Cuesta, 1992), pp. 185–86.

8. The chapter is finely analyzed and connected to the episode of Maritornes at the inn by Frida Weber de Kurlat in "El arte cervantino en el capítulo XXI de

la Primera Parte del *Quijote*," in *Studia hispanica in honorem R. Lapesa* (Madrid: Gredos, 1972), 1: 571–86.

9. Cervantes's use of asyndeton and polysyndeton are noted by Weber de Kurlat, "El arte cervantino," pp. 579–86. Eric MacPhail comments on the use of the future tense in "The Uses of the Past: Prophecy and Genealogy in *Don Quixote*" *Cervantes* 14, no. 1 (1994): 61–74.

10. On the erotic charge of the "white hands" of this imaginary princess and of other female characters in Part One, see Augustin Redondo, *Otra manera de leer el "Quijote"* (Madrid: Castalia, 1997), pp. 165–67.

11. Márquez Villanueva, *Personajes y temas*, pp. 81–92, has shown how the subsequent tale of Leandra in Chapter 51 derives the name of its heroine from the title of an early sixteenth-century Italian chivalric romance, the *Leandra*, that recounts how a Babylonian princess named Leandra frees a Christian knight from captivity. Cervantes's story of Leandra is a parodic version of the Captive's Tale: the charlatan soldier Vicente de la Rosa seduces and carries off Leandra, a rich farmer's daughter who steals her father's possessions for him.

12. The affinity of the practical joke to realism in *Don Quijote* is explored by Alexander Welsh, who further takes the joke of Chapter 43, which once set in motion has no definite goal, as an instance that demonstrates contingency. See Welsh, *Reflections on the Hero as Quixote* (Princeton: Princeton University Press, 1981), pp. 80–100. The sexual overtones of the episode are commented upon by Mary Gaylord in "The Whole Body with All of Its Members: Cervantes, Pinciano, Freud," in *Quixotic Desire: Psychoanalytic Perspectives on Cervantes*, ed. Ruth Antony El Saffar and Diane de Armas Wilson (Ithaca and London: Cornell University Press, 1993), pp. 117–34.

13. On the inns of the novel see Javier Salazar Rincón, "De ventas y venteros: tradición literaria, ideología, y mímesis en la obra de Cervantes," *Anales Cervantinos* 33 (1995–97): 85–116; see especially p. 112 on the inn as the emblem of a fallen world of monetary transactions.

14. See Ellen G. Friedman, *Spanish Captives in North Africa in the Early Modern Age* (Madison: University of Wisconsin Press, 1983). For the Christian selling of Muslim prisoners, see M. Rosi, *Alcuni documenti relativi alla liberazione dei principali prigionieri Turchi presi a Lepanto* (Rome: R. Società Romana di storia patria, 1898).

15. Caroll B. Johnson also reads the Captive's Tale in economic terms, and argues that the tale presents a more conservative economic order countering the new capitalism represented by Captain Viedma's merchant brother. He further offers a feminist-psychoanalytic reading of the story that I find unpersuasive—the cane that Zoraida extends from the window is a phallus, etc.—and takes what I think is an unduly pessimistic view of Zoraida's incorporation into Spanish Christian society. See Johnson, *Cervantes and the Material World* (Urbana and Chicago: University of Illinois Press, 2000), pp. 71–92.

16. A lively account of Cervantes's captivity is presented in William Byron, *Cervantes: A Biography* (Garden City, New York: Doubleday, 1978), pp. 185–247. His fictional avatar, Captain Viedma, had rowed as a slave in a Turkish galley before landing in Algiers; his liberation is contrasted with Don Quijote's freeing of the convict galley slaves in Chapter 22. The degree of sympathy that Cervantes

appears to share with this moment of lawlessness may, in part, be biographically inspired.

17. On Leandra's near rape, see Márquez Villanueva, *Personajes y temas*, p. 144; Combet, *Cervantès*, p. 369; Robert L. Hathaway, "Leandra and That Nagging Question," *Cervantes* 15, no. 2 (1995): 58–74.

18. At the end of Cervantes's play *El trato de Argel*, the redemption of the Christian captives similarly wavers between the miraculous intervention of the Virgin and quotidian monetary transactions; the two come together in the ransoms provided by the Mercedarian friars. One captive comments, "Mi remedio tengo cierto / porque aquí me traen dineros" (I believe that my redemption is certain / because they are bringing me money here, 2480–81), while another proclaims that "Dios nos ha de remediar / hermanos" (God is to redeem us / my brothers, 2486–87), and turns in prayer to Mary, "nuestra luz, nuestro remedio" (our light, our redemption, 2496). Cervantes, *Teatro completo*, ed. Florencio Sevilla Arroyo and Antonio Rey Hazas (Barcelona: Planeta, 1987).

19. See Kim Hall, "Guess Who's Coming to Dinner? Colonization and Miscegenation in *The Merchant of Venice*," *Renaissance Drama*, n.s., 23 (1992): 87–111, 102–3. For a reading of *The Merchant of Venice* that follows carefully the paths taken by money in the play, see Lars Engle, *Shakespearean Pragmatism: Market of His Time* (Chicago and London: University of Chicago Press, 1993), 77–106.

20. The loss of Zoraida's wealth at sea is interlaced with the story of "Princess Micomicona," who, says Dorotea in her disguise as the princess in Chapter 30, lost all the members of her entourage when their ship was in sight of port; her life has been "one continuous miracle and mystery" ["es todo milagro y misterio el discurso de mi vida" (305; 305)]. This romance miracle can be compared to the possible Christian miracle of the Captive's Tale.

21. In "Organic Unity in Unlikely Places: *Don Quijote* I, 39–41" *Cervantes* 2, no. 2 (1982): 133–54), Caroll B. Johnson points out that these Frenchmen are presented as likely Huguenots and hence represent another version of religious difference in the story.

22. This spiritual sense of the Captive's rescue is spelled out explicitly in the liturgy of Our Lady of Ransom (September 24), instituted in the Spanish Order of Our Lady of Ransom, which was founded in the thirteenth century: "O God, who by means of the most glorious Mother of Thy Son, wast pleased to give new children to Thy Church for the deliverance of Christ's faithful from the power of the heathen; grant, we beseech Thee, that we who love and honour her as the foundress of so great a work may, by her merits and intercession, be ourselves delivered from the bondage of the evil one." *Saint Andrew Daily Missal* (Bruges: Abbey of St. André; St. Paul, Minnesota: E. M. Lohmann, 1937), p. 1468.

23. When the Captive, Zoraida, the Renegade, and his fellow captives escape by sea to the promontory of the Caba Rumía, named after the wicked Cava, through whom Spain was lost to the Moors, it appears to the Captive not as the shelter of a prostitute, but as the safe haven of his relief—"no fue abrigo de la mala mujer, sino puerto seguro de nuestro remedio" (424; 426). The language is Marian; see the passages from *El Trato de Argel* cited in n. 18. Cervantes wrote a dedicatory sonnet to the *Grandezas y excelencias de la Virgen*, by Pedro de Padilla,

published in 1587. Canto 9 of Padilla's poem contains the following verses that refer both to the Virgin and to her church of Santa Maria Maggiore in Rome:

> Que este es el puerto donde los que arriben
> Con humilde fe viva en compañia,
> Aunque de la tormenta destrozados,
> Serán bien acogidos y amparados.
>
> Y porque todos acudir pudiesen
> A *puerto* tan *seguro*, y atinasen
> Desde el mar proceloso dó estuviesen
> A saberle buscar y se salvasen,
> Quiso el eterno Rey que una luz viesen,
> Los que tan á peligro navegasen,
> Y como en puertos vemos el exemplo,
> Así en monte á la Virgen trazó templo . . .

(for this is the port where those who put in with live and humble faith, even if battered by storms at sea, will be well sheltered and protected.
And in order that all can have recourse to so sure a port, and to find it after the stormy sea in which they have lived, in order that they may know how to seek for it and to save themselves, the eternal King wished that those who sail in such peril might see a light; and after the example that we see in ports, so here on the mountain he marked out a temple to the Virgin.)

Pedro de Padilla, *Grandezas y excelencias de la Virgen* (Madrid: Vega y Compañia, 1806), pp. 293–94, (my emphasis). The Virgin as a port is to sailors was a familiar part of her litany: "Ut navigantibus portum"; see *Doctrina y piedad Mariana en España: Siglos XVII–XVIII* (Salamanca: Sociedad Mariológica Española, 1984), p. 385. The cult image of "Nuestra Señora del Remedio," brought to Madrid from Flanders in 1593, acquired its name when it calmed a sea tempest en route. See Nazario Pérez, *Historia Mariana de España* (Toledo: Kadmos, 1993), 1: 940.

24. The allusion to Joseph and Mary is the point of departure for a discussion of the Marian elements in the Captive's Tale by E. Michael Gerli in *Refiguring Authority: Reading, Writing, and Rewriting Cervantes* (Lexington: University of Kentucky Press, 1991), pp. 40–60; Gerli argues that the tale preaches racial tolerance not long before the expulsion of the Moriscos. María Antonia Garcés persuasively suggests that the bejeweled Zoraida resembles the manifestation of Mary in the Virgen del Pilar, whose image in Zaragoza was encrusted with pearls and gems; see Garcés, "Zoraida's Veil: 'The Other Scene' of the Captive's Tale," *Revista de estudios hispánicos* 23 (1989): 65–98, 78–79. Garcés *un*persuasively argues that Zoraida's jewelry pieces are so many displaced phallic images that turn her into a version of Freud's Medusa. The Captive's Tale does play on "la joya" (Chapter 41, 427; 429) that Zoraida prizes above all her possessions, her viginity. But sometimes a pearl is just a pearl.

25. Along similar lines see Johnson, *Cervantes and the Material World*, pp. 81–82.

26. See Salvador de Madariaga, *Don Quixote* (1934; reprint, London: Oxford University Press, 1966), pp. 79–93; Márquez-Villanueva, *Personajes y temas*, pp. 24–35, notes Dorotea's economic skills, and sees her, above all, as a woman in love with her "husband," Don Fernando. Stephen Gilman takes a more critical view in *The Novel According to Cervantes* (Berkeley, Los Angeles, and London: University of California Press, 1989), pp. 164–77. See also Robert L. Hathaway, "Dorotea or the Narrator's Arts," *Cervantes* 13, no. 1 (1993): 109–26.

27. One can compare Dorotea's rationalization—that even if she screams and successfully resists Fernando, no one will believe that she did not invite him into her room—to the speech of the rapist Don Diego as he forces himself on the mother of Costanza in Cervantes's *La ilustre fregona*.

28. Gilman, *The Novel According to Cervantes*, p. 172.

29. Ruth Pike, *Aristocrats and Traders: Sevillian Society in the Sixteenth Century* (Ithaca and London: Cornell University Press, 1972), p. 22. See the comments of Tomás de Mercado in his 1569 *Suma de tratos y contratos*, ed. Nicolás Sánchez-Albornoz (Madrid: Instituto de Estudios Fiscales, Ministerio de Hacienda, 1977), p. 62.

30. Don Fernando may actually need Dorotea's money; he is a second son of a Duke, a *segundón*, excluded by primogeniture from the bulk of his family's wealth. I owe this observation to Roberto González Echevarría in his Yale Devane Lectures of 2002, "Love and the Law in Cervantes."

31. One can compare Lope de Vega's respectively comic and tragic treatments of the lady who stoops to conquer, *El perro del hortolano* and *El mayordomo de la duquesa de Amalfi*.

32. The most important critical treatment of the episode of the Canon of Toledo is found in Alban K. Forcione, *Cervantes, Aristotle and the "Persiles"* (Princeton: Princeton University Press, 1970), pp. 91–130. Forcione teaches us not to confuse the Canon with Cervantes, and he is particularly concerned with the ways that Cervantes tests Renaissance theories of literary verisimilitude. See also Riley, *Cervantes's Theory of the Novel*, especially pp. 138–44, 171–78.

33. Along these lines, see the comments on Don Quijote's conversation with the Canon of Toledo in Timothy Hampton, *Writing from History* (Ithaca and London: Cornell University Press, 1990), pp. 264–68.

34. See Forcione, *Cervantes, Aristotle and the "Persiles"*, pp. 114–21, and for a survey of other garden paradises in Cervantes's writings, pp. 212–45.

35. Lope de Vega spells out the norms of the modern stage where the box office overrides Aristotelian rules in his *Arte nuevo de hacer comedias en este tiempo*. For an English translation, see *The New Art of Writing Plays*, trans. William T. Brewster, Papers on Play-Making I (New York: Dramatic Museum of Columbia University, 1914).

36. The connections between the inn of *La ilustre fregona* and the inn of *Don Quijote* are considerable: Maritornes is, of course, no Costanza, but more like the lusty Argüello in the exemplary novella. Her Asturian provenance is taken over, though only in disguise, by "Lope el Asturiano," in real life, the young nobleman Don Diego de Carriazo, whose companion, Don Tomás de Avendaño, in love with Costanza, works as an ostler among muleteers like Don Luis and the harrier-lover of Maritornes. Cervantes is rethinking similar plots.

37. Two chapters earlier, in Chapter 29, the Curate pretends to have traveled "to Seville to collect certain sums of money that a relative of mine, who many years ago went to the Indies, had sent me, and it was not a small sum either, but over sixty thousand pesos" ["a Sevilla a cobrar cierto dinero que un pariente mío que ha muchos años que pasó a Indias me había enviado, y no tan pocos que no pasan de sesenta mil pesos" (299; 299–300)], money that he claims was stolen from him by the convicts that Don Quijote had set free. Seville is thus already associated with the new fortunes that can be made in the New World. This imaginary relative, moreover, anticipates—another instance of Cervantine interlace—the Judge's real brother, the merchant, who has sent money back home to the Viedma family from Peru (435; 437). A similar story of worldly success achieved in the New World is told at the beginning of Cervantes's novella, *El celoso estremeño*.

38. See Hampton, *Writing from History*, pp. 265–66. The issue of the exemplary hero allows Hampton to place *Don Quijote* into a broader study of late-Renaissance literature.

39. A similar observation is made by Nadine Ly, "Don Quichotte: Livre d'aventures et aventures de l'écriture" *Les Langues Néo-Latines* 267 (1988): 5–92, 80–81.

40. Mikhail Bakhtin, *The Dialogic Imagination: Four Essays*, ed. Michael Holquist, trans. Caryl Emerson and Michael Holquist, University of Texas Press Slavic Series, vol. 1 (Austin: University of Texas Press, 1981), p. 7. One passage in the essay, "Discourse in the Novel," seems quite close to the point I am arguing. Bakhtin notes, p. 411, that the inserted genres in *Don Quijote* "serve the basic purpose of introducing heteroglossia into the novel, of introducing an era's many and diverse languages"; then he declares, p. 412, that "this *autocriticism of discourse* is one of the primary distinguishing features of the novel as a genre. . . . Already in *Don Quixote* we have a literary novelistic discourse being tested by life."

41. Gary Saul Morson and Caryl Emerson, *Mikhail Bakhtin: Creation of a Prosaics* (Stanford, California: Stanford University Press, 1990), p. 299.

42. Spitzer, "Linguistic Perspectivism."

43. Bakhtin, in fact, gives relatively little attention to *Don Quijote* in his theory of the novel; see Walter Reed, "The Problem of Cervantes in Bakhtin's Poetics," *Cervantes* 7 (1987): 29–37. See also Anthony J. Cascardi, "Genre Definition and Multiplicity in *Don Quijote*," *Cervantes* 6 (1986): 39–49. Diana de Armas Wilson discusses Bakhtin's concept of "hybridity" with regard to *Don Quijote* in *Cervantes, the Novel, and the New World* (Oxford: Oxford University Press, 2000), pp. 95–103; see also pp. 42–59, on the question of where Cervantes fits in the "rise of the novel."

44. For another mapping of these episodes, see Frank Goodwyn, "The Religious Aspect of the *Quijote*," in *Estudios literarios de hispanistas norteamericanos dedicados a Helmut Hatzfeld con motivo de su 80 aniversario*, ed. Josep M. Solà-Solé et al. (Barcelona: Ediciones Hispam, 1974), pp. 111–17.

45. Cervantes apparently thought that the rosary made from Don Quijote's shirt and the million Ave-Marias risked objections from ecclesiastical censors, and they disappeared from the second edition of the novel. See Marcel Bataillon, *Érasme et L'Espagne* (Paris: E. Droz, 1937), pp. 829–30.

46. The passage is the occasion for one of Miguel de Unamuno's more in-sightful effusions: "There are those who strive to marry Fortune and keep Glory as a mistress, but they lose everything, for Fortune scratches at them out of jealousy, and Glory makes mock of them, wriggling out of their embrace." Miguel dc Unamuno, *Our Lord Don Quixote*, trans. Anthony Kerrigan, Bollingen Series vol. 85, no. 3 (Princeton: Princeton University Press, 1967), pp. 126–27.

47. A discussion of Sancho's plan for his black subjects is found in Redondo, *Otra manera*, pp. 363–80.

48. Luis Andrés Murillo proposed that the Captive's Tale represents the ur-material of *Don Quijote* and that Cervantes invented Don Quijote and Dulcinea as foils to Captain Viedma and Zoraida. Murillo's hypothesis rests on conjecture, but it points to the carefully plotted out opposition between Zoraida and Dulcinea that I am describing. See Luis Andrés Murillo, "El *Ur-Quijote*, nueva hipótesis," *Cervantes* 1 (1981): 43–50.

CHAPTER FOUR
THE GENTLER, WISER DON QUIJOTE

1. Among many critical treatments of the episode, see Alban K. Forcione, *Cervantes, Aristotle and the "Persiles"* (Princeton: Princeton University Press, 1970), pp. 137–44; Helena Percas de Ponseti, *Cervantes y su concepto de arte* (Madrid: Gredos, 1975), 2: 407–583; Ghetin Hughes, "The Cave of Montcsinos: Don Quixote's Interpretation and Dulcinea's Enchantment," *Bulletin of Hispanic Studies* 54 (1977): 106–13; Maurice Molho, "Le paradoxe de la caverne: *Don Quichotte* II, 22, 23, 24," *Les Langues Néo-Latines* 267 (1988): 93–165; E. C. Riley, "Metamorphosis, Myth, and Dream in the Cave of Montesinos," in *Essays on Narrative Fiction in the Iberian Peninsula in Honour of Frank Pierce*, ed. R. B. Tate (Oxford: Dolphin Books, 1982), pp. 105–19.

2. For this suggestion see the chapter on Don Quixote in Ian Watt, *Myths of Modern Individualism* (Cambridge: Cambridge University Press, 1996), p. 86.

3. See Molho, "Le paradoxe de la caverne," p. 148. Molho argues that the "enchanted" Dulcinea is in fact returned to her original identity as Aldonza Lorenzo—though, one would have to add, in a more unattractive form.

4. Don Quijote is quite right to say that there is no comparison between the lady Belerma and the Dulcinea whose fame as Cervantes's literary character in Part One has already eclipsed that of the heroine of the old ballad. Cervantes makes larger claims for his novel just before Don Quijote and Sancho Panza return to their village in Chapter 71. Sancho predicts that he and his master will be depicted on tavern walls just as Helen of Troy and Dido and Aeneas are depicted on tapestries on the walls of the inn where they are staying (1032; 1051). Cervantes places himself alongside Homer and Virgil.

5. Another example of Cervantes's self-conscious rewriting of Part One concerns the episode where Ginés de Pasamonte steals Sancho's ass (Chapter 23), a passage that was inserted into the second edition of the novel and which occasioned a narrative inconsistency, an issue that is raised by Sansón Carrasco in Chapter 3 of Part Two and explained by Sancho in Chapter 4. In Chapters 25–27, Don Quijote's new meeting with Ginés, now disguised as the puppeteer Maese

Pedro, is sandwiched between—and once again associated with—the story of a lost ass and the braying aldermen.

6. Michel Moner, *Cervantès: Deux thèmes majeures (L'amour. Les Armes et les Lettres)* (Université de Toulouse-Le Mirail: France-Iberie Recherche, 1986), pp. 133–36.

7. E. C. Riley, *Don Quixote* (London: Allen and Unwin, 1986), p. 95.

8. On the larger issue of freedom in Cervantes's thought and writings, see Alberto Sánchez, "Libertad, Humano Tesoro," *Anales Cervantinos* 32 (1994): 9–21.

9. For an argument that links Sansón as Knight of Mirrors to Don Quijote's discussion one chapter earlier of the theater that holds up a mirror to life, see Pierre L. Ullman, "An Emblematic Interpretation of Sansón Carrasco's Disguises," in *Estudios literarios de hispanistas norteamericanos dedicados a Helmut Hatzfeld con motivo de su 80 aniversario,* ed. Josep M. Solà-Solé et al. (Barcelona: Ediciones Hispam, 1974), pp. 223–38. See also Timothy Hampton, *Writing from History: The Rhetoric of Exemplarity in Renaissance Literature* (Ithaca and London: Cornell University Press, 1990), p. 275. Robert Alter discusses the issue of mirror figures and doubles more generally as a metaliterary feature of *Don Quijote* in *Partial Magic: The Novel as a Self-Conscious Genre* (Berkeley, Los Angeles, and London: University of California Press, 1975), pp. 1–29, esp. pp. 21–25.

10. See L. A. Murillo, *A Critical Introduction to "Don Quixote"* (New York: Peter Lang, 1990), pp. 215–20.

11. On Sancho's ambitions, see Javier Salazar Rincón, *El mundo social del "Quijote"* (Madrid: Gredos, 1986), pp. 307–9.

12. The critical consensus about the character of Don Quijote in Part Two, which emphasizes his self-doubts and the increased exploration of his inner life and thoughts, is represented by the fine discussion in Riley, *Don Quixote,* pp. 103–15. Salvador de Madariaga presented an influential, schematic reading of the ways in which Don Quijote's and Sancho's characters interact with and influence one another in Part Two in *Don Quixote* (1934; reprint, London: Oxford University Press, 1966), pp. 137–85. Edwin Williamson offers a somewhat different critical take on the issue, arguing for the continuity of Don Quijote's essential madness between the two parts of the novel, in "'Intención' and 'Invención' in the *Quijote*," *Cervantes* 8, no. 1 (1988): 7–22. Howard Mancing argues for continuity of a different type: he contends that the Don Quijote of Part One has already been defeated and to a large extent disillusioned by the end of Part One. See Mancing, *The Chivalric World of "Don Quijote": Style, Structure, and Narrative Technique* (Columbia and London: University of Missouri Press, 1982); for Mancing's quarrel with other critics, see pp. 118–26.

13. Vladimir Nabokov famously created a balance sheet of the victories and defeats, and of the casualties that Don Quijote inflicts and himself receives in his iconoclastic Harvard *Lectures on Don Quixote,* ed. Fredson Bowers (San Diego, New York, and London: Harcourt Brace Jovanovitch, 1983), pp. 89–112.

14. José Ortega y Gasset emphasizes the will of Don Quijote as that which constitutes him as hero in his *Meditations on Quixote,* trans., Evelyn Rugg and Diego Marín (1914; English trans., New York: W. W. Norton, 1963), pp. 148–49.

15. The importance of the Rinaldo allusions and of their connections to Roque Guinart are noted in Henry Higuera, *Eros and Empire: Politics and Christianity in "Don Quixote"* (London: Rowman and Littlefield, 1995), pp. 71–89. Higuera, however, places an unconvincing construction on these allusions, seeing in them Cervantes's reflections on Machiavellian power politics. For the figure of Rinaldo, see Michael Sherberg, *Rinaldo: Character and Intertext in Ariosto and Tasso* (Saratoga, California: Anima Libri, 1993).

16. Miguel de Unamuno, *Our Lord Don Quixote*, trans. Anthony Kerrigan, Bollingen Series vol. 85, no. 3 (Princeton: Princeton University Press, 1967). On Unamuno's place within a romantic tradition of reading *Don Quijote*, see Anthony Close, *The Romantic Approach to "Don Quixote"* (Cambridge: Cambridge University Press, 1977), pp. 136–59. On the Christ-like dimensions of the quixotic hero in the subsequent history of the novel, especially Prince Myshkin in Dostoevsky's *The Idiot*, see Alexander Welsh, *Reflections on the Hero as Quixote* (Princeton: Princeton University Press, 1981), pp. 21–25, 51–60, 203–13; and Eric J. Ziolkowski, *The Sanctification of Don Quixote: From Hidalgo to Priest* (University Park: Pennsylvania State University Press, 1991).

17. This disenchanted world, Georg Lukács argues in some classic pages, corresponds to the world abandoned by God that becomes the subject of the new genre of the novel; writing of *Don Quijote*, he says, "Thus the first great novel of world literature stands at the beginning of the time when the Christian God began to forsake the world . . . when the world, released from its paradoxical anchorage in a beyond that is truly present, was abandoned to its immanent meaninglessness." See Lukács, *The Theory of the Novel*, trans. Anna Bostock (1920; English trans., Cambridge: MIT Press, 1975), p. 103. For a socially inflected discussion that sidesteps Lukács, see Michael McKeon, *The Origins of the English Novel, 1600–1740* (Baltimore and London: Johns Hopkins University Press, 1987), pp. 273–94. Edwin Williamson, *The Half-Way House of Fiction* (Oxford: Clarendon Press, 1984), pp. 110–25, describes Don Quijote's adventures in Part Two in terms of the absence of Providence.

18. The passivity of Don Quijote in Part Two is summed up in Riley, *Don Quixote*, pp. 108–15; and Ruth El Saffar, *Beyond Fiction: The Recovery of the Feminine in the Novels of Cervantes* (Berkeley, Los Angeles, and London: University of California Press, 1984), pp. 81–86.

19. For these social ranks within the nobility see Javier Salazar Rincón, *El mundo social*, pp. 86–159.

20. On the similarity to Cardenio, see Timothy Hampton, *Writing from History*, p. 276.

21. Critics who read Don Diego as a more or less normative figure of the good man leading the good life include Joaquín Casalduero, *Sentido y forma del "Quijote"* (Madrid: Ediciones Insula, 1949), pp. 253–55; A. J. Close, *Don Quixote* (Cambridge: Cambridge University Press, 1990), pp. 47–52; Oscar Mandel, "The Function of the Norm in *Don Quixote*" *Modern Philology* 55 (1957–58): 154–63. On similar lines, see Augustin Redondo, *Otra manera de leer "El Quijote"* (Madrid: Castalia, 1997), pp. 265–89.

22. Hampton, *Writing from History*, p. 279. For a similar formulation, see Luis Rosales, *Cervantes y la libertad* (Madrid: Trotta, 1996), p. 139.

23. Hampton, *Writing from History*, pp. 275–80. Alban K. Forcione sees the opposition of Don Diego and Don Quijote in terms of Cervantes's typically double-edged irony and paradoxical writing; the novel can admire Don Diego's virtues but also acknowledge his limitations. See *Cervantes, Aristotle and the "Persiles"* p. 164 n.61. See also Riley, *Don Quixote*, 143–47. Francisco Márquez Villanueva sees in Don Diego Cervantes's portrait and simultaneous critique of an Erasmian Christian humanism; in this unlikely reading, the wise Don Diego ends up being tinged with his own kind of "madness." See Márquez Villanueva, *Personajes y temas del "Quijote"* (Madrid: Taurus, 1975), pp. 147–227. Still more critical of Don Diego is Charles D. Presberg, *Adventures in Paradox: "Don Quixote" and the Western Tradition* (University Park: Pennyslvania State University Press, 2001), pp. 199–230.

24. Don Diego de Miranda is recalled when the issue of sainthood crops up again much later in Part Two. Among four painted images of "knightly" saints— that is, saints on horseback—that Don Quijote regards in Chapter 58 is one of Saint Martin dividing his cloak with a poor man. He comments that the saint was more liberal than valiant—"más liberal que valiente" (937; 954). This same opposition of liberality and valor is played out, as we shall see, in the contrasting figures of Don Diego and Don Quijote.

Much has happened in the novel by Chapter 58, and in fact all four of the depicted saints—George, Martin, James the Moorkiller, and Paul—now comment on its hero. Like George the defender of damsels—"defendedor de doncellas" (936; 954)—Don Quijote has two chapters earlier championed the cause of the daughter of Doña Rodríguez. Like the liberal Martin—and like Don Diego—Don Quijote has exhibited extreme liberality ["liberal en todo estremo" (720, 737)] at the inn in the aftermath of his destruction of Maese Pedro's puppet show in Chapter 26. Like James wreaking havoc on the Moors—"derribando, atropellando, destruyendo, y matando los agarenos escuadrones" (939; 956)—Don Quijote has annihilated Pedro's puppet Moors ["estos que derriba, destroza, y mata no son verdaderos moros" (716; 734)]. We are made to feel that in his imperfect way Don Quijote has tried to imitate these chivalric saints. But the emphasis is on the imperfection, for Don Quijote ruefully acknowledges that, as a sinner, he does not know what his human actions add up to: "y yo hasta agora no sé lo que conquisto a fuerza de mis trabajos." The implication is that the only perfect imitation that Don Quijote can achieve is a conversion like that of Saint Paul fallen from horseback on the road to Damascus, "a knight-errant in his life and a saint on foot in his death" ["caballero andante por la vida, y santo a pie quedo por la muerte" (937; 954)]: that is, a conversion away from chivalry itself to a pedestrian holy death as a Christian. This is, of course, the conversion effected in the last chapter of the novel.

Don Quijote's failure to emulate these Christian knights except in death is consonant with Lukács's characterization of the novelistic universe as a world forsaken by God or a guiding providential plan; see note 17. On the episode, see Hampton, *Writing from History*, pp. 281–84, who points out the connection to Don Diego de Miranda. It occasions one of Unamuno's characteristic meditations in *Our Lord Don Quixote*, pp. 246–59.

25. Marcel Bataillon, *Érasme et L'Espagne* (Paris: E. Droz, 1937), pp. 834–35. Redondo, *Otra manera de leer*, pp. 283–89, returns to Bataillon and offers a powerful rebuttal to those like Marquez-Villanueva and Presberg, who see Don Diego's religiosity as merely conventional; to the contrary, Redondo insists upon the simplicity, rationality, and freedom that separates it from the sacramentalism of the Counter-Reformation.

26. *Adages*, trans. R.A.B. Mynors, in *The Collected Works of Erasmus* (Toronto, Buffalo, and London: University of Toronto Press, 1989), 32:55, 61; references are to book, century, and adage. Edwin Duval has discussed this section of the *Adagia* in his indispensable study of the fiction of Rabelais, *The Design of Rabelais's "Tiers Livre de Pantagruel"*, Etudes Rabelaisiennes t. xxxiv (Geneva: Droz, 1997), pp. 122–28.

27. The prophecy uttered at the moment of Don Quijote's imprisonment in his cage in Chapter 46 of Part One refers to him as the "furious Manchegan lion" ["el furibundo león manchado" (469; 472)]. One should note in this episode how the exchange of glances between the lion ["miró"] and Don Quijote ["lo miraba"] (643; 656) recalls the meeting of Don Quijote and Don Diego de *Miranda* one chapter earlier.

28. For Don Diego as a figure of a new bourgeois sensibility that has substituted money for arms and hungers for peace during a period of religious war, see Casalduero, *Sentido y forma*, pp. 253–54.

29. Forcione, *Cervantes, Aristotle and the "Persiles,"* pp. 162–64; Casalduero, *Sentido y forma*, p. 256.

30. The victory of love is, of course, not surprising: it is a literary cliché. As Redondo points out in *Otra manera de leer*, p. 388, the cards are stacked against Camacho and he cannot win. John Sinnigen sides with the winner Basilio in "Themes and Structures in the 'Bodas de Camacho,'" *Modern Language Notes* 84 (1969): 157–70. My reading of the way the episode also defends the behavior of Camacho shares the approach of Kathleen Bulgin, "'Las bodas de Camacho': The Case for *el Interés*," *Cervantes* 3, no. 1 (1983): 51–64.

31. For such traditional rituals of mating in medieval and Renaissance culture, see Thomas M. Greene, *Besieging the Castle of Ladies*, Occasional Paper no. 4 (Binghamton, New York: Center for Medieval and Early Renaissance Studies, 1995). Charles Dempsey describes a fifteenth-century Florentine version, organized by one Bartolomeo Benci in honor of Marietta degli Strozzi in 1464 in *Inventing the Renaissance Putto* (Chapel Hill and London: University of North Carolina Press, 2001), pp. 77–86.

32. Bulgin, "'Las bodas de Camacho,'" p. 53 n.4, notes some of these parallels.

33. Bulgin, "'Las bodas de Camacho,'" pp. 52–53; Casalduero, *Sentido y forma*, pp. 257–67.

34. In a brilliant discovery, Redondo has found a link between this false miracle and the "miracles" carried out by the so-called "familiares de santa Quiteria." See *Otra manera de leer*, pp. 390–401.

35. Bulgin, "'Las bodas de Camacho,'" p. 61: "If one judges the episode from the point of view of orthodox Christian morality, Camacho would seem to come out ahead. In any event, he is certainly not a villain."

36. Albert O. Hirschman, *The Passions and the Interests: Political Arguments for Capitalism before Its Triumph* (Princeton: Princeton University Press, 1977), pp. 41–42.

37. Don Diego wants well-written books that keep him wondering and in suspense by their invention—"admiren y suspendan con la invención" (634; 647)—though he ruefully asserts that there are few such books in Spain. We are to assume that *Don Quijote* itself is just the book to fit his bill. On the valorization of *suspense*, the creation of the desire to read, among Renaissance literary theorists, and for the role of the concept in developing a purely secular (versus an allegorical) idea of reading, see the important essay of Terence Cave, "'Suspendere animos': Pour une histoire de la notion de suspens," in *Les commentaires et la naissance de la critique littéraire, France/Italie (XIVe–XVIe siècles)*, ed. Gisèle Mathieu-Castellani and Michel Plaisance (Paris: Aux Amateurs de Livres, 1990), pp. 211–18. Cave shows that the theorists responded to two texts not accounted for by Aristotle's *Poetics*, the *Ethiopica* of Heliodorus and the *Orlando furioso* of Ariosto; these were two of Cervantes's favorite authors and models.

38. Hampton, *Writing from History*, p. 280; Riley, *Don Quixote*, p. 146: "With Don Diego, Cervantes opens a path leading directly to the nineteenth-century novel."

39. The scene anticipates the episode in Chapter 54, which will be discussed in the next chapter, where Sancho Panza joins the Morisco Ricote and the German "pilgrims" in drinking wine and eating bread. For a critical discussion, see Alban K. Forcione, "Sancho Panza and Cervantes' Embodiment of Pastoral," in *Literature, Culture, and Society in the Modern Age: In Honor of Joseph Frank*, ed. Edward J. Brown et al. (Stanford, California: Department of Slavic Languages and Literatures, Stanford University, 1991), 1: 57–75.

40. See Bataillon, *Érasme et L'Espagne*, p. 836.

41. Compare the condemnation of the "diabolical engines of artillery" that brings Don Quijote's speech on arms and letters to an ironic conclusion in Chapter 38 of Part One.

42. For the modern, bourgeois novel as the genre of compromise—and therefore, for him, the genre emblematic of the function of literature itself—see Franco Moretti, *The Way of the World: The "Bildungsroman" in European Culture* (London: Verso, 1987), esp. pp. 3–13, 159–61.

43. On the episode, see Alison Weber, "Don Quijote with Roque Guinart: The Case for an Ironic Reading," *Cervantes* 6, no. 2 (1986): 123–40; Casalduero, *Sentido y forma*, pp. 346–48; Robert L. Hathaway, "Claudia Jerónima (*DQ*, II, 60)," *Nueva Revista de Filología Hispánica* 36 (1988): 319–32.

44. Hampton, *Writing from History*, pp. 286–88.

45. The connection between the two stories is noted in passing by Riley, *Don Quixote*, p. 100.

CHAPTER FIVE
ARISTOCRATS

1. Sebastián de Covarrubias Orozco, *Tesoro de la lengua castellana o española*, ed. Felipe C. R. Maldonado, rev. Manuel Camarero (Madrid: Castalia, 1994), p.

796: "En éstos [palafrenos], según los libros de caballerías, caminaban las doncellas por las selvas" (On these palfreys, according to the books of chivalry, damsels went about through the woods).

2. In two essays, Anthony Close shows that the chivalric masquerades that the Duke and the Duchess put on for Don Quijote and Sancho Panza do not differ much in kind from actual courtly festivities of Cervantes's day that featured chivalric themes, and which could be taken quite seriously. Spanish aristocrats still liked to dress up and play at being knights. The figure of Don Quijote himself began to appear in these court amusements after the publication of Part One in 1605. See Close, "Fiestas palaciegas en la Segunda Parte del *Quijote*," in *Actas del Segundo Coloquio Internacional de la Asociación de Cervantistas: Alcalá de Henares, del 6 al 9 noviembre de 1989* (Barcelona: Anthropos, 1991), pp. 475–84; "Seemly Pranks: The Palace Episodes of *Don Quixote*, Part II," in *Art and Literature in Spain, 1600–1800: Studies in Honour of Nigel Glendinning*, ed. Charles David and Paul Julian Smith (London and Madrid: Támesis, 1993), pp. 69–87. For analyses and documents of some of these noble entertainments, see Teresa Ferrer Valls, *Nobleza y espectáculo teatral (1535–1622)* (València: UNED, Universidad de Sevilla, Universitat de València, 1993). Close in time to *Don Quijote* were the festivities for the marriage of the Duke of Braganza in 1603, which featured the embassy of a Moorish princess (with a story not unlike that of "Princess Antonomasia" in Chapter 38 of Part Two), a tourney in defense of her cause, and the intervention of a prophetic Arthurian enchantress, "la sabia Brisenda"; for a description, see pp. 225–33.

3. See Javier Salazar Rincón, *El mundo social del "Quijote"* (Madrid: Gredos, 1986), p. 150.

4. Vladimir Nabokov, *Lectures on Don Quixote*, ed. Fredson Bowers (San Diego, New York, and London: Harcourt Brace Jovanovich, 1983), p. 53; see Nabokov's third chapter, "Cruelty and Mystification," pp. 51–74.

5. A. J. Close, *Don Quixote* (Cambridge: Cambridge University Press, 1990), p. 14. Close has expanded this critical viewpoint in a book-length study, Anthony Close, *Cervantes and the Comic Mind of His Age* (Oxford: Oxford University Press, 2000). It is certainly helpful to contextualize the fiction of Cervantes within the literary theory and practice of his time, but Close's work is subject to the criticism that it cannot allow Cervantes any distance from his contemporaries. See also P. E. Russell, "'Don Quixote' as a Funny Book," *Modern Language Review* (1969): 312–26.

6. Close, "Seemly Pranks." The Duke and the Duchess are defended against Nabokov by Thomas Hart in *Cervantes and Ariosto: Renewing Fiction* (Princeton: Princeton University Press, 1989), pp. 102–14. Both critics seem to identify Cervantes with the most powerful characters in his book, but it is precisely aristocratic abuse of power that these episodes are calling into question.

7. Close, *Don Quixote*, pp. 86, acknowledges that Cervantes can be critical of the excesses of the Duke and Duchess, but adds, "In any case, his eventual condemnation of the Duke and Duchess seems tainted by double standards; he blames the doer, but relishes the deed." I would understand that Cervantes includes himself as a target for criticism in his reflections on the cruelty of slapstick: unlike the Duke and Duchess, he is self-aware.

8. On Cervantes's working of Avellaneda's continuation into his fiction, see E. C. Riley, *Cervantes's Theory of the Novel* (1962; reprint, Newark, Delaware: Juan de la Cuesta, 1992), pp. 212–19. For a reading of the Prologue to Part Two and some reflections on how Avellaneda is a kind of double of the satirist Cervantes, see Michael Seidel, *Satiric Inheritance: Rabelais to Sterne* (Princeton: Princeton University Press, 1979) 78–94.

9. On the Duke and the Duchess as readers, see L. A. Murillo, *A Critical Introduction to "Don Quixote"* (New York: Peter Lang, 1990), pp. 178–80.

10. Along different lines, Ruth El Saffar shows how the various jokes that the Duke and Duchess play keep developing beyond their original intentions and control. El Saffar, *Distance and Control in "Don Quixote": A Study in Narrative Technique* (Chapel Hill: University of North Carolina Press, 1975), pp. 92–98.

11. See Salazar Rincón, *El mundo social*, pp. 56–63.

12. Margaret Mann Phillips *The "Adages" of Erasmus: A Study with Translations* (Cambridge: Cambridge University Press, 1964), pp. 317–20. See also Robert M. Adams, *The Better Part of Valor: More, Erasmus, Colet, and Vives on Humanism* (Seattle: University of Washington Press, 1962), pp. 43–54.

13. More, *Utopia*, ed. Edward Surtz, S.J., and J. H. Hexter, in *The Complete Works of St. Thomas More*, vol. 4 (New Haven and London: Yale University Press, 1965), p. 171.

14. Michel de Montaigne, *The Complete Essays of Montaigne*, trans. Donald Frame (Stanford, California: Stanford University Press, 1965), p. 316. I have used the dialogue between Sancho Panza and the Duke to gloss, in turn, this passage in Montaigne in David Quint, *Montaigne and the Quality of Mercy: Ethical and Political Themes in the "Essais"* (Princeton: Princeton University Press, 1998), pp. 61–65.

15. For the role of Sancho's donkey, see Giuseppe di Stefano, "—Venid, mochachos y veréis el asno de Sancho Panza . . . ," *Nueva Revista de Filología Hispánica* 38 (1990): 857–73.

16. Alban K. Forcione offers a beautiful critical discussion of this scene in "Sancho Panza and Cervantes' Embodiment of Pastoral," in *Literature, Culture, and Society in the Modern Age: In Honor of Joseph Frank*, ed. Edward J. Brown et al. (Stanford, California: Department of Slavic Languages and Literatures, Stanford University, 1991) 1: 57–75.

17. One can compare Sancho's explanation to the Duchess in Chapter 33 of his love and loyalty for a Don Quijote he knows to be mad: he has eaten his master's bread—"he comido su pan" (768; 784).

18. In chapter 70 Sancho suggests that the disenchantment of Dulcinea that Love has consigned to the punishment of his body might just as well have been assigned to his donkey: "Bien pudiera el Amor—dijo Sancho—depositarlos en los de mi asno" (1024; 1042). His sentiment underscores the analogy that the novel makes between beating servants and mistreating animals.

19. For the motif of flagellation in *Don Quijote*, see Augustin Redondo, *Otra manera de leer el "Quijote"* (Madrid: Castalia, 1997), pp. 171–203.

20. I am indebted to Sherwin Nuland for this medical diagnosis.

21. For an analysis of this beginning and of a new social orientation of the novel, see Joaquín Casalduero, *Sentido y forma del "Quijote"* (Madrid: Ediciones

Insula, 1949), pp. 215–35. José Angel Ascunce Arrieta discusses how Part Two depicts the spectrum of Cervantes's Spanish society in *Los Quijotes del "Quijote": Historia de una aventura creativa* (Kassel: Reichenberger, 1997), pp. 424–78.

22. Lawrence Stone, *The Crisis of the Aristocracy, 1558–1641* (Oxford: Oxford University Press, 1965); Norbert Elias, *The Civilizing Process*, vol. 1, *The History of Manners*; vol. 2; *Power and Civility*, trans. Edmund Jephcott (1939; English trans. New York: Pantheon Books, 1982).

23. For a European-wide survey of literature critical of court life and courtiers, see Claus Uhlig, *Hofkritik im England des Mittelalters und der Renaissance* (Berlin and New York: Walter de Gruyter, 1973). For Spain, see chapter 6, pp. 224–56.

24. Baldesar Castiglione, *The Book of the Courtier* (4.4), trans. Charles Singleton (Garden City, New York: Anchor Books, 1959), p. 289. See also Leonard Mades, *The Armor and the Brocade: A Study of "Don Quixote" and the "Courtier"* (New York: Las Americas Publishing Co., 1968); J. G. Fucilla, "The Role of the *Cortegiano* in the Second Part of *Don Quijote*," *Hispania* 33 (1950): 291–96.

25. The germs of the polemic against courtiers are already present in Part One. Don Quijote awakens in Chapter 7 after having been put to bed on his return from his first sally; he is preoccupied in his delirium that the courtier knights— "caballeros cortesanos' (93; 76)—are getting the better of the knights-errant in the tourney. To his fellow traveler Vivaldo in Chapter 13, he declares that "ease, luxury, and repose were invented for soft courtiers, but toil, unrest, and arms were designed and made for those whom the world calls knights-errant" ["El buen paso, el regalo, y el reposo, allá se inventó para los blandos cortesanos; mas el trabajo, la inquietud y las armas sólo se inventaron e hicieron para aquellos que el mundo llama caballeros andantes" (130; 117)].

26. For the central role of ladies in the court society designed by the *Book of the Courtier*, see Claudio Scarpati, "Osservazioni sul terzo libro del *Cortegiano*" *Aevum* 66 (1992): 519–37; David Quint, "Courtier, Prince, Lady: The Design of the *Book of the Courtier*," *Italian Quarterly* 37, nos. 143–46 (2000): 185–95.

27. *El caballero puntual* of Alonso Jerónimo de Salas Barbadillo (1614) contains a letter from Don Quijote to the titular hero, an impostor nobleman, asking him how to succeed as a courtier. See Leonard Brownstein, *Salas Barbadillo and the New Novel of Rogues and Courtiers* (Madrid: Colección Plaza Mayor Scholar, 1974), pp. 95–99. See also "El Mundo por de dentro" in the *Sueños y discursos* (1627) of Francisco de Quevedo, ed. Felipe de C. R. Maldonado (Madrid: Castalia, 1972), pp. 165–66 where a tailor dresses himself as a hidalgo, a hidalgo as a caballero, a caballero as a lord, the lord as a king.

28. The Italian humanists had already exhausted the issue of the relationship of virtue to nobility in the fifteenth century: see the collection of their writings on the subject in Albert Rabil, Jr., *Knowledge, Goodness, and Power: The Debate over Nobility among Quattrocento Italian Humanists* (Binghamton, New York: Medieval and Renaissance Texts and Studies, 1991). In the "Sueño del infierno" in Quevedo's *Sueños y discursos*, pp. 122–25, devils inform a haughty nobleman, who insists that his damnation must be some mistake and who has all his patents of nobility ready to show them: "el que en el mundo es virtuoso, ése es hidalgo"

(p. 123). See Salazar Rincón, *El mundo social*, pp. 71–85, who begins by restating the aristocratic belief in the power of birth and blood in determining nobility.

29. Antonio de Guevara, *Menosprecio de corte y alabanza de aldea: Arte de marear*, ed. Asunción Rallo (Madrid: Catedra, 1984), p. 155 (Capitulo 4).

30. Riley, *Don Quixote*, pp. 145–46, notes how Don Quijote incongruously lumps the provincial homebody Don Diego with the idle courtier class to which he opposes himself as a doughty knight-errant. But Don Quijote later seems to make a distinction at the end of Chapter 36, where he distinguishes himself from "the knight who has never ventured beyond the boundaries of his town, nor from the lazy courtier" ["ni al caballero que nunca ha acertado a salir de los términos de su lugar, ni al perezoso cortesano" (795; 809)]. The first of these presumably refers to Don Diego de Miranda.

31. On aristocratic indebtedness in Cervantes's Spain, see Charles Jago, "The 'Crisis of the Aristocracy' in Seventeenth-Century Castile," *Past and Present* 84 (1979): 60–90.

32. Castiglione, *The Book of the Courtier*, p. 165 (2.65) for Serafino, pp. 40–41 (1.24) for grace. See Redondo, *Otra manera de leer*, pp. 421–38, for the obscene joke on Don Clavijo's name—Sir Key.

33. Casalduero, *Sentido y forma*, p. 317.

34. I think that it is untenable to see Cervantes embracing a "conservative ideology," as Michael McKeon maintains in *The Origins of the English Novel 1600–1740* (Baltimore and London: Johns Hopkins University Press, 1987), pp. 285–94. McKeon acknowledges, pp. 289–90, how ambiguous is his main evidence: Sancho Panza's renunciation of ambition in the name of liberty after the fall of his government in Chapter 53 (909–10; 926–27), a passage that—McKeon does not note—is an interlaced parallel to Don Quijote's celebration of liberty when he leaves the castle of the Duke and the Duchess at the opening of Chapter 58. The indignation of the novel against the aristocratic order does not allow it to embrace the social status quo, and Don Quijote and Sancho Panza finally escape their noble patrons. Far more untenable is Anthony Close's "Seemly Pranks," which views, p. 86, the Duke as pestered by Doña Rodríguez's "extravagantly silly and immodest parading of her grievances" and, poor man, forced to endure the "indignity" of Tosilos's "affront to his authority." For a view of the episode of the Duke and the Duchess as a satirical attack on the nobility, see Ludovik Osterc, *El pensamiento social y político del "Quijote"* (México: Ediciones De Andrea, 1963), pp. 123–31; Osterc connects, as I do, the Duke and the Duchess to Don Fernando in Part One. The value and limitations of Osterc's study, which attributes modern democratic sentiments to Cervantes, are discussed by Salazar Rincón, *El mundo social*, pp. 13–14.

35. One can compare the rhetoric of peasant honor in Lope de Vega's *Peribañez* and *Fuenteovejuna*. See Walter Cohen, *Drama of a Nation* (Ithaca and London: Cornell University Press, 1985), pp. 311–27.

36. The Duke's refusal to grant a comic solution to the story of Doña Rodríguez's daughter will be papered over in an early-eighteenth-century rewriting of this episode, the opera *Don Chisciotte in corte della Duchessa* of the noted Italian librettists Apostolo Zeno and Pietro Pariati, performed in Vienna in 1719. In their version, which actually manages to follow *Don Quijote* with considerable

fidelity, the noble lovers Alvaro and Doralba play out the parts and plot of the disguised Tosilos and the daughter of Doña Rodríguez, and the two are happily married at the opera's end, as are Altisidora and Laurindo, Alvaro's onetime rival for her hand. This double aristocratic wedding that concludes the opera takes the place of the disputed marriage of the real duenna's daughter, whose fate is simply left up in the air: the Duke is neither guilty nor innocent. The librettists' invention underscores just how far comic decorum is violated in Cervantes's episode. For the text, see Andrea della Corte, ed., *Drammi per musica dal Rinuccini allo Zeno* (Turin: UTET, 1958), 2: 375–520.

37. The extent of the Duke's tyranny is further emphasized by the interlacing of Chapters 44–57, where the appearance of Doña Rodríguez and her daughter as appellants for justice in Chapter 52 is juxtaposed in the same chapter with the letter that Teresa Panza writes to Sancho. In the news of their village, Teresa writes both of Pedro de Lobo's son, who intends to become a priest in order to escape marrying Minguilla, whom, rumor has it, he has put in the family way, and of some girls who went off with a company of soldiers. She withholds the names of the latter because they may come back, "and there are sure to be fellows who will marry them, for better or for worse" ["no faltará quien las tome por mujeres, con sus tachas buenas o malas" (904–5; 921)]. In the village, some comic solution will be available for the plight of seduced young women; at the castle of the Duke and the Duchess, the Duke's injustice will block just such a solution when Tosilos falls in love with the daughter of Doña Rodríguez.

38. The parallel between Tosilos and Andrés is noted by Edwin Williamson, *The Half-Way House of Fiction* (Oxford: Clarendon Press, 1984), pp. 191–92. For Williamson's comments on the episode of Andrés, see pp. 99–100, 167–68. See also Timothy Hampton, *Writing from History: The Rhetoric of Exemplarity in Renaissance Literature* (Ithaca and London: Cornell University Press, 1990), pp. 251–52; Redondo, *Otra manera de leer*, pp. 307–23.

39. Alexander Welsh has analyzed Don Quijote's encounter with the convicts in Chapter 22 of Part One, and discussed how concerns about justice characterize later novels that model their heroes after Don Quijote. See Welsh, *Reflections on the Hero as Quixote* (Princeton: Princeton University Press, 1981), pp. 37–80.

40. I am indebted for this observation to Maria DiBattista, "Don Quixote," in *Homer to Brecht: The European Epic and Dramatic Traditions*, ed. Michael Seidel and Edward Mendelson (New Haven and London: Yale University Press, 1977), p. 116.

41. See Murillo, *A Critical Introduction*, pp. 198–99.

42. A blown-up version of this idea is the theme of Henry W. Sullivan, *Grotesque Purgatory: A Study of Cervantes's "Don Quixote," Part II* (University Park, Pennsylvania: Pennsylvania State University Press, 1996).

43. This is the contention of A. J. Close in *Don Quixote*, p. 27.

44. Caroll B. Johnson, *Cervantes and the Material World* (Urbana and Chicago: University of Illinois Press, 2000), pp. 15–36. For a negative reading of the disenchantment of Dulcinea through money, see Ghetin Hughes, "The Cave of Montesinos: Don Quixote's Interpretation and Dulcinea's Disenchantments," *Bulletin of Hispanic Studies* 54 (1977): 107–13, 110–12.

45. Karl Marx and Friedrich Engels, *The Communist Manifesto*, in *Essential Works of Socialism*, ed. Irving Howe (New York: Bantam, 1970), p. 33.

46. Johnson, *Cervantes and the Material World*, p. 38.

47. Literature is included. Cervantes gently pokes fun at himself in the figure of the author in the printing shop in Chapter 62 who seeks profit to go along with a fame that he says is worthless without it (980; 999).

INDEX